Participation Pays

Praise for this book

'Praxis is known for its work among disadvantaged communities over the decades, and I congratulate them on the publication of this book.'

Amina J. Mohammed, UN Assistant Secretary-General, Special Advisor of the Secretary-General on Post-2015 Development Planning

'Here are amazingly powerful stories and great frameworks and tools for citizens' empowerment. This book should be a must-have for practitioners, trainers, or decision-makers working in the fields of social justice, democracy or accountability. This should not only re-root and re-energize participation discourse and practices but also give the post-2015 generation a lot to work with to get the implementation, monitoring, evaluation and reporting of the next goals right.'

Ramesh Singh, International Organisation Director, Greenpeace International

'*Participation Pays* is a very timely reminder of the necessity of participation as India moves from a 65-year old system of centralized and top-down planning through the Planning Commission to a hopefully much more decentralized and bottom-up system. It is a reminder that perhaps the only thing that can truly bring about transformation is if we start listening to the voices of poor and marginalized people and include them in policy, planning and resource allocation decisions.'

Nisha Agrawal, CEO, Oxfam India

'Community-based practitioners, researchers and students alike will appreciate this rich collection of cases about marginalized citizens producing and owning knowledge to fuel social change. It will reinvigorate a commitment to participation and set a new standard for its practice.'

Alison Mathie, Coady International Institute, St Francis Xavier University, Nova Scotia, Canada

Participation Pays
Pathways for post-2015

Edited by Tom Thomas and Pradeep Narayanan

Practical Action Publishing Ltd
The Schumacher Centre,
Bourton on Dunsmore, Rugby,
Warwickshire, CV23 9QZ, UK
www. practicalactionpublishing. org

A catalogue record for this book is available from the British Library.
A catalogue record for this book has been requested from the Library of Congress.

ISBN 978-1-85339-869-8 Hardback
ISBN 978-1-85339-870-4 Paperback
ISBN 978-1-78044-869-5 Library Ebook
ISBN 978-1-78044-870-1 Ebook

Thomas, T. , and Naryanan, P. , (2015) *Participation Pays: Pathways for post-2015*, Rugby, UK: Practical Action Publishing, <http://dx. doi. org/10. 3362/9781780448695>

Since 1974, Practical Action Publishing has published and disseminated books and information in support of international development work throughout the world. Practical Action Publishing is a trading name of Practical Action Publishing Ltd (Company Reg. No. 1159018), the wholly owned publishing company of Practical Action. Practical Action Publishing trades only in support of its parent charity objectives and any profits are covenanted back to Practical Action (Charity Reg. No. 247257, Group VAT Registration No. 880 9924 76).

Cover design by Mercer Design
Indexed by Elizabeth Ball
Typeset by Allzone Digital Services Limited
Printed and bound in India by Replika Press Pvt. Ltd.

Contents

List of figures and tables vii

Foreword
Robert Chambers ix

Preface xiii

List of acronyms xv

Glossary of terms and how they are used xvii

1 **Introduction: powering knowledge from the margins** **1**
Tom Thomas and Pradeep Narayanan

2 **Breaking the barriers to information: community-led land mapping in Bihar** **5**
Anindo Banerjee, Rohan Preece, and Anusha Chandrasekharan

3 **Building consensus methodically: community rebuilding in the Maldives** **25**
M. J. Joseph, Ravikant Kisana, and Mary George

4 **Knowledge base: towards a community-owned monitoring system** **41**
Rohan Preece, Stanley Joseph, Gayathri Sarangan and Sowmyaa Bharadwaj

5 **Lost policies: locating access to infrastructure and services in rural India** **63**
Tom Thomas, Moulasha Kader and Rohan Preece

6 **A new deluge? People and aid in the aftermath of disaster** **85**
Moulasha Kader, Ajai Kuruvila, and Shireen Kurian

7 **Subverting for good: sex workers and stigma** **101**
Sowmyaa Bharadwaj, Shalini Mishra and Aruna Mohan Raj

8 **Making people count: from beneficiaries to evaluators** **113**
Anindo Banerjee, Rohan Preece and M. J. Joseph

http://dx.doi.org/10.3362/9781780448695.000

9 **Reimagining development: marginalized people and the post-2015 agenda** 137
Pradeep Narayanan, Sowmyaa Bharadwaj, and Anusha Chandrasekharan

10 **Conclusion: pathways to post-2015** 163
Tom Thomas and Pradeep Narayanan

Index 165

List of figures and tables

Figures

2.1	Major milestones in land reform in Bihar	8
2.2	Hierarchy of land use	10
2.3	Land mapping: from individual knowledge to shared knowledge	11
2.4	Scaffolding critical thinking about land	12
2.5	Example of a map showing unauthorized encroachments	13
2.6	Example of a map showing one individual's unauthorized occupancy of land	14
2.7	Land mapping: from shared knowledge to public knowledge	15
2.8	Maps as a lobbying tool	16
2.9	Towards empowerment: the land mapping and redistribution cycle	17
3.1	Conceptual and methodological framework of the beneficiary identification process	30
3.2	Steps undertaken for the beneficiary identification process	31
5.1	Social map illuminating proximity of key infrastructural services to forward caste households	69
5.2	Frequency of distribution of certain kinds of infrastructure in sample villages	71
5.3	Composition of sample villages based on availability of infrastructure	71
6.1	Mind map of how aid agencies and government squeezed community interests in the name of development	89
7.1	Causal loop analysis (participatory tool) facilitated with sex workers	104
7.2	Stakeholder analysis	104
7.3	Analysis of ease of engagement with stakeholders for stigmatized members of communities	105
7.4	Mapping engagement with stakeholders	108
7.5	Scale of progression of engagement with stakeholders	108
8.1	The process of the evaluation from the perspective of the community representatives	118
8.2	Cobweb analysis of one of the teams of community representatives	122
8.3	Known Indian languages of community representatives	127
9.1	The Voice for Change Advocacy Campaign	141
9.2	Process followed by the GLP	145
9.3	Representation of panel identities	146
9.4	The Ground-Level Panel's alternative approach to goal-setting	147

Tables

2.1 Operational landholdings: comparing Bihar and national figures 6
2.2 Introducing Bihar 7
3.1 Towards transformative engagement 37
4.1 Stages of community mobilization in the Avahan initiative 44
4.2 Self-monitoring: parameters and indicators 48
4.3 Action plan for Namakkal CBO: August to November 2013 50
5.1 Flagship schemes introduced by the Government of India 64
5.2 Auditing process overview 70
5.3 Distribution of infrastructure facilities across social habitations in sample villages 73
5.4 Extent of inequity of infrastructural provision in the sample villages 74
5.5 Access ratings of eight services by different caste and religious groups 75
5.6 Group-wise ranking of infrastructure based on attitude of service provider 76
5.7 Group-wise rating of service at different types of village infrastructure, according to location of infrastructure 83
7.1 Terms used to describe the communities 106
8.1 Participatory tools used during the evaluation process 123
9.1 Goals of the High-Level Panel 140
9.2 The Ground-Level Panel's Goals 148

Foreword

Robert Chambers

It is an honour to have been invited to write a foreword for this remarkable, important, timely and inspiring book.

It is remarkable because it presents key experiences and learning of remarkable people in a remarkable organization. Praxis is an NGO which has been at the forefront of participatory practice for over two decades. It is deeply committed to ideals of equity and justice: as this book illustrates so eloquently through reflective accounts of eight of its major activities, it has aligned itself with those who are poor, marginalized and discriminated against, working with them, and enabling them to gain for themselves respect, their rights and a better life. Praxis has engaged mainly in India and with some of India's most intractable problems; and with the exception of the Maldives, all the chapters draw on Indian experience. What the book does not mention is that Praxis funds itself through commissioned projects like those recounted here, and uses its income not to reward staff but to build up a corpus to fund other activities, such as its participatory training work in Afghanistan. Also what cannot be shown here is the behaviour, attitudes, commitment, resolution and courage without which the experiences in these eight chapters would never have been achieved.

Participation Pays is important because it opens up and demonstrates frontiers for development practice. The authors describe much of what they do as subversive (latin *sub*, below and *vertere*, to turn). Consistently the actors in these pages are from *below*, the powerless, those on the social, economic, spatial and political margins. So here we can learn from subaltern, subordinated groups – the landless in Bihar, those robbed of homes, livelihoods and land by the tsunami in the Maldives and Tamil Nadu, transgendered people, LGBTs, sex workers, injecting drug users, men having sex with men, and pervasively again and again in different contexts women and those facing caste discrimination. We read how Praxis *turns* normal top–down power relations on their heads. Those 'below' are sought out, respected, listened to, facilitated to do their own appraisal and analysis, and their priorities and realities are then put first. And when this is done, again and again, they show capabilities – in participatory mapping of land, in conducting their own censuses, in wellbeing ranking, in analysing power relations, designing and building their own new homes, in carrying out evaluations, in facilitating their peers to do likewise – far beyond what many development professionals suppose.

Participation Pays is timely because it is being published in the watershed year of 2015 when the MDGs come to an end and the SDGs (sustainable development goals) start. The MDGs 'picked the low-hanging fruit', that is, the targets could most cheaply and conveniently be achieved through gains by those whom it was easiest to reach, not through those who were less easy, weaker, more marginal and worse off. SDG rhetoric stresses equity and equality, holding promise that the focus will shift to those who are poorest, most stigmatized, excluded and marginalized, least able to help themselves, and most isolated; in short, those who are 'last'. These are precisely those with whom Praxis has been engaged for two decades, opening up and exploring pathways to 2015, making this book so timely and the subtitle *Pathways for post 2015* so apposite.

How participation pays fits the new goals. For empowering those who are powerless, participation is both indispensable and cost-effective. There is no substitute. But it is not a solution to be taken off the shelf. It has to be lived. It has to be part of a mindset and a way of life. So let those who read this book not be misled. It is all too easy and common for those who talk of participation to neglect power and the personal dimension. NGOs widely adopt participatory rhetoric and write nice proposals, but many are gatekeepers and claim to speak for those who are poor and marginalized rather than enabling and empowering them to act and speak for themselves. Power relations have to be reversed through personal and institutional commitment and action, and resisting the top–down reporting and accountability demands of donors. If downward accountability is not part of the SDGs, then in the interests of those the SDGs are meant to serve it must be fought for. Participatory non-negotiables, like those of Praxis, need to be debated, agreed and asserted, to become stronger and more accepted in balancing development relationships.

Participation Pays is inspiring because it gives us hope that we can make our world a better place. The barrage of bad news that assaults us daily neglects the good news. And here the good news is evidence that much can be achieved against the odds if only we have the guts and vision to try. Those who illegally controlled land in Bihar could be confronted. Those who sought to exploit the post-tsunami opportunity to seize land and water for hotels and shrimp farming could be opposed. Poor, marginalized and stigmatized people could do much more than most professionals would have supposed. Again and again, asking who? and whose? questions – whose knowledge, whose appraisal, whose analysis, whose priorities, whose indicators,whose monitoring and evaluation, whose realities, whose theory of change? – these and many other questions can be answered by 'theirs' rather than 'ours'. And 'we' often have power to empower, not least by convening occasions, and bringing poor people and those with power together, showing how their values and priorities differ, as with the Ground-level Panel which Praxis convened to influence the post-2015 agenda.

Praxis deserves praise for what it has shown can be done, for its self-critical modesty, and for sharing what it has learnt. May the pathways it has opened up, explored and shared encourage and embolden others, not to follow in their footsteps, but to blaze their own trails and to do this with the similar courage and commitment. Another world is possible. As President Obama so memorably said before his first election, 'Yes we can'. What Praxis has shown is that what we can do is more than many have believed.

Professor Robert Chambers is a research associate of the Institute of Development Studies, University of Sussex, UK

Preface

Paulo Freire defines praxis in *Pedagogy of the Oppressed* as 'reflection and action directed at the structures to be transformed'. Through praxis, oppressed people can acquire a critical awareness of their own condition and, with their allies, struggle for liberation. Praxis Institute for Participatory Practices through its engagements with communities living in poverty has been striving to give essence to the Freirian concept of Praxis since its inception in 1997. The years have raised our individual and collective critical consciousness through the innumerable dialogues that were enriched by the experiences of different communities living in poverty. This book is an attempt at capturing, documenting, and sharing some of those lived experiences. The authors and editors in this book have merely shared these experiences – the knowledge belongs to the people.

We are grateful for the tremendous support and inspiration from many people without which this book would not have been possible. While with some communities, the engagements have been shorter, there were others with whom we were fortunate enough to have dialogues for nearly a decade. These dialogues, both short- and long-term ones, convinced us and the communities, that participation does pay rich dividends, in the short and in the long run. This book is the outcome of that collective conviction of both the communities and us that there is a lot that can be and needs to be shared, to deepen participation and to realize the power of praxis.

This compilation would not have been possible without the hard work of all the researchers, village volunteers and Praxis colleagues who facilitated these dialogues over the years. We are thankful to the Avahan programme of the Bill and Melinda Gates Foundation for providing us the opportunity for some critical and long-term engagement with sex workers, sexual minorities and people using drugs. A special thanks is extended to Rohan Preece and Sowmyaa Bharadwaj who helped in coordinating and drafting sections of this book.

We also extend our thanks to Helen Wishart and Clare Tawney at Practical Action for their tireless help in making this book see the light of day.

Finally, we want to thank organizations and campaigns whose struggles have been penned here and are grateful to the girls, boys, transgender persons, women, and men who shared inspiring insights about their lives, struggles, aspirations, and assessments of contemporary development interventions.

Tom Thomas and Pradeep Narayanan

List of acronyms

ART	Anti-retroviral therapy
BC	Backward class
BRCS	British Red Cross Society
CBG	Community-based group
CBO	Community-based organization
CBPPI	Community-based pro-poor initiatives
CFAR	Centre for Advocacy and Research
DAPCU	District Aids Prevention and Control Units
DLSA	Delhi State Legal Services Authority
FGD	Focus group discussion
FSW	Female sex worker
GoM	Government of the Maldives
ICTC	Integrated Counselling and Testing Centre
ICDS	Integrated Child Development Services
IDC	Island Development Council
IDPs	Internally displaced persons
IDU	Injecting drug user
PRSC	Partner Representative Steering Committee
MIDP	Maldives internally displaced person
MSM	Men who have sex with men
MoU	Memorandum of undertsanding
NIEA	National Infrastructure Equity Audit
NFHS	National Family Health Survey
NREGS	National Rural Employment Guarantee Scheme
NRHM	National Rural Health Mission
OBC	Other backward class
PHC	Primary health centre
PLHA	People living with HIV/AIDS
RCM	Red Cross Maldives
RCS	Red Cross Society
RGNDWM	Rajiv Gandhi National Drinking Water Mission
SACS	State AIDS Control Society
SC	Scheduled caste
SHG	Self-help group
SIFFS	South India Federation of Fisherman Societies
SNEHA	Social Need Educational and Human Awareness
SSA	Sarva Shiksha Abhiyan
ST	Scheduled tribe
STI	Sexually transmitted infection
TAI	Tamil Nadu Aids Initiative
TG	Transgendered people
TI	Targeted intervention

UNDP	United Nations Development Programme
VLPP	Village Level People's Plan
VPA	Vulnerability and Poverty Assessment
VPT	Village public telephone
WDC	Women's Development Council

Glossary of terms and how they are used

There are many words used in this book which mean quite different things in different contexts. Most of these words abound in other literature on participatory development, and have been frequently defined, so our intention is not to provide *definitions* but rather to serve as a guide to how, very broadly, some of the most frequently occurring of these words are used here, and what we mean by them.

To get a fuller picture, the reader is encouraged not to stop with this very brief list, but to refer also to the index and to the chapter contexts within which they are used. If the reader finds any words that are not on this list, but wants a further explanation, (s)he is warmly encouraged to get in touch with the Praxis team via email.

Community

The term 'community' is used here in a number of different ways. Most often in this book, it refers to a group of people identified as beneficiaries of a development project who share common characteristics. These common characteristics can include a shared residence (e.g. those who reside in the same village, hamlet, or habitation); a shared identity (e.g. transgender, female sex workers, people with HIV, people with common livelihoods such as fisher people, a religious minority group, a tribe, a caste group, or people who share a residential area that may be larger than a single village or habitation) or a shared experience (e.g. of a natural disaster, of socio-economic marginalization, of exclusion, or of stigmatization). The use of the term 'community' within this volume, does not therefore, imply homogeneity amongst members, indeed, more often than not, it embodies great diversity.

Participation

Participation is always discussed with reference to a community (as described above) or otherwise to a member of a marginalized or excluded group. Reflective of their agency to make decisions, it refers to such kind of engagement by community members in the activities that are the focus of the case study within each chapter, such as planning, monitoring, mapping and evaluating that help them make informed decisions. In other words, it also often refers to community involvement in knowledge generation, knowledge management and knowledge creation.

Tool

This is a general term to describe a particular method used in the context of programmatic activities, monitoring, evaluation and research, in order to facilitate a certain set of processes and outcomes. In this volume reference is frequently made to 'participatory tools', which enable community involvement in work initiated by outsiders, and which may also enable community facilitation or even leadership of a process.

Data

This refers to information generated and identified through the course of programmatic activities, monitoring, evaluation, or research. It is of interest because it contributes to an understanding of: (1) one or more of the aforementioned four processes, (2) their impacts and (3) the communities that they involve. Data is therefore constitutive of knowledge about development work as well as being the fruit of research and other forms of enquiry. Typically the subject of aggregation and scrutiny, in this volume it frequently refers to information that has been generated, collected and used by community members themselves and for their own purposes.

CHAPTER 1

Introduction: powering knowledge from the margins

Tom Thomas and Pradeep Narayanan

Over the past two decades Praxis has witnessed the trials, tribulations and glories of 'participation', not as a bystander or uninvolved commentator but from inside the ring as a practitioner. Praxis' initiation came at a time of frenzied activity with the explosion of tools, field innovators, writers, and authors – a time when the development world was smitten by the participation bug. Everyone was adapting, modifying or innovating tools, renaming them as appropriate to specific theatres of participative action. The push was to adapt, innovate, document, and share. Praxis (in its previous avatar as a unit of ActionAid India) became the clearing house for much of these activities of the early 90s. Then came the scale-up and the big push by the World Bank through its 'Voices of the Poor' project that spanned continents. We joined that effort too by undertaking the India segment of the study. Participation became the buzzword and no project, be it of the World Bank, UK Department for International Development (DfID) or other donors/non-governmental organizations (NGOs)/international NGOS (INGOs), was worthy without a 'participatory' tick in the checkbox. Participation was written into all donor-funded government programmes. Of course, scaling up comes with its share of problems and criticisms. The decade that followed saw a slew of these, and participation was then declared the new orthodoxy and the new development tyranny.

We agree and identify with most of the criticism, and looking back, we wonder whether it is the price we paid for the move from the margins to the mainstream – or whether there is something inherent in the approach that couldn't stand up to the expectations? The answer probably lies somewhere at the intersection of these two. There is no denying that the approach was a huge paradigm shift for aided developmental interventions. Knowledge creation has been problematic since time immemorial – at best it attempted neutrality and at worst, it was a blatant display of power by the dominant class or caste. What got buried deep beneath all this is the struggle of people living in poverty: people who are stigmatized and excluded. Within development circles, participation for the first time opened its doors to a more systematic and equitable inclusion of the pariahs in knowledge creation through the pioneering work of Robert Chambers and others. People living in poverty were for the first time being asked their views and their

http://dx.doi.org/10.3362/9781780448695.001

priorities. Through *Whose Reality Counts?* and similar work, their reality was being given a premium. They were being heard rather than being told, for a change. The sites for exercise of power were loosening up. However, the liberating potential of this experience remained limited because much of these interactions were one-offs, confined to the Western philosophical tradition of knowledge for its own sake rather than being founded in the history of struggles of the marginalized. This defect slowly began to be challenged by many practitioners from the global South, and the addition of 'Action' to the terminology reflected this shift (Participatory Reflection and Action/Participatory Learning and Action). Somewhere along this stage in the history of participatory approaches came the intersection with the scaling up by the big players. The scaling up was resourced by proponents of neoliberal ideology that encouraged and supported the utilitarian aspects of participatory approaches, focusing on stakeholder engagement for faster implementation and better efficiency. It saw in the approach a quick way to gain access to a new community, get (and often set) their expectations, forge consensus and allocate roles – thereby reducing costs, managing crowds better, and increasing project efficiency. The governments that adopt this approach often view community engagement as one-dimensional and yearn for depoliticized forms of participation that are sanitized, clinical and conflict-free (Whitfield, 2012). A good part of participatory approaches got pushed back into the fold of knowledge for its own sake, with no particular accent on dialogue to raise critical consciousness or probe deeper into structural causes of poverty. This made it easy for the new financiers (and hence self-assumed managers) of the approach to cherry-pick whatever suited their scheme of things – the prime example being the World Bank's 'Voices of the Poor' initiative. Fairly soon along this trajectory, a mockery of the approach also came in the form of compartmentalization of community participation as a separate component. It was often sanctioned long after the planning and programme roll out phases were under way – making do without even the need for cherry-picking! The likes of the World Bank, The Asian Development Bank and DfID excelled in this.

Even when the political left dabbled with participation at scale (such as in the People's Plan Campaign, Kerala), it failed to go beyond the party's attempt at community outreach. Even here it continued to focus on surface-level issues and skimmed over structural causes of inequality and marginalization. It also almost completely failed to reach out to the poorest – the *adivasis* (tribal communities) of Kerala.

Why participation? It owes much of its intellectual heritage to the Western philosophical construct of knowledge for its own sake that assumed political neutrality of knowledge. It was resourced and scaled up by neoliberals who, at best, used it as a mechanism for project management. Even the left used it mainly as an outreach programme. Though this remained the mainstreamed paradigm, many continued to explore the subversive potential that participation offered. Some saw its potential for conscientization, infusing some of Paulo Freire's thinking into it, while others used it to explore the local power dimension more deeply. David Archer's REFLECT (Regenerated Freirean Literacy through Empowering Community Techniques) and John Gaventa's Power Cube are some examples of these explorations. We in Praxis, in the two decades of our work, continued our search for ways of re-politicizing participation to give it the edge, to subvert for good, in the continued struggle for a democratic basis for state power, without which addressing structural causes of poverty would be a near impossibility.

What you will find in this book is an assortment of explorations of the subversive potential of participation, particularly by powering knowledge from the margins. It explores ways of tackling some of the challenges posed to powering knowledge from the margins through challenging dominant data; tackling myths; and showcasing alternatives. The chapters 'Breaking the barriers to information'; 'Lost policies', and 'Building consensus methodically' address the tyranny of existing data by creating alternate data that clearly show the gaps and blind spots in the so-called 'official' data. The chapters 'A new deluge?' and 'Subverting for good', bust the myths that dominate development practice. 'A new deluge?' challenges the myth perpetuated by development practitioners and governments that communities do not have the inclination or capacity to participate in planning for their relief and rehabilitation, and that all interventions in the aftermath of disasters need to be top-down. This pioneering work showed that disaster-affected communities are fully capable, and that preventing them from participating could misguide the entire intervention. It demonstrated that participation in post-disaster situations was not a luxury but non-negotiable and eminently achievable. Similarly, the work with sexual minorities challenged the myth that stigma is only a by-product of their HIV status rather than a cause of it. Communities from across six states in India in unison argued that stigma is one of the biggest challenges that affect their mobility, choices and health-seeking behaviour and are a cause of their discrimination, rather than a manifestation of it. The chapters 'Knowledge base', 'Making people count' and 'Re-imagining development' showcase alternative paradigms and possibilities that demonstrate how people living in poverty have the ability to engage in spaces that were hitherto reserved for academics, civil society organizations and consultants. The community-led evaluation of a UNDP programme in 'Making people count' demonstrated that communities can take on the role of evaluators and produce a very grounded and informed take on the state of affairs, often offering insights that external evaluators will not be capable of. It offered practical ways of dealing with questions of subjectivity and offered alternative pathways to evaluations. The Ground-Level Panel showed that people living in poverty have the ability to engage with matters beyond their immediate needs, by critiquing the UN High Level Panel recommendations and suggesting their vision for a post-2015 framework. Both of these experiences put forth alternative paradigms that show that communities are capable of direct talk and no longer need interpreters to talk on their behalf.

The chapters also offer much richer subtexts on processes, dilemmas, and power-plays within the development sector itself, as well as nuanced accounts of people's existence and development practices. For example, 'Lost policies' reveals disparities in the location of and access to public services depending on who you are, which god you pray to and which caste you belong to. 'A new deluge' shows the entire development sector and the Indian Government's complete misreading of the local political economy and design of thoroughly faulty recovery programmes. 'Breaking the barriers to information' deals with the struggles over one of the most contested resources – land. The struggles of sexual minorities against the use of stigma as a tool to push them into sub-human existence are a dominant thread in the chapter 'Subverting for good'. The chapter 'Knowledge base' also outlines the subtle power struggles between civil society organizations and community-based organizations, and the liberating potential of access to data.

This book zeroes in on experiences that bring subaltern voices into the reckoning while discounting those that showcase 'participation' as a panacea. It addresses both practitioners as well as those more inclined to theorizing. Both might find experiences that resonate with their own experiences or theories of change. The thread that connects all of the chapters is the attempted subversion of existing power relations in favour of communities.

About the authors

Tom Thomas has over 20 years of experience in the development sector and has led Praxis on several tasks that have provided critical inputs into development policy and thinking on social development, in India and in several countries across South Asia.

Pradeep Narayanan has close to two decades of experience working Government and non-government institutions as a rights-focused activist-researcher on community mobilization and participation across several thematic spheres.

References

Chambers, R. (1997) *Whose Reality Counts? Putting the first last*, Rugby: Practical Action Publishing.

Whitfield, D. (2012), *In Place of Austerity: Reconstructing the Economy, State and Public Services,* Nottingham: Spokesman Books.

CHAPTER 2

Breaking the barriers to information: community-led land mapping in Bihar

Anindo Banerjee, Rohan Preece, and Anusha Chandrasekharan

Abstract

[1]Inequities in rights over land in Bihar, simmering disputes, and years of frustrated attempts to secure justice form the backdrop to a grassroots land-mapping exercise undertaken in 38 villages in 2008. This chapter charts steps made by landless and land-scarce people to map land within their own villages and achieve local ratification for them. It cites examples of how these maps were used to claim access to land. The process is understood as a journey of conscientization leading in many cases to praxis and even, in a few cases, to land justice. Land mapping of this kind involves various subversions of knowledge and practice: some of these are discussed, as well as some enduring challenges.

Keywords: social justice, land rights, casteism, Bihar land records, commuity-owned data

Setting the scene

In contexts of land scarcity, disagreements over who owns what sometimes escalate into disputes, especially when land is perceived as being encroached on or unfairly obtained. Bihar, a state in northern India bordering Nepal, is a case in point. Home to more than 100 million people, it has been affected by disputes over land in recent decades. In the 1990s, regular battles were waged between upper-caste militias, who often enjoyed political patronage, and left-leaning anti-establishment groups claiming to represent the interests of disadvantaged people. Violence scarred the landscape as tensions boiled over into bloody attacks and reprisals. The situation has now simmered down, but the inequity – a disturbing union of land ownership and caste privilege – remains.

For some time now, ever since British rule and the exaltation of the *zamindars* (landowners) who kept millions of labourers in a state of peasantry, Bihar has been marked by severe disparities in land ownership. Land is also in relatively short supply: almost 30% of the land in this densely populated state is uncultivable. Unsurprisingly, Bihar has a much higher share of marginal farms (agricultural land up to 1 hectare/2.5 acres) than other states in India. The 2010–11 Agricultural Survey, which categorizes land into marginal, small, semi-medium, medium, and large, found that 91.06% of operational holdings

http://dx.doi.org/10.3362/9781780448695.002

in Bihar were marginal – more than 24 percentage points higher than the share in the country as a whole. Disparities in holdings are particularly significant between scheduled castes and more privileged social groups.[2]

In Bihar, extreme poverty lies at the thick end of daunting inequality. The state has the lowest levels of household expenditure in India and chronic levels of malnutrition (Dreze and Sen, 2013, Statistical Appendix). Yet, despite social problems and inadequate steps for reform, progressive legislation and policies have been passed in attempts to heave the state out of semi-feudalism and into a more contemporary – if still exploitative – landowner-centric, yield-oriented system of production. The abolition of the Zamindari Act was implemented as a law in 1948, and the Land Reform Act was passed as long ago as 1950. The *Bhoodan* social movement that took hold in Bihar, as elsewhere in India, in the early 1950s, held the promise of landless and land-poor people accessing land offered to them by the land-rich, but without the security of ownership. It was given legislative backing in 1954, though it achieved limited success in realizing its transformational potential.

Table 2.1 Operational landholdings: comparing Bihar and national figures

	Percentage distribution of operational landholdings		**Average size of operational landholdings (hectares)**	
Size	Bihar	India	Bihar	India
Marginal	91.06	67.04	0.25	0.38
Small	5.86	17.93	1.25	1.42
Semi-medium	2.56	10.05	2.59	2.71
Medium	0.50	4.25	5.09	5.76
Large	0.02	0.73	14.45	17.36

The average size of a landholding in Bihar is considerably smaller than in India as a whole: 0.39 hectares in Bihar as opposed to the national figure of 1.16 hectares. Scheduled tribes in Bihar have, at 0.5 hectares, less than a third of the size of scheduled tribe landholdings at the national level of 1.53 hectares (Agriculture Census, 2010-11). People from scheduled castes fare particularly badly in Bihar, with average landholdings of just 0.3 hectares: less than half the size of the national average landholding for scheduled castes of 0.8 hectares.

Box 2.1 Introducing Bihar

Bihar is a north Indian state bordering Nepal, and is the third most populous state in the country (see Table 2.2). 33.7% of people in Bihar live below the national poverty line, compared with the Indian average of 21.9% (Planning Commission, 2013). The vast majority of Bihar's population live in rural areas, and have been largely excluded from India's growth since economic liberalization in 1991. Although roughly 60% of India's labour force is occupied in agriculture (Ministry of Agriculture, 2002), this sector's share in gross domestic product (GDP) declined significantly between 1984 and 2004. The major part of the growth has been in the service sector, benefiting urban areas rather than the rural areas found in most areas of Bihar.

Table 2.2 Introducing Bihar

Indicator	Figure
Population	104,099,452
Area (hectares)	94,163
Decadal population growth 2001–11 (absolute)	20,806,128
Decadal population growth 2001–11 (percentage)	25.10%
Population density (per square kilometre)	1,106
% Scheduled caste* population (2001)	15.7
% Scheduled tribe* population (2001)	0.90
Literacy rate (7+ years)	61.8%
Male literacy rate (7+ years)	71.2%
Female literacy rate (7+ years)	51.5%
Rural population (absolute)	92,341,436
Urban population (absolute)	11,758,016
Percentage of population 'multi-dimensionally poor' (2005–06)	79.3%
Proportion of undernourished [weight-for-age] children below 5 (2005–06)	55.9%

Sources: Census of India, 2011; Dreze and Sen, 2013

* These are official designations recognized by the Constitution of India, given to various groups of historically disadvantaged people

In 1961 – after some resistance – an act was passed to prevent excessive private ownership. This, the Bihar Land Reforms (Ceiling, Land Allocation and Surplus Land Acquisition) Act, allowed any individual to own up to 30 acres of land. By 1973, it had been changed to entitle ownership to a family rather than to an individual, stipulating a limit of 45 acres for each family.

However, administrative inefficiencies and delays played into the hands of the landed, as in the years that followed, the slow rate of implementation of these acts allowed time for the land to be divided amongst family members or other individuals loyal to them. Many also took advantage of legal loopholes enabling landowners to retain excess land provided that it was used for specific purposes, such as homestead land or land for commerce.

Today, the inequity continues, with over a third of rural households in Bihar entirely landless. At the same time, numerous individual landowners sit on vast tracts of land. In certain districts as many as 70% of households are landless. This usually means they have to work on leased land, handing over more than half of their gross output to the landowners, almost double what is normally paid elsewhere.

With most land records dating from before independence, and with land inequities between the landed and the landless aligning closely with multiple

Bihar Zamindari Abolition Act, 1948

- Under the *zamindari* system, large landowners *(zamindars)* collected tax from peasants working on their farms. The system kept multitudes in a state of landlessness and economic dependency.
- The Zamindari Act was passed initially in 1947 and then amended in 1948. It was a step in the direction of land justice for the peasant classes, although the wide representation of *zamindars*, like many dominant groups in the state machinery, did not necessarily bode well for its thorough enforcement.

Bihar Land Reforms Act, 1950

- This act sought to abolish intermediaries tenures (such as *zamindars*): it thus brought *raiyats* (tenants and cultivators) into direct contact with the state.
- The implementation was slowed down by opposition in the early years. Preparation of new land records required consultation with and approval of different parties.

Bihar Land Reforms (Ceiling, Land Allocation and Surplus Land Acquisition Act) 1961; amended 1973

- The Bihar Land Reforms (Ceiling, Land Allocation and Surplus Land Acquisition) Act 1961 allowed any individual to own up to 30 acres of land.
- By 1973, it had been changed to entitle a family rather than an individual to ownership, stipulating a limit of 45 acres for each family.

Figure 2.1 Major milestones in land reform in Bihar

Box 2.2 Government action

The Government of Bihar has shown itself to be aware of the need for reforms, and set up the Land Reform Commission (LRC) in 2007 to look into land distribution in Bihar and provide recommendations to the government. The LRC, chaired by D. Bandhyopadhyay, submitted its report to the government in April 2008. The LRC's recommendations included setting a ceiling on land ownership of 15 acres, and suggested:

1. Allotting between one acre and 0.66 of an acre of land defined as surplus under the Bihar Land Reforms Act 1961 to the lowest quintile of agricultural labourers, consisting of 16.68 lakh (1,668,000) households.
2. Allotting at least 10 decimals of land to shelter-less households of 5.84 lakh (584,000) non-farm rural workers.
3. Enacting legislation to ensure the rights of sharecroppers to at least 60% of the produce they cultivate.

Source: *Mainstream*, XLVII: 33, August 1, 2009.

economic, social and political inequities, those who most need to make their voices heard typically struggle to do so. They struggle amid an informal system, as most arrangements of share-cropping are based on oral agreements in which legal protection of tenants is often elusive.

As a high-level commission, the LRC was not specifically set up to involve communities who were themselves experiencing conditions of land scarcity. Furthermore, existing records detailed ownership, but were silent on the question of control – Who is actually in day-to-day charge of the usage of the land, and for how long? They revealed nothing about whether or not land was contested between two or more parties, despite the fact that considerable swathes of the Bihar landscape were under dispute. Extant records were also not disaggregated to indicate distribution of land ownership amongst different social groups.

Clearing the ground

With the system of land records inadequate and inaccessible to most people in rural areas who depend on it for their survival, a need was felt by Ekta Parishad (a people's movement dedicated to non-violent action, aiming at social and land reform in India), to break through the opacity and create a transparent understanding of land distribution at the grassroots level. Developing a knowledge base such as this, it was calculated, could act as a starting point for sustained advocacy and a resource for campaigns for proper redistribution according to the promises enshrined by legislation.

Given these considerations, the Bihar unit of Ekta Parishad, together with Praxis, decided to undertake an exercise to identify specific issues related to land distribution and the prospects for allotment of land to the huge number of landless households in the state. To address the inadequacy of existing records, it would be necessary to create a database that provided more insight into the question of who has what stake over a certain area of land.

An analytical framework was developed, incorporating indices on land distribution, control, disputes, and disparities in ownership. This was designed to generate maps with layered indicators that would allow an understanding of patterns of distribution.

Whose maps?

A key decision facing the action team comprising members from Praxis and Ekta Parishad was *whom* to engage in the land-mapping process. There would be no shortage of potential participants in the villages of Bihar. However, a conscious decision was made to seek to involve those on the edges of land – sharecroppers and landless labourers – to ensure that their voices were mainstreamed. Ekta Parishad identified the facilitators, who also belong to marginalized sections of society.

At a residential workshop, village representatives from Gaya and Jamui districts came together to participate in a pilot land-mapping exercise. The idea was to build up a group of villagers who would be able to anchor the process in selected locations, with the support of local people. Soon after the initial workshop, the team of villagers carried out the first land-mapping exercises across seven villages in Jamui. This group evolved to become the facilitators of the entire process. Most were landless themselves.

Locations for land mapping were chosen based on disparities in land ownership and also an interest in testing the land-mapping process out across different areas. There was an attempt to reach out to communities where there was a demonstrated enthusiasm for taking forward the outcomes of a land-mapping process for campaigns and advocacy purposes. The entire process lasted around six months across 38 villages in the districts of Gaya, Jamui, Nawada, Patna, and West Champaran.

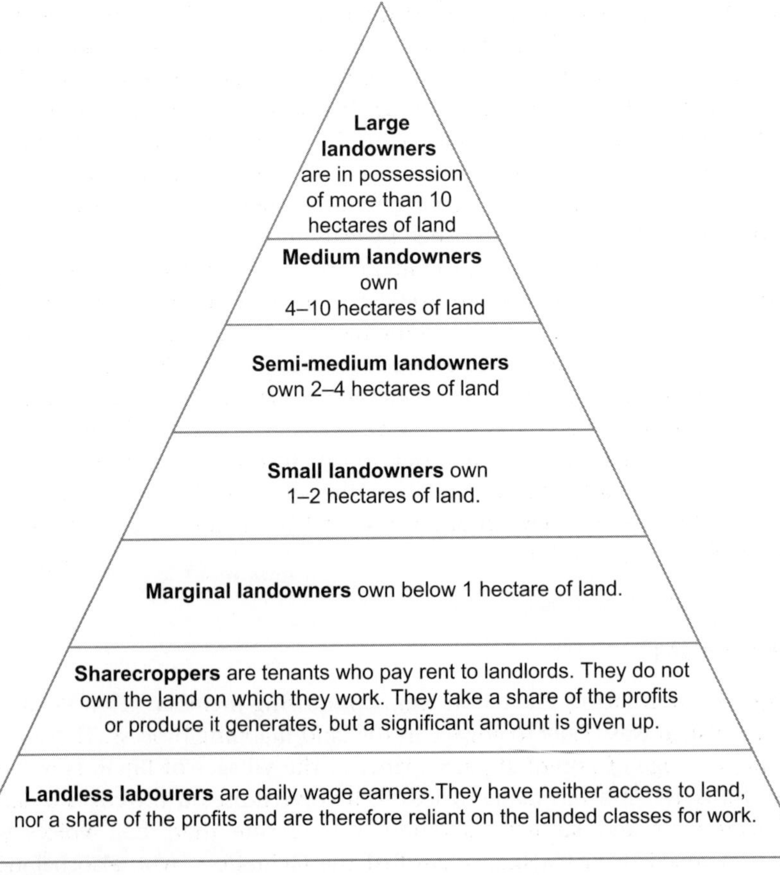

Figure 2.2 Hierarchy of land use

Village teams were identified based on their familiarity with distribution of land in the village. Many were agricultural labourers; some were sharecroppers; and some were themselves landless. Training included orienting participants on the aims and methods of the mapping process, as well as on components of the data collection framework (see Figure 2.4).

Making the maps

This section attempts to represent the land-mapping process as it took place within villages. Within this representation, a key interest is in data use at the village level. Data, for our purposes, means information represented in maps and in recording sheets used to help develop maps. It locates understanding about land in three different zones: individual, shared and public. It locates data within three partly distinguishable but overlapping zones and tracks the movement of data about land from an individualized zone to a shared zone, where it is made known to the mapping team.

At this stage some of the knowledge that individuals possessed about land was yet to be shared with other members of the cartography team. As indicated in Figure 2.3, this knowledge began to be shared as individual members of the team pooled information about the local area into maps. Each and every plot of land in the village was drawn – either on the ground, using chalk, or on large sheets of paper, using pencil. Each plot was assigned a unique reference number. The team then recorded a range of information related to each piece of land on a recording sheet: the reference number for the plot; the name of the person currently in control or possession of the plot; their father's name; their caste, whether the land was irrigated or un-irrigated (to ascertain the quality of the land); the name of the legal owner; whether the land has been subject to disputes; type of land (according to its legal status); duration of control over the plot; the basis of control or possession of the plot; the size of the plot; the plot number as per official records, and any other remarks.

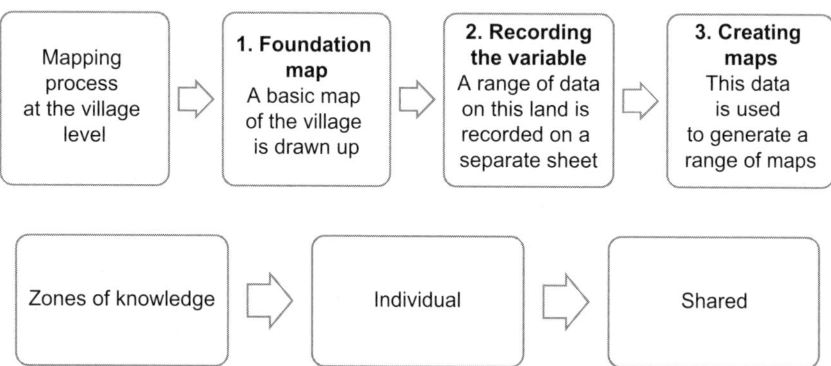

Figure 2.3 Land mapping: from individual knowledge to shared knowledge

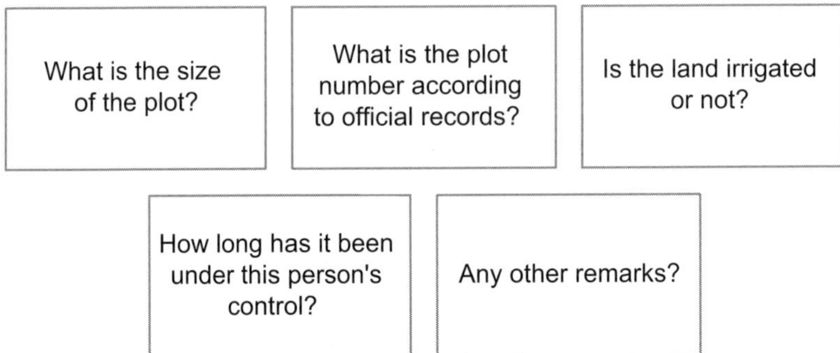

Figure 2.4 Scaffolding critical thinking about land

Filling the recording sheet out supported villagers' thinking about land-related issues in the village as they considered the broad range of variables connected to a certain piece of land, The process enabled the development of a multi-layered understanding of land, incorporating, for example, the ability to make distinctions between who owns it and who controls it and – probing further – to consider the basis of this control. Questions such as 'Who controls the land?' and 'What is the basis of this control?' not only call for some analytical thinking but are also potentially subversive, as they invite participants to pay attention to any injustices in the way in which control over land has been secured and consolidated within their community. When the participants are themselves – as in this case – largely landless and land insecure, the value of land mapping as an exercise in developing a critical consciousness becomes increasingly apparent, as inequity in control over land is brought into focus.

The initial process, which mentioned the area of homestead land for each household, had ensured that no household was omitted from the land-mapping exercise. Using data on the recording sheet, it was then possible to generate a number of different maps about each village. The land mapping brought to the fore some significant information, encouraging some sensitive and critical conversations about land occupancy and ownership. One area that came up for discussion was *benaami* holdings.[3] These typically relate to instances where an owner would register land under fictitious names to circumvent their seizure of land beyond the ceiling stipulated by law. The process also brought up conflicts on account of incomplete execution of the process of government land allotment, and stories of longstanding injustice. In one village in Gaya district, an outsider was issued a revenue receipt for a plot of 1 acre and 11.5 decimals for a plot that had been under the control of a local family for more than 100 years. Despite 10 applications being filed in the local circle office (an administrative office within a geographical jurisdiction that facilitates land registration) to attempt to settle the resulting dispute, and costs paid to service land measurement, no remedial steps had been taken at the time of the land-mapping exercise.

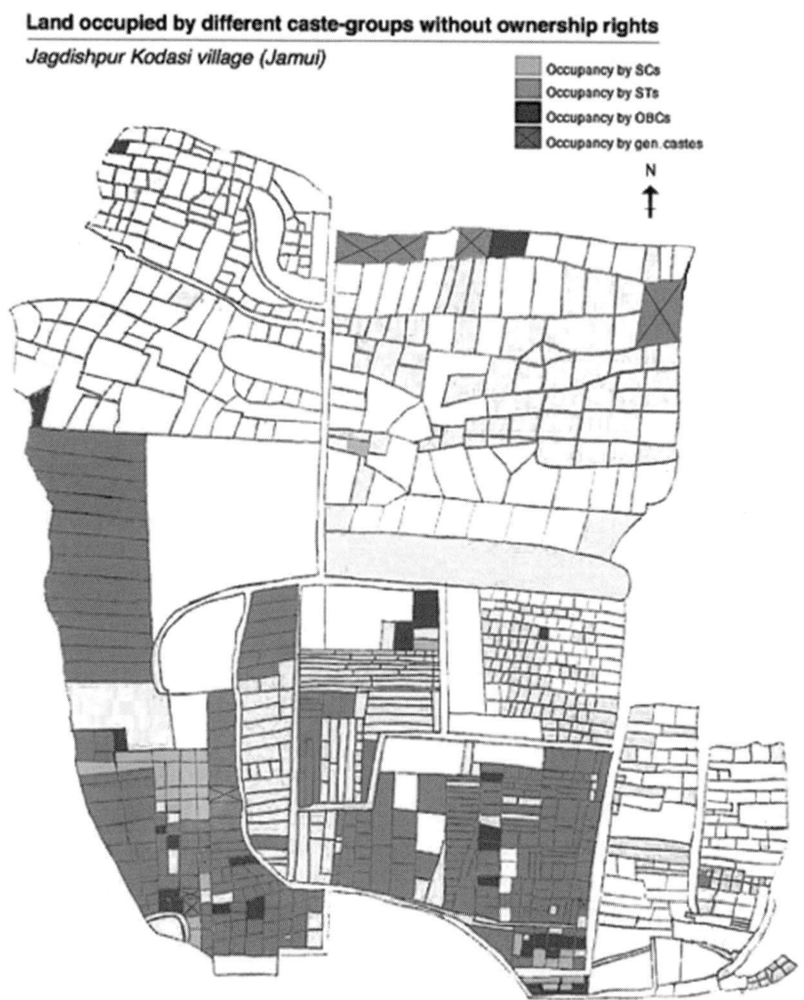

Figure 2.5 Example of a map showing unauthorized encroachments

In the same village, a large landowner was able to obtain a document legitimizing his right to a four-decimal plot on land being tended to by the family of Munshi Thakur for more than two centuries. Munshi Thakur has unsuccessfully been trying to get this landowner's document cancelled for almost 20 years, but to no avail. The local Gram Panchayat (village council) even came together to discuss the issue, but this did not help. Multiple other stories emerged of families who had lived on plots of land for many years without being able to register it in their names (cf. Praxis and Ekta Parishad, 2009: 19-21).

Figure 2.5 focuses on differences in the extent of unauthorized encroachments according to caste. It shows that in Kodali village of Jamui

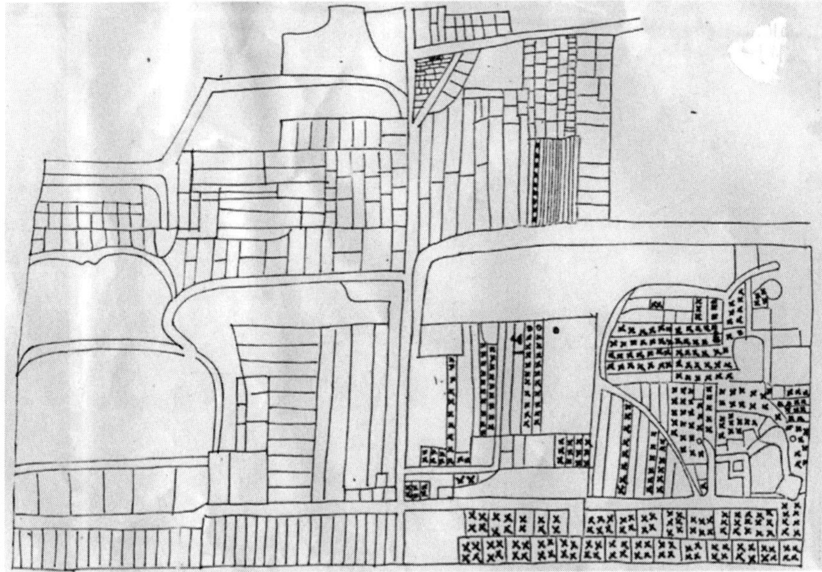

Figure 2.6 Example of a map showing one individual's unauthorized occupancy of land

district, most unauthorized encroachments were by other backward classes (OBCs) and other castes (excluding scheduled castes and scheduled tribes). Scheduled castes, the least land secure community, encroach considerably less than, for example, OBCs.

Figure 2.6 illustrates the relative scale of one individual's land occupancy in a particular village in Jamui district. It is indicative both of the power of certain privileged individuals within the iniquitous context of Bihar, and of the way this power is often predicated on assertion rather than any substantive legal foothold.

In this process of applying community data about a village to a map, individual knowledge about the village also entered a shared domain, to which the village mapping team, as well as the research teams from Praxis and Ekta Parishad, had access. Many were of course very intimate with the injustices they had experienced, and working with others through issues of ownership, control and other questions helped to bring close attention to the details of these issues as they affected others. But discussing these issues amongst land-poor villagers and invested NGO teams is quite a different matter from raising them amongst those who might have been implicated by the mapping process itself. It was when the maps were brought to a public location within the village that the subversive potential of the exercise was at its height (see Figure 2.7).

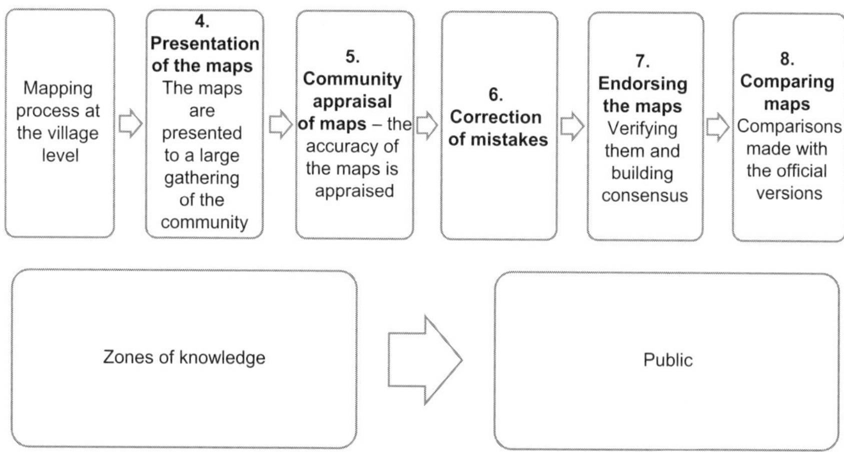

Figure 2.7 Land mapping: from shared knowledge to public knowledge

As the maps became the concern not just of the dedicated village team but of the community at large, they became objects of scrutiny, discussion, and verification. They included the landowners – especially the medium-to-large landowners – who, until now, had not participated in the land-mapping process. Moving the maps into a public space brought them into the domain of these more powerful interests within the community who may have had a vested interest in curtailing their use.

Here, members of the wider community – typically around 50 adult villagers – were called upon to understand data the maps yielded and also, significantly, to appraise it, checking their understanding of reality against that conveyed through the maps. Where appropriate, corrections were made to the maps. The final endorsement of the maps was thus made contingent on collective approval of their accuracy: villagers attending the meeting fingerprinted their assent to the maps presented before them. The records generated through this exercise were then compared with government records. In some cases these up-to-date, locally generated maps recorded information not available on existing government maps, such as the latest occupants or users. The contours of the newly developed village maps were drawn, along with the contours of the 'official' government maps, on a separate sheet of paper.

Power mapping: glimpses of justice for land-poor people

The villagers used the maps in various ways. In a number of villages, they have been a tool for lobbying for the distribution of unused public lands. In villages such as Mircha Kodasi in Jamui district, the maps gave credence to campaigns against the illegal occupancy of land above stipulated ceilings. In Bagaha block in West Champaran and other locations, the mapping exercise facilitated the identification of households without homestead land. These

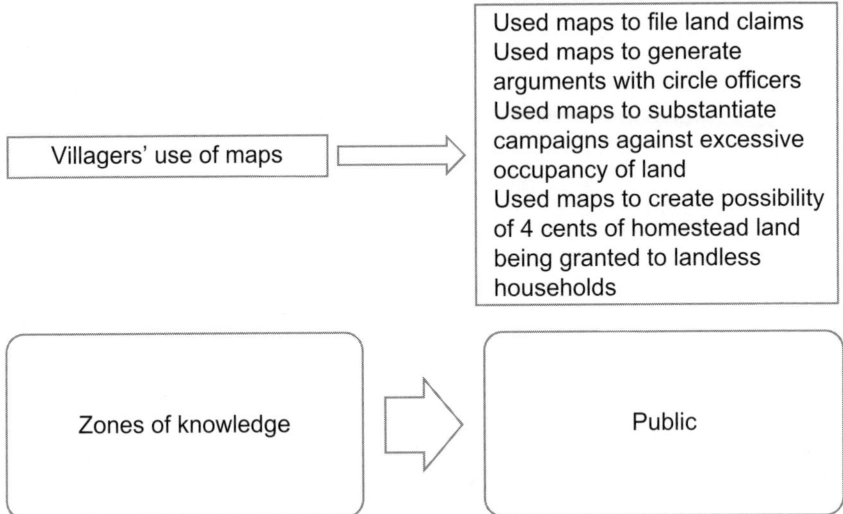

Figure 2.8 Maps as a lobbying tool

households were eligible to be granted 4 cents (approximately 162 square metres) of homestead, as per the state government's policy. There were also reports of villagers using land maps to file claims and buttress their arguments for land with circle officers. In several instances the land maps helped villages identify and wrest control over available government land.

Box 2.3, Case 1: landless families in Khanpura stake their claim

In Khanpura village of Paliganj block of Patna, the land-mapping process helped in identifying 57 acres of government land eligible for redistribution. 51 acres of this land were acquired by 150 families, and 30 of these families also managed to secure formal possession with the issuance of a *parcha* (paper) that established the name of the owner of land in revenue records.

The process helped families like those of Bhola Manjhi and Shobhana Bacharwa identify land donated under *Bhoodan* but not subsequently distributed. Of late, 120 families have staked a claim over *gair majarua* (unallocated government land) in the village, identified from the land-mapping exercise. The local circle office has already initiated a formal assessment of their claims.

The collaborative nature of the data generation process meant that it built knowledge that could serve as a platform for collective learning, reflection and action. The process cultivated a core team of village mappers, who were what what Paulo Freire describes as 'conscientized' about land issues and able to share their knowledge with others. Culminating in public endorsement of the maps in a community setting, it activated social exchanges around questions of land justice. The land mapping exercises also enabled the building of a cadre of skilled facilitators.

Box 2.4, Case 2: encroachment exposed, justice enabled

In Mircha Kodasi village of Sikandra block in Jamui district, Rupan Koda, son of Kesar Koda, was able to wrest control over 6 acres and 62 decimals of land (around 6.6 acres) belonging to his ancestors. The land had been misappropriated by a village landlord, but the land-mapping process brought clarity regarding the particulars of encroachment of land in the village. In a similar way, the maps enabled Thiru Koda, a man from the same village, to stake a claim over 5 acres and 68 decimals of land (around 5.7 acres) that an influential village landlord had encroached upon. While the claims are currently in progress, both Rupan and Thiru are in control of the land.

By developing accessible information on who owns land, and who has control over it, government records about land – to which only the state and landowners previously had access – were brought into the community domain. For example, villagers identified areas of government land that could be made available for distribution to landless households and also helped to identify homeless households. This provided a platform to press for the right to homestead land. Villagers also identified those who, for a considerable period of time, had occupied land under dispute. These occupiers were now entitled to argue for formal ownership of this land.

In this process, community members retained possession of the original maps created on pieces of cloth or large sheets of paper, and often used them in their drives for land justice. Praxis digitized them and developed A4 versions that were then returned to the community.

The land-mapping process increased the bargaining power of land-poor communities in a range of ways. The villagers developed resources with which to critically analyse their situation in relation to land and then

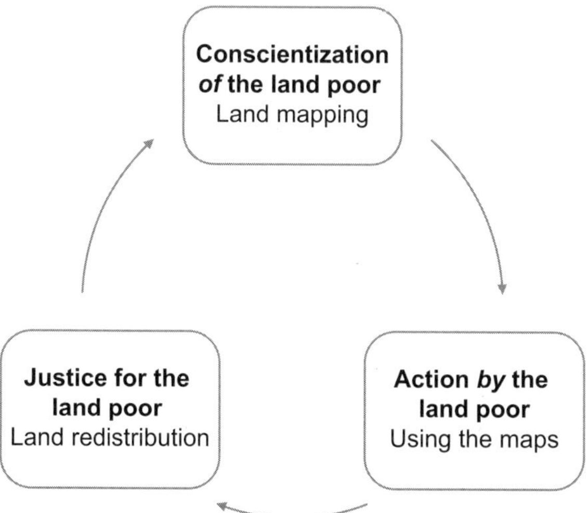

Figure 2.9 Towards empowerment: the land mapping and redistribution cycle

do something constructive about it. There were concrete achievements: examples where villagers successfully secured land rights in their favour following a land-mapping process and with use of land maps. Where land mapping did not lead directly to successful claims for land, it opened up avenues through which these claims could be pursued. It left behind land maps with disaggregated data for every local plot, indexed in terms of ownership, control, nature of disputes, type of land, etc. These maps were left with community-based organizations to use in their own campaigns and advocacy activities.

Locating challenges and limitations

Evidently, the marginalization of a sizeable section of the population became entrenched in the contexts of corruption, indifference and the presence of an inefficient administration and insensitive bureaucracy. It is notable that the representation of socially marginalized sections of society has been extremely limited among government officials, which come in the way of a concerted movement towards land justice. Across the state, larger landowners are disproportionately represented in positions of power – and not just in politics. It is essential to implement strict punitive actions against people encroaching upon land in an illegal manner, barring those belonging to the deprived and eligible sections (e.g. landless people from socially disadvantaged categories of society), but this has not transpired into reality. There appears to be a lack of political will among the political and administrative class to enable land justice on a significant scale.

On the ground, some of the more immediate operational challenges included trying to avoid possible backlashes from local land sharks. With the process anticipated to expose all cases of excessive and illegal land holdings, this was not a risk to be taken lightly. The risks were mitigated by developing strong links with local community-based organizations, which meant that village mapping teams were not acting in isolation but, rather, in concert with the broad-based critical mass of deprived people struggling together for their rights. In fact, even the larger landholders had an interest in making a claim on holdings under their control – even if illegal holdings – to prevent any rival claims on the same land.

Contextual challenges did not just affect the scale of impact, but also shaped the initial intentions behind the process. Given the sluggishness of the state bureaucracy, an exercise like land mapping would require an enormous push from 'above' to catalyse and quicken resolution of issues related to provision of land, ensuring possession and grievance redressal for all just claimants. Nor, indeed, could the ground level process be undertaken on sufficient scale to impact the vast millions of people in Bihar who remain on the fringes of land. With these constraints, a more modest strategy was in order, focusing on demonstration of the potency of land mapping as an exercise.

Contesting norms of knowledge and practice

Many of the official land records in Bihar are out of date, some by up to 40 years. One contribution of this process was to expose the inadequacies in existing records. In doing so, the process helped to show that popularly generated knowledge could be more accurate, and more relevant, than official knowledge.

Mapping also enabled recognition of those people in a community who owned more land than is permissible under the amended version of the Bihar Land Reforms (Ceiling, Land Allocation and Surplus Land Acquisition) Act 1961. Verification and endorsement of the maps at the community level brought this kind of information into sharp relief.

The land-mapping process also created 'unusual' data that challenged conventional knowledge paradigms – data, for example, on who controls land rather than simply who owns it – which has explosive political potential because conventional mapping systems either happen to not look at it or have a vested interest in not looking at it.

Delving into the use of land meant exposing those using land that they did not own. Revealing the extent to which larger landowners occupy the land of the land-poor, the exercise helped to rewrite the debate on encroachment, eliciting new answers to questions such as 'Who are the encroachers?' and 'Who are the parasites on public and state resources?' In the context of Bihar, scarred by a recent history of conflict and violence over land, these are loaded questions.

Established practices of map-making were also challenged. Here, it was not elites, but landless and marginalized people who created knowledge and then used it for their own ends. In doing so, the village mappers also invoked an alternative paradigm as to what counts as being worthy of being mapped. In the making and sharing of these maps, the social group of the person in control or possession of the land, together with questions such as the basis of control, and whether the land is disputed (see Figure 2.4), suddenly became relevant. The message was clear: ordinary people need not rely on elite or conventional versions of reality, but can help to create their own.

Whilst this chapter has focused on the community-level mapping process and use of the data, other outputs were delivered through a parallel process of consolidation of community-level data. Ekta Parishad documented and disseminated the findings. The maps emergent at the village level also helped to expose some of the limitations of the *Bhoodan* movement and, in so doing, implicate some of the more powerful, landed members of the community. As village-level data was collated centrally and analysed by Praxis, the extent of this failure became increasingly apparent. The process also uncovered uncomfortable truths about weaknesses in the legal system: the lack of mechanisms to secure speedy resolution of land disputes had put families' livelihoods in serious jeopardy.

The disaggregation of data on ownership according to social group and gender contributed to a level of detail missing from official government records (cf., for example, Agricultural Survey, 2011). The lenses provided by the land-mapping process also showed how land poverty intersected with social exclusion. It was found, for example, that many landless families from dalit and tribal communities have been unable to make use of land that was allotted to them by the state government because of an inability to establish control over holdings (cf. Praxis and Ekta Parishad, 2009: 24).

Disaggregated data thus contributed to an understanding of land inequity as part of a larger narrative of social exclusion. This, in turn, called into serious question the legitimacy of existing patterns of land ownership and use, and encroachment on to the land of the land-poor by those relatively better off reared its ugly head. The average size of unauthorized possession for different social groups illuminates this problem: 0.46 acres for scheduled castes, compared with 2.04 acres for general castes (cf. ibid: 17). The key difference here is their starting point: the more privileged typically own considerably more land.

The data also provided evidence on women's contribution to farming, a factor that is typically underplayed, as well as abiding disparities in land ownership between women and men. Women made up just 1.85% of all the landholders covered under the land-mapping study (Praxis and Ekta Parishad, 2009: 27). The study provided a resource for advocating that the government should take a proactive approach towards allocation of land in the names of women.

The claims did not simply go unheard. At a state-level event in Bihar's capital Patna on 5 February 2010, attended by senior functionaries within the Bihar government, it was promised that henceforth land ownership would be in the name of women or jointly with women. The process of establishing mechanisms to support land justice was also accelerated. Initially proposed in 2009, the twin legislations – Bihar Land Tribunal Act and Bihar Land Disputes Resolution Act – sought to reduce the caseload of courts in Bihar and transfer them to specially set up land tribunals, with the intention of resolving disputes more rapidly. The Acts were finalized, with several amendments, in 2013.

Conclusions

The impulse to bring to light micro-level issues and possibilities relating to land distribution was borne of a desire to make those villages in Bihar more just: economically, recognizing the economic value of land; socially, recognizing the social status attached to land ownership; and politically, recognizing the political power of land. The efforts created resources – human and cartographical – and momentum that could be channelled to secure land for the landless in challenging and sometimes volatile contexts.

The land-mapping process showed how a participatory grassroots initiative can generate powerful statistics on a vital political issue, and open up new avenues of analysis. At the release event for that study, the Bihar Minister for Revenue and Land Reforms promised to take forward one of its recommendations that land titles should be in the name of women. This kind of promise gave the community members hope and confidence that their work could contribute to larger policy change.

Generating robust data on all of these areas created considerable potential for advocacy and campaigns in favour of the poor and landless. With the policy commitments the Government of Bihar made following the release of the study at the event in Patna in 2010, the process may have also made a contribution to change at that level.

The land-mapping exercise democratized information and analytical thinking about land. It enabled disaggregated data to be collected, adding insight, for example, into gender-based disparities in rights over land. It also accorded lenses to analysis of land within academic, political and, to some extent, wider public discourse, and generated a valuable resource for policy advocacy in the direction of land justice. Highlighting the contestability of existing arrangements, it placed knowledge about land and tools of critical analysis in the hands of land-poor people, enabling them to raise questions about land and assert their right to it. In doing so, it left a legacy of critical consciousness around land issues, opening up pathways towards self-mobilization for land justice.

About the authors

Anindo Banerjee, Praxis. Anindo has over a decade's experience in international social development, particularly in conducting participatory assessments, policy analysis and capacity-building processes.

Rohan Preece, Praxis. Rohan has worked with development sector organizations in different parts of the world and has experience in social research, teaching and monitoring and evaluation.

Anusha Chandrasekharan, Praxis. Anusha has a background in journalism, later moving to communications work in the development sector.

Endnotes

1. This chapter is based largely on *Landlessness and Social Justice: An assessment of disparities in land distribution and prospects of land reforms* (Banerjee, 2009), a book that detailed the land-mapping process that was facilitated in five districts in Bihar, India. This was a joint initiative of Ekta Parishad and Praxis. A list of participants and contributors is in Annex 1.
2. For example, in a survey conducted in 1999–2000, the data for which we believe is unlikely to have since undergone significant change, 94% of scheduled castes across the four districts of Nawada, Jamui, Gaya and West Champaran were marginal landholders (owning less than 1 hectare of land), compared with 60.5% of other caste communities (also known as general castes – in other words, those who are not from scheduled tribes, scheduled castes, other backward castes, or minorities (Muslim in this context)); 82.5% of scheduled castes were virtually landless (owning less

than 0.4 hectares of land), compared with 49.5% of communities from other castes; and 53% of scheduled castes were facing near total landlessness (owning less than 0.1 hectare of land), compared with 30.5% of other castes. (NSSO, 1999–2000 in Banerjee, 2009).

3. The word *benaami* is used to define a transaction in which the person in whose name a property is purchased is a mask of the real beneficiary. In these cases, the question of who provides the finance does not affect the *benaami* status.

References

Asian Development Research Institute (2008), Monograph 2, Current Agrarian Situation in Bihar (Submitted to the Bihar Land Reforms Commission).

Banerjee, A. (2009) *Landlessness and Social Justice*, Delhi: Praxis – Institute for Participatory Practices and Ekta Parishad.

Banerjee, A. (2010), 'Participatory Land Mapping for Social Equity' in *Deepening Participation for Social Change, Case Studies from Africa and Asia*, International Institute for Environment and Development <http://pubs.iied.org/G02726.html> [Accessed January 2015]).

Census of India 2011 <www.censusindia.gov.in/2011census/censusinfodashboard/index.html> [Accessed 1 June 2014].

Dreze, J., and Sen, A. (2013) *An Uncertain Glory: India and its Contradictions*, London: Penguin – Allen Lane.

Ducker, C. (2005) 'Faith with Deeds: The Priority of Praxis in Liberation Theology' <http://www.theduckers.org/media/the%20priority%20of%20praxis%20in%20liberation%20theology.pdf> [Accessed on 10 July 2014].

Human Rights Watch (1999) 'The Pattern of Abuse: Rural Violence in Bihar and the State's Response' <www.hrw.org/reports/1999/india/India994-06.htm> [Accessed 5 June 2014].

Jha, D.K. (2013) 'The Great Betrayal of Bihar's Landless,' *Open Magazine*, 28 December 2013, <www.openthemagazine.com/article/nation/the-great-betrayal-of-bihar-s-landless> [Accessed on 5 June 2014].

Kabeer, N. (1999) 'Resources, Agency, Achievements: Reflections on the Measurement of Women's Empowerment', *Development and Change* Vol. 30.

Mainstream (2009), 'Bihar: Implement Bandyopadhyay Commission's Recommendations for Land Reforms', Mainstream 48 <http://www.mainstreamweekly.net/article1547.html> [Accessed on 6 June 2014].

Ministry of Agriculture, Government of India (2011), Agriculture Census 2010–11, <http://agcensus.nic.in/document/agcensus2010/agcen2010rep.htm> [Accessed 5 June 2014].

Planning Commission, Government of India (1966) 'Implementation of Land Reforms: A Review by the Land Reforms Implementation Committee of the National Development Council', New Delhi: Government of India <http://planningcommission.nic.in/reports/publications/pub1966land.pdf> [Accessed 6 June 2014].

Kamat, S. (2007) 'Walking the Tightrope: Equality and Growth in a Liberalising India', in Green et al. (2007), *Education and Development in a Global Era: Strategies for Successful Globalisation*, Department for International Development: Educational Papers.

Kennedy, J. and King, L. (2014) 'The political economy of farmers' suicides in India: indebted cash-crop farmers with marginal landholdings explain state-level variation in suicide rates', *Globalization and Health* 10:16 <www.globalizationandhealth.com/content/10/1/16> [Accessed 4 June 2014].

Ledwith, M. (2005) *Community Development,* Portland: Policy Press.

Misri, B.K., Country Pasture/Forage Resource Profiles – India, Food and Agriculture Organization of the United Nations, Romeat: <www.fao.org/ag/agp/AGPC/doc/Counprof/India/India.htm> [Accessed 5 June 2014].

Planning Commission, Government of India (2013), Press Notes on Poverty Estimates, 2011–12, <http://planningcommission.nic.in/news/pre_pov2307.pdf> [Accessed 6 June 2014].

Annex 1: List of contributors

Ekta Parishad: Manju Dungdung, Pradeep Priyadarshi, Ajai Choudhuri, Kapileshwar

Praxis: Jay Kumar Verma, Roma Dey, Anindo Banerjee

With significant support from: Ajai Manjhi, Varsha Jawalgekar, Sanjay Kumar Pradad, Mary Pinakattu, Mohd. Ali Anwar, Manjusha ET, Mukta Ohja, Rajendra Ram, and Ranjit Kumar Jha.

CHAPTER 3

Building consensus methodically: community rebuilding in the Maldives

M. J. Joseph, Ravikant Kisana, and Mary George

Abstract

In the year 2004, the island nation of the Maldives was devastated by a massive tsunami that caused destruction across the Indian Ocean region. Only nine islands of the Maldives escaped flooding, while more than 50 incurred massive destruction, 13 had to be completely evacuated and 6 were entirely destroyed. Vilufushi, also known as Thaa Atol, was one of the islands that had to be evacuated. Land reclamation undertaken as part of the subsequent recovery programme almost tripled the size of the island, creating an opportunity to provide additional housing to the island community. Instead of following a standard, top-down approach to identifying beneficiaries, it was decided to empower the island community itself to collectively take the decision. This chapter follows the facilitation process and seeks to document how community voices were brought together in a participatory manner. The results challenge the conventional narrative that in a post-disaster context, affected communities are too fragmented by conflicts of interest to be able to find common agreement.

Keywords: tsunami, Maldives, relief and rehabilitation, planning, beneficiary identification, mapping

Context

In December 2004, the island nation of the Maldives was struck by a massive tsunami that caused untold destruction to coastlines along Southeast Asia, India, Sri Lanka and as far afield as the east coast of Africa. The damage to the Maldives, comprising nearly 1,200 islands (190 of which are inhabited), was particularly severe. The Maldives is the world's lowest lying nation: the average height is a mere 1.5 metres above sea level. Only nine islands escaped flooding, with more than 50 incurring massive destruction, 13 having to be completely evacuated and six completely destroyed.

The Government of Maldives (GoM) immediately began the tough task of reconstruction. With prominent international agencies stepping in to provide aid and expertise, the GoM embarked on its recovery process. One initiative undertaken as part of this process was the British Red Cross Society (BRCS)'s three-year Maldives Recovery Programme (MRP), which was launched

http://dx.doi.org/10.3362/9781780448695.003

in partnership with the GoM in May 2005. The programme worked in six Maldivian islands, aiding the recovery process by building houses on the plots where they originally stood. The GoM's general reconstruction policy involved providing 'a house for a house', however, Vilufushi presented some unique challenges.

Vilufushi was one of the 13 islands that had to be completely evacuated. The subsequent recovery of Vilufushi via land reclamation in the aftermath of the tsunami almost tripled the size of the island. Previously, Vilufushi had 230 registered plots of land. However, the island was relatively densely populated and the government decided that during the reconstruction, 250 new houses would need to be developed. In this context of 'building back better' and contributing to rebuilding a community on the island, BRCS invited Praxis, a non-governmental organization specializing in participatory methods and approaches, to initiate a participatory beneficiary identification process to identify 250 internally displaced persons (IDPs) who would be entitled to receive a house. BRCS planned to initiate a participatory process to identify with the IDPs who would receive a house as part of the BRCS recovery programme based on transparent, agreed criteria for prioritizing households. The key challenge was to strike a balance between the BRCS criteria, the GoM's 'house for a house' policy, and community needs and aspirations.

'Normal' practice in the case of disaster relief

When natural disasters occur, rebuilding and reconstruction represent an enormous challenge for agencies responsible. Given the dynamic nature of the situation on the ground and the urgent need for action, there is typically very little time available for methodical planning and organized implementation. Several variables must be taken into account because every disaster, natural or man-made, presents a unique scenario. The planning agency may draw a parallel from a different experience in the past, but it cannot replicate the same model because the context is always different.

Disaster relief has typically developed structures that are top-down in orientation. This is often because a relief effort responds to an emergency situation in which the need to ensure a speedy response, that can be managed effectively by donor agencies and governments, dominates the agenda. In such cases, community participation may be deemed desirable but unfeasible, with government and relief organizations in the fray instead building and providing an apparatus in which the community is a passive recipient of relief. In these circumstances, the community rarely has a say in determining the scope and extent of the kind of relief extended to them. Furthermore, the process of allocation is hardly ever based on a community consensus, but is instead usually engineered from an externally formulated logic and protocol.

In these contexts, the locus of decision-making remains distanced from members of the affected community. The widely held view among international organizations is that an affected community, reeling under the effects of a disaster, is in no position to pool and mobilize the resources to lobby for the relief they need. Indeed, the effect of a disaster often causes a breakdown in the community's command and outreach ability (Petrucci, 2012). Yet external players tend to identify a breakdown in certain community systems as justification for a *wholesale* neglect of community voices during moments of critical decision-making.

Authorities outside the affected community itself – from government to NGOs at varying distances from the community – often make most critical decisions at such times. This is because disasters are often viewed as one-off events needing external 'experts', who are presumed to have greater expertise – sometimes because they have experience dealing with previous disasters in other contexts. However, many external agencies also arrive at a disaster ignorant of the affected community's specific cultural and social mix, but are nevertheless given responsibility for determining the shape of their rehabilitation. Perhaps to compensate for this ignorance of ground realities, external agencies bring their own ideological biases into determining the best courses of action. The resulting approaches often exclude the demands and needs of the affected community, whose perspectives consequently remain unheard and unregistered. Community members therefore remain outside the scope of the official decision-making apparatus.

Some scholars have critiqued the dominant top-down disaster relief model as ineffective (Hossain, 2013: 161). Despite good intentions, relief work in many disaster contexts frequently fails to benefit the community as much as it should have (cf. Chapter 5 in this volume, 'A New Deluge?'). Indeed, in some cases, it actually does more harm than good. Existing approaches to disaster relief have failed to acknowledge or address this problem.

When the locus of decision-making is removed from the community, external agencies cannot depend on being guided by community voices and concerns. Instead of working according to the basis of the needs and priorities of the affected community, agencies rely on official data and other sources such as local political and institutional bureaucratic wisdom. There are many limitations to such an approach. Official data often contains considerable invisible spaces, and so will not necessarily be representative of the entire community in all its diversity. For instance, the most vulnerable and marginalized members of a community are not always represented specifically, and are instead merged into the larger data set. This creates a more homogenous picture in which diversity and difference are often lost in aggregation. Yet diversity and difference matter. For instance, the data might be silent about the particular conditions of the most marginalized groups most likely to be negatively affected by a disaster and typically least equipped to rebuild. Any decisions based on such databases are therefore more likely to further exclude such groups' concerns from the decision-making variables.

Furthermore, over-reliance on official data records and narratives means that external agencies' relief efforts often perpetuate the social status quo seen before the disaster. In addition, the absence of grassroots community perspectives from decision-making processes, and their limited influence over the design of the relief apparatus, may aggravate inequality. The most powerful disaster survivors are likely to have interests more closely aligned with those in positions of authority, meaning that they are often able to ensure that relief and rehabilitation processes prioritize their needs.

One of the fundamental ways in which this can occur is through the very basic logic of relief itself. If the external agency's idea of intervention is to rebuild the community as it was, then it follows logically that it wants to rebuild existing social inequalities. As mentioned above, disasters' impact is rarely felt equally across different communities: socially excluded groups tend to experience a heavier burden of the disaster than more privileged communities because they are affected by the collapse of even the most basic safeguards of their everyday existence. Even in the event that relief work aims to build the community back better, the way in which this is done can raise its own problems. For example, external agencies often attempt to treat all claims equally, in an attempt to ensure that no claimant is left behind or marginalized. However, in an inequitable social structure some people are able to shout louder than others. This creates a particular problem in the context of relief mobilization. When all claims are treated equally without taking into account existing power structures, external authorities can unwittingly deepen inequalities.

The manner in which claims are handled creates similar problems. To maintain a sense of bureaucratic neutrality, external authorities often attempt to introduce systems that do not seem to further social inequalities. The idea here is to promote equity so that the most vulnerable among the affected will receive as much relief as possible. However, despite good intentions, the reality may be different. As explained, the 'neutrality' of the relief distribution mechanism and the relief apparatus is typically built on data sourced from official records and narratives. This source itself is not necessarily a neutral or inclusive foundation for such an endeavour. Furthermore, the grievance redressal system put in place may not be inclusive or equally accessible to all members of the community. It may be cumbersome and prohibitive. There is a risk that more powerful voices – on whose narratives official records are likely to be based – have better access to the grievance redressal system. Ultimately, groups with more agency within the pre-disaster system, as mentioned previously, are likely to be more easily able to access post-disaster support systems because of the generally higher quality of their dwellings, livelihood, overall health and social capital (DANIDA, 2000). On a related point, wealthier individuals are likely to be able to rebuild faster in the event of a disaster, as they might have better access to certain means of coping and will also be more likely to have more agency within the geographical community affected (Wisner et al., 2003: 92–93). Disaster relief can therefore often contribute to the mobilization of bias (Gaventa and Cornwall, 2001), at the expense of the mobilization of justice.

In the context of Vilufushi, this standard approach towards disaster relief created a situation in which several deserving households could have been excluded from the rebuilding process. There would obviously be a conflict of interest within the community. As mentioned earlier, the process of reclaiming Vilufushi added more land to the existing island. The more powerful voices could sideline the more marginalized ones and appropriate the new land made available. The participatory process sought to address such concerns and place the mantle of decision-making on the community itself.

Engaging the community

The aim of the engagement was to design and facilitate a participatory process that would generate a list of beneficiaries of the reconstruction programme on Vilufushi. Post-process, it was envisaged that the MRP team would be well positioned to initiate its construction programme based on a clear beneficiary list agreed upon by both the community and the GoM. This would help BRCS to work with known and consenting families on the design of houses to be constructed. The initial identification of beneficiaries would lead to further participatory consultation on house design and on sanitation requirements.

Keeping these challenges in mind, the following steps were conceptualized to engage the community:

a) Setting up a representative community decision-making unit that would work with the leadership but be accountable to everyone.
b) Setting up a time-bound process to take the community through a series of steps, starting with beneficiary identification but also addressing other areas requiring participation, such as plot allocation on a new land use plan and the design process.
c) Setting up a system of roles and responsibilities between the community and the committee so that there was a clear mutual understanding of decision-making authority and suitable checks and balances in place.
d) Setting up a system of documenting decisions taken and displaying them to the community.

The Praxis team began working with the idea that beneficiary identification should be a participatory decision-making process and that this warrants a systematic approach. Decision-making would also have to take into account all the stakeholders' interests and constraints mentioned previously. In lieu of that understanding the team from Praxis saw its role in the entire process as that of a facilitator. The primary investment and leadership in the process would be the office of the PRSC (Partner Representative Steering Committee) and the community at large.

The conceptual framework above demonstrates that the creation of a database of indigenous knowledge about patterns of land use on the island by the community was at the core of the process of determining the final beneficiary list. This knowledge base would need to be verified and reviewed for

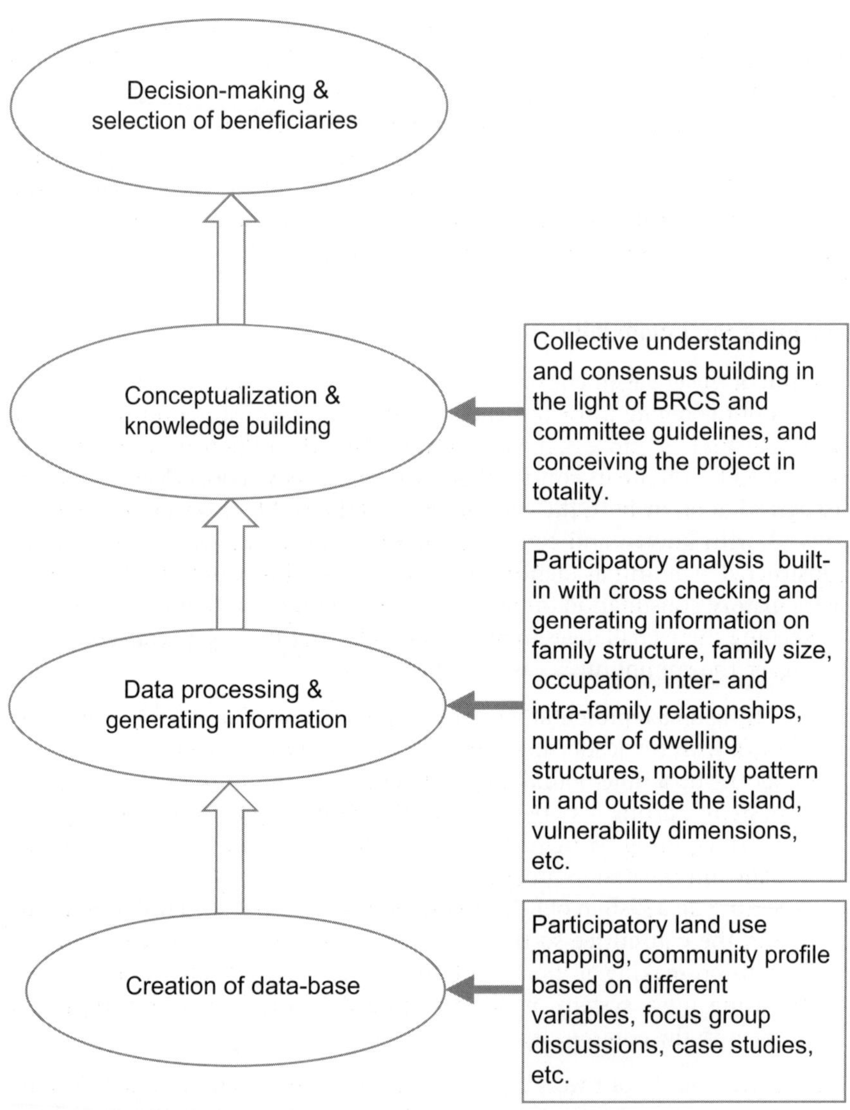

Figure 3.1 Conceptual and methodological framework of the beneficiary identification process

validation. This process would be undertaken through seeking accreditation from the community, in addition to the GoM and BRCS.

Hence it was envisaged by Praxis and BRCS that facilitating a knowledge-building process would allow informed decision-making. In the context of the beneficiary identification process it was important to generate data and create a legitimate information base. Beyond the fact of the knowledge base, the question of who makes decisions was also important. In this context, the PRSC was the primary agent taking decisions on behalf of the community, BRCS and the GoM. It was therefore important to provide members of the GoM, the BRCS and the community outside the PRSC with opportunities to review, question, scrutinize and endorse their decisions.

Beneficiary identification process

The facilitation process would have to follow a step-by-step process. Each of the new steps was identified in the light of the critical analysis carried on the results generated from the preceding steps. This laddering was done to eventually arrive at the beneficiary list for the reconstruction programme on Vilufushi.

This step-by-step laddering process is summarized in the following diagram:

Figure 3.2 Steps undertaken for the beneficiary identification process

To begin with, the process was initiated by the election of a 16-person team that would make up the PRSC from among members of the community and they were given an orientation by the Praxis team. The PRSC then made a map of the pre-tsunami land usage in Vilufushi, based on an older map from the Island office. The completed map, 14 feet by 8 feet, was put up in a hall for community members to review and verify.

After the community verified the land usage map, the task of creating a comprehensive database about the profiles of families was undertaken by Praxis. These profiles pertained to land usage already registered on the community map.

The community was issued cards, two per family, one each for the pre-tsunami and post-tsunami expected situation. These cards were meant to record information pertaining to land usage such as the number of people living on the land and land ownership details. Praxis attempted to reach out to all the members of the community and make this process as inclusive as possible. The cards were then placed on the social map corresponding to each plot.

Following this data processing was also undertaken in a participatory manner. Analysis was carried out on family structure, family size, occupation, inter- and intra-family relationships, types of houses, mobility patterns in and outside the island, and vulnerability dimensions. Necessary modifications were made to the matrices in consultation with family members. Data cross-checking was done with the help of new community members, who were brought in as volunteers. Official documents, such as the VPA list, MIDP list, census data and Island Office's lists, were considered for reference and integrated with the experiential knowledge of the committee members and other key informants (such as island chiefs, IDC and WDC members).

Additionally, the committee identified procedures to review the collected data and deal with any inconsistencies. It also compiled a database of vulnerability amongst the community members. Following this a second round of data processing was undertaken for family 'cards' (physical cards that contained information about families, used while facilitating participatory tools) which had been set aside in the previous round for further review. Taken together, all of these presented a comprehensive pre-tsunami land status for Vilufushi.

Following this, three rounds of screening were conducted, in keeping with the RCS guideline, and a beneficiary identification list was drawn up. The list developed with the community was handed over to the GoM and BRCS with a presentation on the process and outputs. A grievance management system was set up and forms issued to the community. Community validation was sought on the outputs of the beneficiary identification process and a review of the same. The registered grievances were addressed and an attempt was made to finalize settlement of existing disputes.

Lessons from the field

The facilitating team faced the challenge of balancing between BRCS criteria, the GoM for house policy and the needs of the community. However, there were also plenty of ground-level implementation challenges.

To begin with, the GoM did not have an established housing policy. Most policy-related issues were mediated by the government agencies through very brief and topical circulars. Furthermore, even the BRCS policy on the matter was a generic one which called for simply providing a 'house for a house'. In Vilufushi, the lack of locally relevant policy proved deeply problematic.

Firstly, the government had taken an inadequate account of the actual, pre-tsunami land-use pattern of Vilufushi. Several families from the island had been living in the capital Malé because it offered better living conditions, including more promising education and livelihood prospects for their children. In their absence, they had rented out dwellings on Vilufushi to others. A simple house for a house policy could not possibly account for this complexity because there was a question of whose ownership of the house the policy and reconstruction programme would honour. Would it consider actual inhabitants who were renting the house for the new housing that would be developed, or would the absentee landlords, who actually owned the house in a pre-tsunami context, be accommodated?

This problem was further complicated by the fact that, in many cases, those renting were already Vilufushi residents who owned houses elsewhere. The GoM owned all land on the islands, and new couples could not buy or set up housing without presenting their marriage certificate to the GoM to be considered for a separate dwelling. When clearance from the GoM was delayed, families tended to live together in large groups in the same house or rent a property from another person residing on another island. Some families would rent out one room of their house to couples waiting for a marriage clearance. In many cases, the facilitating team therefore faced a challenge. They could not dismiss tenants' claims using ownership records alone because local governance, and land and cultural practices gave them as strong a claim as the actual, absentee owners of the houses.

The facilitating team also had to deal with discontent in the community along occupational lines. After the tsunami, Vilufushi's inhabitants were temporarily housed on a separate island called Buruni while land on Vilafushi was being reclaimed. The facilitating team was conducting the participatory exercise on Buruni itself. While most of Vilafushi's inhabitants supported and participated in the exercise, those who earned their livelihood from fishing were dissatisfied because they were only available to participate on weekends. Many of this group became anxious that their interests would not be well represented, particularly as the reconstruction was not limited to housing, but also focused on building other amenities like a hospital, a park, and a madrasa. The point about geographies in the context of the rehabilitated Vilufushi was particularly sensitive to fishing communities because closer proximity to the sea enabled them to take their boats out much more easily. Even the inhabitants of Vilufushi who lived on Malé were not initially happy with the process, as they felt underrepresented.

Finally, there was also an issue of understanding how representative the constituent members of the PRSC were. The island administrative machinery was co-opted into the PRSC, including the island chief and the island committee members. Only a handful of the members were elected. Even so, the facilitating team had to deal with attempts by some PRSC members to appropriate housing by falsifying information. Some instances of ethnic tension were also encountered.

On the ground realities and resolutions

The situation in Vilufushi presented a series of challenges to the facilitating team. While each was rooted in a particular social and cultural context, the solution was evolved through constant engagement with the community. The important thing to keep in mind is that problems did not originate at one specific point of time. There was no one bottleneck in the process where anomalies had been concentrated. Instead they emerged at every step of the way, with different stakeholder groups intervening with their concerns at different moments in the decision-making process.

This was where the methodological framework proved its credibility. Breaking down the task into smaller parts proved to be the key. Each small step arrived on the back of a feedback mechanism from the community on the previous step. This ensured that even though challenges emerged at every step, there were mechanisms to deal with them.

While there was no explicit housing policy, it was decided that the beneficiary identification process would honour the claim of the people actually living on the island as opposed to the people away from the island. Furthermore, undeveloped plots from the pre-tsunami scenario would not be developed in the post-tsunami context. All decisions were taken with the community's consultation.

Communities unhappy with the process were given a forum to air their concerns. The process accommodated their feedback and everyone had the nature of the process explained to them.

To overcome these discrepancies, the PRSC created a matrix that covered family profiles and the land use information for the island as part of the framework. The matrix covered the following questions:

- Information on details of the registration of the house/plot, the owner or rights-holder of the plot/house; and construction status of the houses;
- Use or purpose of the house and details of other dwelling structures;
- Details of other building structures in the plot used for non-dwelling purposes;
- Number of families residing in the house.

Along with these, a set of questions pertaining to the family members' individual profiles was covered. The idea was to match individual demographic profiles to the land-use matrix and issue all family members with two individual profile cards for the land covered under the matrix data. One card was for pre-tsunami demographic context while the other was for the post-tsunami demographic development. This was because, in some cases, family members lived outside Vilufushi before the tsunami, but might want to return to the registered land plot after the event (and vice versa). The cards were issued to the family members, after a formal signature, to ensure transparency. In this matter, all people dependent on each registered plot (whether residing in Vilufushi or not at the time of the tsunami), were accounted for.

All the family information was carefully documented and verified via the community map and analysed. Repetitions and errors were cleaned out. The PRSC also developed guidelines for handling policy disputes by synthesising the BRCS directives and information from the local community. The guidelines were shared with the community, and a vulnerability index was prepared for this purpose.

Finally, the PRSC grouped the families into different groups based on construction status (under construction or inhabited), dwelling status (rented or occupants of houses), family sizes, plot status (empty or vacant), and registration status according to RCM guidelines. The family cards were then put into these different groupings. Three rounds of screening were held and the community was involved in each stage to answer questions and provide feedback. This complex mechanism of regular feedback ensured that the framework was sufficiently flexible to incorporate the different challenges that occurred.

Empowerment through subversion of standard practice

In disaster relief, the 'normal' process of relief and reconstruction is not an inclusive process at all. Rather, it is a top-down structure in which best practices from previous experiences are extrapolated onto the current scenario in the hope that learning from one disaster context will be applicable in another. This approach is fraught with possibilities of exclusion, especially amongst those who are the most vulnerable (see Chapter 6, on the relief effort following the tsunami in Tamil Nadu).

Instead, the Praxis team decided to empower the community of Vilufushi. Rather than leaving it to government officials to identify beneficiaries, the Praxis and BRCS mobilized the community to bring about an inclusive methodology for beneficiary identification and work out a mechanism for grievance management.

The important elements of this unorthodox approach were the following.

Empowering the community to lead critical decision-making

One of the most important dynamics in the process was the PRSC's participation throughout the stages of beneficiary identification. Constituting the committee at the very beginning contributed much to this participatory process. The leadership of the 16-member team of community representatives was crucial to the creation of a social map of the island as well as the analysis of data to evaluate community members' eligibility for land and house entitlements. Under 'normal' practice, the community representatives would have little or no role in determining relief and reconstruction beneficiaries.

Their initiative and participation ensured the process had the will of the community behind it. It also meant that critical decision-making was not left in the hands of authorities removed from the community.

Participatory process to decide on beneficiaries

The process of identifying beneficiaries itself bypassed several conventions of more frequently followed practices.

Firstly, to ensure that only the most deserving benefited, the Praxis team guided PRSC to evolve a sequence of activities in a step-by-step manner. Each step was reached based on lessons from the preceding steps, meaning that it was built on actual results (experiential knowledge). This meant that the PRSC could address any mistake or decision that caused a roadblock by revisiting the last step at which things were functioning smoothly. This meant that the committee did not have to start from scratch every time it hit a roadblock.

Secondly, the participatory creation of a social database, involving the entire community, was the main pillar of the process. The focus on creating an adequate database made the beneficiary identification process more scientific and systematic.

Thirdly, community validation had to be built in with the same processes, as it was essential to the success of the programme. Information that was part of the database was given serious scrutiny through cross-checking with the community itself using transparent processes such as community hearings and the accessible public display of data. This ensured that the compiled database was truly representative of the reality on the ground.

Taking 'vulnerability' into account

Another feature of the 'normal' procedures undertaken in the context of disaster relief work is to generally consider all claims for support and rehabilitation on equal terms. While in principle this may sound correct, it ignores the pre-existing vulnerability index of the affected community. Wealthier and stronger voices in the community have better coping structures and agency in a post-disaster context, and are therefore likely to have greater influence on proceedings. By treating all claims on an equal footing, marginalized people are more likely to get excluded.

While the PRSC was working on the beneficiary identification process, it took care not to neglect the various vulnerability indices of community members. The team collected data on the entire community and identified particularly vulnerable community members and units. Some of those identified as vulnerable included: widows with a single child who remained the primary income earner; households in which the main income-earner was adversely affected by the tsunami; families with chronically sick members; families with orphans; elderly people without anybody to take care of them; widows with too many dependents; and families with a large number of members.

These were factored into the process while evaluating claims for land and housing allocation.

Development of community guidelines

The Praxis team guided the PRSC towards the formulation of clear community guidelines and development of a grievance management system. There is often a lack of clarity among affected communities in the context of disaster relief and rehabilitation about the terms and conditions of the engagements and relief available to them. However, in the case of Vilufushi, the PRSC ensured that there was clarity across the board.

The PRSC developed committee-specific procedures with clauses pertaining to the claims process, including the terms on which the beneficiary identification would be based. This was essential to inform the community of the criteria on which the PRSC was evaluating their claims. These guidelines included points such as: only the inhabitants of Vilufushi would be considered; plots given to people before the tsunami or reclaimed and legally registered but empty at the time of the tsunami would be replaced with plots and not houses; and if a house was given on loan to a caretaker or friends the people living there would be given priority over the owner.

The PRSC also ensured that it followed RCM guidelines for beneficiary selection and vulnerability. A grievance management system was created to deal with disputes and grievances that arose during the claims process to manage community members' expectations and ensure that a path of least possible conflict was agreed upon. Since claims involved land and housing allocation in a small island community, there were bound to be some disputes about claims that would not be accommodated. However, these procedural

Table 3.1 Towards transformative engagement

Normal context	'Subversive' empowerment
Officials and experts are the best decision-makers of the fate of the community. Often creates more tension in the community.	The community themselves take over the locus of decision-making, ensuring the will of people is behind the decision. More likely to be accepted.
Top-down resource allocation, relying on 'official' data sources. Assumes community is incapable of allocating resources equitably.	Participatory resource distribution, from 'community' data sources and validation. More reliable and demonstrates community's ability to allocate resources for itself.
Seeks to perpetuate 'equality' by trying to treat all claims as 'equal'. Attempt at social engineering – often leads to perpetuating the same inequalities in a reinforced fashion.	Takes vulnerability into account by not treating all claims as equal, seeking to avoid reinforcing local inequalities.
Often unaware of local strategic needs, with decision-making based on 'best practices' from a different context.	Responsive to strategic needs of the local population and in keeping with the organic community fabric.

guidelines followed and made transparent by the PRSC ensured that there was consensus around its decisions.

Responsive to strategic needs

Vilufushi is a small island with its own organic community fabric. The nature of a community's inherent social structure tends to get ignored in many decision-making processes, whose approaches towards resource allocation tend to create social rifts. By contrast, the 'subverted' process used on Vilufushi empowered the community as a whole to decide resource allocation, ensuring that the process was in keeping with the community's social fabric and avoiding turning community members against each other. The larger community was also consulted on the individuals identified in the index of vulnerability. In keeping with the agreed norms and guidelines, the allocation was responsive to the community's strategic needs and avoided socially alienating the inhabitants of the island.

Learning

Participatory decision-making is generally considered to be difficult to achieve in communities affected by disaster because the community is reeling under the effects of the disaster and is usually desperate for urgent relief measures. The priority in such cases is speedy extension of relief rather than inclusive decision-making experiments. However, the experience of allocating land resources to the inhabitants of Vilufushi demonstrated that it was possible to consider inclusive and participatory methodologies, even in the context of disaster relief and rehabilitation. It also showed that such a process of participatory and inclusive decision-making, whilst subverting much standard practice, could actually empower communities and avoid the exclusion and alienation that more frequently employed procedures can cause.

There are some general lessons that may be considered as learning for further such initiatives. These are as follows:

a) The criticality of investment of quality time for conducting such sensitive exercises cannot be underestimated. The facilitators from Praxis stayed on the island for nearly 90 days over a six-month period to support the PRSC. The continued presence of the facilitating team ensured that the community representatives were not left adrift and had guidance for every step of the process. It also ensured that the PRSC was able to handle moments of crisis or community resistance in an inclusive and consensual manner by sticking to its mandated guidelines.
b) Local community representatives' stewardship of the process was absolutely critical in dealing with sensitivities encountered during the consultations. It ensured that the spirit and will of the community was taken into account. The community representatives also brought to the table their local knowledge and experience, significantly improving the beneficiary identification process.

c) The case study proved that the community can work together within a framework of limited means in which all its demands may not be met. This goes against the standard belief that in matters of resource allocation, all community members would make claims to maximize their benefit. That was not the case in this exercise.
d) The gaps or disconnects between community aspirations and the quantum, and nature, of aid offered, need to be discussed at the highest level to contribute to a more responsive housing provision policy in similar situations.

About the authors

M J Joseph, Praxis. Joseph has over two decades of experience in social work research and practice, with a major part of the experience in development research across various themes.

Ravikant Kisana, Praxis. Ravikant had a background in advertising and the media industry before making his transition to the development sector.

Mary George, Praxis. Mary has over two decades' experience in the development sector, with a focus on gender and equity.

References

DANIDA (2000), *Who Suffers? Identifying the Vulnerable Groups*, Workshop Papers: Improving the Urban Environment and Reducing Poverty <http://web.mit.edu/urbanupgrading/urbanenvironment/issues/vulnerable-groups.html> [Accessed January 2015].

Gaventa, J. and Cornwall, A. (2001), 'Power and Knowledge', in P. Reason and H. Bradbury (eds), *Handbook of Action Research: Participative Inquiry and Practice*, pp. 70–80, London: Sage Publications.

Hossain, A. (2013) 'Community Participation in Disaster Management: Role of Social Work to Enhance Participation', *Antrocom Online Journal of Anthropology*, 9:159–168.

Petrucci, O. (2012) 'Assessment of the impact caused by natural disasters: simplified procedures and open problems', in Tiefenbacher, J. (ed.) *Managing Disasters, assessing hazards, emergencies and disaster impacts*, <http://www.intechopen.com/books/approaches-to-managing-disaster-assessing-hazards-emergencies-and-disaster-impacts/assessment-of-the-impact-caused-by-natural-disasters-simplified-procedures-and-open-problems> [last accessed 4.2.15] Open Access Publisher.

Seymour, R. (2013) 'The real story of 'looting' after a disaster like typhoon Haiyan', *The Guardian*.

Wisner, B., Blaikie, P., Cannon, T., and Davis, I. (2003) *At Risk: natural hazards, people's vulnerability and disasters*, 2nd edn, Routledge, London and New York.

CHAPTER 4

Knowledge base: towards a community-owned monitoring system

Rohan Preece, Stanley Joseph, Gayathri Sarangan and Sowmyaa Bharadwaj

Abstract

This chapter tracks the evolution of community data production and use within the context of the Avahan HIV prevention initiative in India, from its origins as community consultation, towards its fruition in a self-administrable community-owned monitoring system. Female sex workers (FSWs), transgender people (TGs), men who have sex with men (MSMs), and injecting drug users (IDUs) have piloted, tested, and refined tools to measure the progress of their own community-based organizations (CBOs). The chapter highlights three important characteristics of the transition to community monitoring: a community-responsive approach, data use by those who generate it, and the CBO's greater accountability to its members. After discussion of some of the challenges and limitations associated with CBO self-assessment, the chapter closes with an analysis of ways in which community-led monitoring can be leveraged as an instrument of CBO independence.

Keywords: community-based organizations, monitoring and evaluation, HIV/AIDS, community mobilization measurement, community-owned data, self-assessment tools

Monitoring, power and sustainability

In the context of large-scale aided development, project information systems have predominantly served as mechanisms to facilitate the 'upward' transfer of knowledge about communities to project management. Whilst this may suit agencies interested in planning and managing programmes, the effect has often been to consolidate a system of externally driven intervention, wherein beneficiaries do not influence the programme beyond a contribution to the planning stage. Typically, neither the indicators nor the data that is created have meant very much to the beneficiaries. Such target-oriented project management information systems (MIS) have tended to operate in an extractive way, draining time from CBO activities yet not creating information the community can actually use for themselves (cf., for example, Jacobs et al., 2010).

Scenarios such as these are not yet a thing of the past. Monitoring often remains an obligation imposed from above, requiring compliance but being

http://dx.doi.org/10.3362/9781780448695.004

of little recognizable benefit to community members. In such contexts, the community – as the yielder of data, but not the user of data – is likely to learn only minimally from the process, and remains dependent on outsiders for their skills of monitoring and planning, for key knowledge about the project, and so on. The imperative to measure up to externally driven standards thus risks disempowering communities through perpetuating systems of dependency.

The contradiction becomes prominent in long-term projects, especially those that engage with structural issues aimed at community empowerment where the objective is to create a beneficiary-owned programme through community mobilization. Even when there is an articulated promotion of community ownership, a substantial body of wisdom about the progress of a project often lies outside the domain of community members, preventing participation in crucial decision-making and the realization of a truly community-owned organization. In such programmes, a participatory approach to monitoring and evaluation is often the missing link. A key challenge is therefore to ensure that even where the project has been externally initiated in the first instance and over the period of time the project transcends towards community organisations, the capacity to sustain it is cultivated from within the community. Such sustainability requires community ownership. Core to ownership is decision-making and local initiatives, which require a flow of information, ways of analysing this information, and some control over the means through which it is obtained.

Typically, embedding these processes requires a good deal of effort from NGOs and CBOs. Yet development of monitoring capabilities amongst the community is often neglected. Clearly, getting it right is difficult. Monitoring systems need to be rigorous and information empirically measurable; but indicators need to be authentic to the experience of community members. Donors demand some stake in how their money is spent, but beneficiaries should be able to set their own priorities. Projects are designed to be empowering; but systematic monitoring can reinforce dependency. These were some of the challenges facing designers of the Avahan initiative to address HIV-AIDS in six higher-prevalence states in India.

The Avahan initiative

In October 2003, the National Aids Control Organization (NACO) had declared that there were 5.1 million people living with HIV/AIDS, with infection rates particularly high in the states of Tamil Nadu, Karnataka, Andhra Pradesh, Maharashtra, Manipur, and Nagaland. Certain groups were also identifiable as sharing a common exposure to HIV risk. Avahan facilitated a programme of interventions for people living and working in contexts of higher risk of HIV/AIDS in 82 districts.

Set up by the Bill and Melinda Gates Foundation, Avahan has focused on a strategy of community mobilization. 'Community' is understood here as a group of people who have some common priorities and who are prepared to act together in the common interest (Praxis, 2009: 3). For the purposes of the Avahan programme, the term community was also understood as those sharing a common identity. This identity was linked to a certain kind of life practice (such as sex work, homosexuality, or drug use) perceived to put them at higher risk of HIV/AIDS than the surrounding population. By 2009, Avahan was mobilizing prevention strategies for around 321,000 people, including 221,000 female sex workers (FSWs), 82,000 high-risk men who have sex with men (MSMs) and transgendered people (TGs), and 18,000 injecting drug users (IDUs). Capitalizing on already existing informal networks, the programme usually, though not always, brought together local people who shared a particular life practice in common. This became a point of unity amid the diversity of individual members. Sometimes, mixed groups (for example of TGs and MSMs) emerged.

Within the context of the Avahan intervention, setting up community-based groups (CBGs) which are collectives of community members committed to taking action in the common interest through chosen representatives, was the first stage. CBOs which are a more evolved and organized community group, with a formal democratic process for selecting leaders and, typically, a legal identity of its own as a basis for independent functioning, were also set up across many Avahan programme locations.

Community members would meet in various ways. For many, interactions happened through informal gatherings of no fixed frequency at drop-in centres or at hotspots. Once a community-based group was formed, it would then conduct localized but formal meetings of community representatives, at which the programme or community initiatives could be discussed. Where CBOs had been set up, elected representatives would meet monthly at the district levels and take responsibility for matters such as membership fees and, ultimately, for strategic planning (cf. Thomas et al., 2012).

The approach taken by Avahan was consistent with the third phase of the Indian government's National AIDS Control Programme (NACP) Phase III (2006–11), which envisaged a community-centred intervention model. This was predicated on:

- greater uptake of services when communities make HIV prevention a priority *for themselves*;
- already existing informal networks within communities providing a supportive environment in which good practices, like accessing information, have an opportunity to multiply;
- community capability to mobilize demand for good quality services;
- the indispensability of community ownership for long-term project sustainability. (NACP-III, in Praxis 2009: 8)

The programme aimed at transitioning a targeted intervention (TI) project to its natural owners – members of the intended beneficiary community. Under this objective, developing community-based organizations was a strategy that

Table 4.1 Stages of community mobilization in the Avahan initiative

Stage	Description	Time Frame
I	Strengthening a sense of common identity and fostering involvement in the intervention	Years 1–4 (2003–07)
II	Fostering community structures and action	Years 5–7 (2008–10)
III	Sustaining impact and ownership	Years 8–10 (2011–13)

Source: Praxis 2009: 5

would enable community members to manage the HIV interventions through a sustainable model of community participation. Community ownership was seen as necessary to securing long-term HIV risk management and HIV risk reduction.

Beyond the transitioning of the TI project to the community, another concern was to enable groups and organizations to finally take ownership of the agenda for change. In the context of these impending transitions, a challenge for Avahan was to develop effective methods of measuring community mobilization. This would require investigation of a range of domains, such as the intensity of activity, the process of mobilization and the changes that could be attributed to community mobilization. Set against this backdrop, Praxis, an organization that has participation as its core mandate, was commissioned by Avahan to evolve a design to monitor community mobilization within the scope of its HIV/AIDS prevention project. The approach was different from a traditional MIS in the way that it involved beneficiaries of the Avahan project in the design and process of monitoring.

Monitoring community mobilization

Two community members were part of the study's core design team for the Community Ownership and Preparedness Index (COPI) from the outset. Initial discussions had led to the identification of good leadership, inclusion, legitimacy, and capacity to take a broad approach (flexibility to use not only methods that strengthen HIV prevention but also focus on vulnerability reduction, empowerment, and sustainability) as important features of a strong community-based group. After further collaborative investigation into areas of change to be anticipated through the mobilization processes, a four-day workshop was held to develop parameters to assess community mobilization. The following emerged:

1. Leadership;
2. Governance;
3. Decision-making;

4. Resource mobilization;
5. Community collective networks;
6. Risk management;
7. Engagement with the state;
8. Engagement with other key influencers.

A total of 22 indicators were distributed across the parameters, with between one and four indicators attached to each. A Community Ownership and Preparedness Index (COPI) was evolved as a set of participatory tools and processes (for a more detailed explanation of the development of COPI, see Narayanan et al., 2012). Facilitated by Praxis in concert with SLPs and the NGOs and communities with whom they work, community mobilization monitoring (CMM) through COPI was instituted on an annual basis from 2009. Questionnaires were the predominant data collection tool, with a few blocks of questions being facilitated by using some participatory tools. Researchers would visit CBO representatives and related stakeholders on an annual basis and collect a range of relevant data from them to ascertain the CBG's position in relation to the identified parameters.

Results were shared with community members in a dialogic way, enabling them to offer objections, to discuss and, through the process, to reflect on their own progress (Praxis, 2009: 6). Overall, 40 CBOs were involved in community mobilization monitoring across six states.

Beyond consultation: the transition to a new model of monitoring

Community mobilization monitoring provided a platform for understanding CBG development and growth as they transitioned into semi-independent CBOs. The involvement of community representatives at each major step of the evolution of the COPI apparatus ensured some relevance and applicability; it also created opportunities for exchanges around progress and development between community members and external resource persons from NGOs. Over the course of monitoring, CBO representatives became increasingly familiar with the framework and with what they were being monitored against.

However, in the context of ensuring long-term community ownership of HIV prevention, the arrangements put in place through the use of COPI could not stand independently. As a largely consultative space (Pretty, 1995), it was not providing CBO members with opportunities to take over leadership and be accountable for monitoring and all the information it generated. This is more than a technical point, as the monitoring itself was creating rich fields of understanding that, though shared with communities, was ultimately analysed outside the domain of community. This missing link is something that required addressing for the community to build on their knowledge and was critical to their future development.

With these limitations in mind, the Avahan programme aimed to evolve informed community leadership through transitioning the monitoring system to the CBO. Praxis worked with CBOs facilitated by Tamil Nadu Aids Initiative in Tamil Nadu and Project Orchid in Manipur to evolve a community-based self-assessment process. The following section visits key stages of the process followed in Tamil Nadu.

Developing a framework for self-assessment

At a meeting in Chennai of 23 CBOs from Tamil Nadu, leadership teams participated in discussions about self-assessment. A key objective of the session was to reach some consensus on the value of self-assessment in the context of community mobilization and organization strengthening. Parameters, indicators and sub-indicators were discussed, words and terminology debated, and benchmarks considered for each sub-indicator.

Subsequently, in Vellore, discussions with community leaders led to the evolution of indicators and parameters that would reflect the strength of a CBO and also measure changes occurring due to activities being organized. The process included some discussions of community members' aspirations for their CBOs. This led to the setting of benchmarks and the creation of a knowledge bank of good practice to be drawn on, to shape the contents of the self-monitoring toolkit.

For example, to establish means of verifying the 'presence of second-line leadership in CBOs', a range of sub-indicators were identified, including the number of required leadership qualities found in at least half of CBO members; the percentage who pay the annual fee; the percentage who regularly attend meetings and events; the number of regular volunteers; the number who have contested or won elections at any level; and the number of potential leaders outside the leadership team. Then, to develop the part of the toolkit measuring the leadership qualities sub-indicator, relevant qualities were discussed and suitable benchmarks identified for the required number of community leaders with at least some of these qualities. Overall, the benchmarks set suggested that many CBO leaders had high expectations for their CBO's development.

Based on the indicators, questions, and benchmarks suggested by the community leaders for a range of parameters, a final toolkit was developed.

Empowering CBOs to monitor themselves

The framework that emerged was then shared with CBO teams in different locations in Tamil Nadu. Ultimately, nuanced understanding of eight parameters was arrived at: leadership, governance, decision-making, resource mobilization, network and project management, engagement with the state for realizing rights and engagement with larger society for addressing isolation and stigma – with indicators aligned with each of these. Teams were oriented both on how data had to be collected and how it was to be analysed at the CBO level. Based on this training the participants returned to their own CBOs and used the toolkit to collect information about their CBOs from members. The scope of the toolkit was broad, incorporating measurement of community preparedness, mobilization and quality of service delivery, as well as the CBO's capacity to address issues of disenfranchisement, discrimination in access to ration cards (which provided eligibility for subsidized food and fuel rations), and support of police and legal systems in times of crisis. In total, 23 CBOs completed a self-assessment process.

CBO teams assessed themselves on all the indicators and, based on the responses, arrived at a band or stage of progress for each: basic, foundation, promising, or vibrant. The process of self-assessment was not externally monitored. It was done internally by the CBO members so as to obtain a realistic picture of where they stand in relation to different indicators.

Box 4.1 Conversations with communities

Needless to say, the tools were not developed overnight.

A shortcoming of the first version of the toolkit had been that though CBO members assessed their CBO's progress, they were not *themselves* called to make inferences about what the measurements meant. After the meeting in Vellore, the self-assessment data was handed over to Praxis to be analysed. Praxis took responsibility for identifying the capacity-building needs of CBOs in the different areas as had been measured by each indicator. The responses of CBO members were linked to predefined benchmarks, aggregated at the indicator level, and then accorded one of three bands: basic, promising or vibrant. Praxis therefore used the self-assessment results to work out whether certain inputs were needed and, if so, what these were. The bands suggested the extent of support the CBO required in that particular domain. Indicators at the basic level suggested a need for specific training, technical support, guidance, and advisory inputs; those at the promising level implied a requirement for technical support, guidance, and advisory support; those at the vibrant level suggested that only advisory support was needed. A separate 'analysis' tool was used to enable this process.

Following feedback from CBO representatives the decision was made to build a component of 'analysis' into the assessment toolkit. This would enable CBO members to match results to one of three bands: green for vibrant, yellow for promising, and red for basic. (The colours selected were easy to identify with as they appeared in traffic lights that all CBO members were familiar with, and the significance of the colours drove the point home quite efficiently). As the data had emerged from the first round, and in the light of feedback of community members, a decision to add two parameters, on engagement with the state for realizing rights and engagement with larger society for addressing isolation and stigma (see Chapter 8 and Table 4.2, below) was taken. A set of 15 tools were then finalized for assessing CBOs along the eight parameters. Responses, matched to colour-coded bands, enabled an overall presentation of where CBOs stood at the time of assessment.

With CBO representatives oriented on the new framework, a second round of assessment was held six months later. Using this evolved framework, community members were more easily able to identify which areas of activity were progressing well and which were not. Table 4.2 shows the parameters and indicators of the evolved self-assessment toolkit.

Disseminating data and evolving a capacity needs assessment plan

At a meeting in Chennai in January 2013, three representatives from each of the CBOs presented their data across all indicators and parameters. They

Table 4.2 Self-monitoring: parameters and indicators

Parameters	Indicators
Leadership	LT has internalized its vision, mission and objective. Leadership sets CBO's agenda independently. Presence of second-line leadership in CBOs. Leadership is leading a functional crisis response system. Leadership involves community in events and mobilization.
Governance	Clear, regular and participatory selection process for leadership. Leadership is accountable to wider community.
Decision-making	Leadership is making strategic decisions with community participation. Committees formed and functional for making emergency or urgent decisions.
Resource mobilization	Quantum of resources mobilized exceed INR 20,000. Systems for effective resource mobilization.
Networking	Strong networking with civil society groups. Strong networking with government.
Project management	Targeted intervention (TI) project management. CBO Management. Financial and legal risk management (understanding the essentials of managing a collective)
Engagement with the state for realizing rights	Claiming rights and entitlements for community members.
Engagement with larger society for addressing isolation and stigma	Making the community visible and addressing isolation and stigma through engagement.

disseminated self-assessment data from the previous year to fellow CBO members and others including the State Lead Partner NGO, Tamil Nadu Aids Initiative (TAI) and Praxis. They shared experiences and used the platform for mutual learning. They also revisited some of the information they collected to look at each issue in an objective way and ensure that CBO leaders had not exaggerated their progress. After discussing each of the indicators, they indicated the appropriate colour codes corresponding to their band scores on a chart to enable visibility.

The experience of sharing the data led to discussions about reliability. One area of discussion was the tendency to exaggerate progress along certain indicators to avoid being perceived as having performed badly. The group exercise was helpful in forcing consideration of the *implications* of the scores they had given themselves. An exaggerated high performance signalled transition to a stage of independence, which in effect meant that external support in that area was no longer required.

In an attempt at converting the assessments into capacity needs assessments, it was agreed that all areas marked red would require rigorous training and all yellows would require guidance and advice, whereas all areas in green meant an ability to perform independently of support. TAI used this dataset to inform the training programme that they organized for all CBOs in districts across Tamil Nadu.

In addition to sharing data they had collected, the CBO representatives also discussed their experiences of using the self-assessment tool. The overall framework was reviewed and found still to be relevant in that all indicators were reflective of all activities. In those cases where activities along a certain indicator had not been carried out, some CBO teams identified a need to prioritize those activities in the next quarter. For other CBO teams, leaving one or two indicators out of the overall analysis was not a concern, since those corresponding activities had not featured on their agenda. A drawback would be an incomplete overall analytical picture, but this principle of flexibility was operative from the outset: it was up to the CBO to decide what indicators to use, as the system allowed customization.

Using analysis to activate the planning cycle

A central purpose of self-assessment lay in enabling CBOs to plan with greater understanding and certainty. For their planning, they were encouraged to refer to the existing project MIS, which focused more specifically on the TI – including activities such as condom distribution, whereas the self-monitoring toolkit was oriented around organizational development. The action plans identified monthly and quarterly targets.

Data generated was also used by TAI, the state-level partner NGO, to develop its capacity-building plan. A toolkit developed in the local language, that was used to facilitate this process and enter data into in a structured form, had a column where CBO members could state in detail the kind of support (if any) they needed from the state-level partner (in this case, TAI). The data was later used by TAI to aggregate areas where they could play a more supportive role to the CBOs, and record those in which the CBOs were performing well.

Community representatives later reviewed these earlier prepared action plans. For example, in August 2013, members of the leadership team of a CBO of female sex workers based in Namakkal, Tamil Nadu, reviewed progress in every activity that they had proposed to carry out in April, May and June that year. Against each activity, they marked one of three symbols, representing 'not done', 'done' or 'exceeded expectations.' Advocacy for securing rights and entitlements, internal auditing and fundraising were three activities that had not been done as planned; however, most activities had been completed. The review led to discussions of reasons why certain activities had not been performed.

In the feedback session they stated that they found the process helped them to stay focused on what needed to be achieved. It created a shared understanding of what was happening and was also a way of bringing attention to issues being deprioritized, as well as areas of weakness. The whole

Table 4.3 Action plan for Namakkal CBO: August to November 2013

	Activities	Target	Aug-13	Sep-13	Oct-13	Nov-13
1	Number of local community events (capacity building initiatives) organized by CBO against planned in the next four months	8	2	2	2	2
2	Number of CBO members who will participate in local capacity-building initiatives organized by CBO (hotspot/block level)	150	40	40	40	30
3	CBO participated in community events or trainings organized by implementing partners (TAI) (Yes=1; No=0)	8	2	2	2	2
4	Number of community members who will participate in community events or trainings organized by implementing partners (TAI)	150	40	40	40	30
5	Number of functional primary groups (such as SHGs, hotspot level groups, or any other informal groups at the primary level) formed by CBO	100	25	25	25	25
6	Number of CBO members who will be organized into functional primary groups (such as self-help groups, hotspot level groups, or any other informal groups at the primary level)	1,300	325	325	325	325
6a	Number of key population individuals who will become active members of CBOs	950	500	450		
7	Number of trainings/support events on financial management systems (including bylaws, legal compliance, etc.) to be organized by implementing partner (TAI)	4	1	1	1	1
8	Number of CBO members (CBO staff/leadership team/second line leader) who will participate in the trainings on financial management systems (including bylaws, legal compliance, etc.) (TAI)	120	30	30	30	30
9	CBO accounts to be audited internally (Yes=1; No=0)	4	1	1	1	1

Table 4.3 Action plan for Namakkal CBO: August to November 2013 (Continued)

	Activities	Target	Aug-13	Sep-13	Oct-13	Nov-13
10	Number of non-TI projects or activities to be handled by the CBO (e.g., savings, children's education, and any other community welfare activity)	8	2	2	2	2
11	Amount of funds to be raised by CBO (in INR) in upcoming months	200,000	50,000	50,000	50,000	50,000
12	Number of key population of individuals in the area in which CBO operates, who have savings accounts, in community-run banks or community SHGs, community cooperatives or any other bank form. ('Key population' refers to high-risk communities that are the beneficiaries of targeted interventions)	1,100	300	300	300	200
13	Number of key population individuals in the area in which CBO operates, to have taken out a loan or insurance services from community-run banks or community SHGs, community cooperatives or any other bank form.	1,500	350	450	350	350
14	CBO has fully functional 'report cards' of HIV services for the community (Yes=1; No=0)	4	1	1	1	1
15	CBO will initiate a minimum of three actions with key stakeholders (TI, DAPCU, SACS, healthcare providers for ICTC, STI services etc.) (Yes=1; No=0)	4	1	1	1	1
16	Number of key population individuals in the area in which CBO operates, who have obtained at least one formal identification document.	300	100	100	50	50
17	CBO formally linked/recognized at block or district level (Yes=1; No=0)	4	1	1	1	1

(Continued)

Table 4.3 Action plan for Namakkal CBO: August to November 2013 (Continued)

	Activities	Target	Aug-13	Sep-13	Oct-13	Nov-13
18	CBO has functional crisis response systems (Yes=1; No=0)	1	1	1	1	1
19	Number of paralegal workers who will be trained in district legal service authority (DLSA) with the support of Centre for Advocacy and Research (CFAR)	80	20	20	20	20
20	CBO conducts at least one sensitization programme or training for police, perpetrators, media and healthcare providers (Yes=1; No=0)	4	1	1	1	1
21	Number of positive media articles on CBO's activities	1	1	1	1	1

process was useful in preparing them for the next activity: the development of a new action plan. With some guidance, the CBO leadership team evolved the plan – they enlisted activities and also assigned targets for different activities. The team were advised that the plan should reflect indicators in the self-assessment framework and any other relevant work, such as that done with SHGs. The action plan of the CBO for August to November 2013 (Figure 4.1) shows quarterly and monthly targets for 24 activities.

Owning community history: creating and sharing digital stories

During the process of generating information using the COPI, one could say that the CBO members were closer to the periphery of the reporting process – sharing relevant knowledge which was synthesized, owned, and communicated. An emerging concern was therefore to enable the CBO members to become co-creators of knowledge through more personal and meaningful participation in the processes of communicating their work.

For this it was necessary to use a medium accessible to community members, a significant share of whom were not functionally literate. Digital Storytelling (DST) emerged as an appropriate medium since it utilized contemporary audio-visual technologies to provide platforms for people to tell their stories, and crossed the barrier of reading and writing requirements. In September 2013, a workshop was held in Mettupalayam, Tamil Nadu, in which representatives from these CBOs were trained on the techniques of digital storytelling.

The digital story takes the form of a five-minute video illustrating the CBO's development. The key episodes that CBO members selected were synthesized into a single story. Members were encouraged to use images and pictures to draw a journey of their CBO and identify the various stages along the journey when things changed. They were advised on elements that they could add to their representative journey, based on a reading of the report that had been developed using data generated through the COPI tool. Additions were then woven into the story. Next, the CBO members were asked to identify four important moments in the CBO's journey. They represented these using drawings, which were then fine-tuned. Once all the images were in place, a story of the CBO was narrated and recorded. Key highlights of some stories include their work on crisis cases emerging from dealings with police, thugs, and the media; the CBO's internalization of these cases and decisions to hold sensitization drives about some of these; and the holding of cultural events to further build social capital and raise visibility in a positive way. Stories emphasized the training of members in various employable skills and acquisition of assets for the CBO office; their registration under law; the obtaining of entitlements for their members; the advocacy work they did with government officials; and the building of networks of state and national level significance.

Using data trends for strategic planning

By the time the third round of self-assessment had been completed, the CBO leadership had enough data to be able to observe trends. Teams recorded the band scores against each indicator across the three rounds. After identifying trends, they suggested exploring the explanations for these to collectively arrive at ways of leveraging and sustaining successes and overcoming barriers. For example, if an indicator showed the level of resources mobilized as low, the members analysed why it was low and tried to find out ways to improve it in the next implementation period. Next, they organized indicators into different categories according to the kind of trends they had shown, ranging from very weak (indicating no progress) to strong (indicating good and steady progress). Based on the data that they had collected, CBOs developed action plans. TAI then used the data to develop a capacity building plan for each CBO.

Transitioning to a paradigm of CBO leadership and accountability

In the transition from CMM to a community-centred MIS, three major shifts are observable:

The monitoring framework is more responsive to communities

Self-measurement enabled CBO members to evolve indicators of specific relevance to their contexts. In some cases, community members decided which indicators were relevant to their development needs and prioritized them.

CBOs of IDUs in Manipur and Nagaland, for example, developed a different set of indicators to those of FSWs and TGs in Tamil Nadu. For example, some FSW CBOs working with savings linked self-help groups wanted to monitor the programme in their communities, so they developed specific indicators for the same under the project management parameter. This enabled them to shift the monitoring agenda from the predefined project to problems facing the community (see Chapter 8).

Through the digital storytelling medium, CBO representatives synthesized currents of knowledge and understanding that they saw as important. Though the stories themselves were largely descriptive – not analytical or evaluative – in nature, the digital storytelling platform provided CBO members with an opportunity to select information and to present it in a way that made sense to them. The final product was a consolidation of key moments from within the CBO's history. Unlike previous narrative reports used within the project context, it was very much a joint creation of the CBO members and Praxis, yielding institutionally relevant and accessible information for the wider community. The digital stories were also useable for fundraising purposes.

Data is now being used by those who generate it

Though the data that community members generate is used by facilitating organizations to understand where the CBO stands on various indicators and to organize specific capacity building programmes to address issues, it is now available for community consumption too. Rather than data being created by communities and then analysed by outsiders, the communities now have control not only of the means of production of data but also the means of its analysis. The requirement to provide explanations for observed trends invited the participants into a domain of greater ownership of the CBO's journey, characterized by a deeper insight and understanding.

The involvement of community representatives in monitoring – from the design stage to the point of data use – has, over time, also enabled more informed decisions regarding the CBO's future development. As CBO members themselves became interpreters of data, they were able to diagnose whether or not their CBOs had made progress in specific parameters. Crucially, this information has been used to shape action plans for future months, as they decided on targets and set priorities for themselves and their community. The leadership team, which is the executive body of the CBO, typically did this planning. Through self-assessment and change mapping over three years, members said they had a clearer idea of what progress the CBO was making. As one member in Namakkal, Tamil Nadu said, 'the process helps us understand the entire functioning of the CBO in a systematic way.'

With communities themselves facilitated to interpret the data, the need for support from external staff from NGOs has been reduced. Yet the embedding of self-monitoring has also led to a situation where the original facilitating

NGO (in this case TAI) is now dependent on CBOs for knowledge about their progress. The transitioning of the MIS started under the Avahan initiative to CBO leadership teams has made them the go-to resource on data.

The CBO leadership teams are more accountable to the wider community

Does self-measurement empower the CBO, or does it empower the leadership team of the CBO? This critical question needs to be asked; and the most powerful justification of self-measurement here is in its contribution to a culture of greater accountability. Involvement in monitoring has made them agents of data production. And their productive investment has not been alienating: the data production process was generative and even a matter of personal and professional pride. As one CBO member said, 'The idea that we have to be transparent and account for every rupee is something very important and we would do this. We have no problem in sharing this information, for we are very honest.'

With greater ownership of the toolkits used to produce data, and the means with which to conduct analysis, the CBOs' responsibility to the wider community has deepened. The growth of knowledge and understanding about a CBO's organizational development has raised questions of transparency that all democratic institutions face. And, in contexts of increased institutional accountability, opportunities for more participative forms of scrutiny have arisen. CBO leadership teams have had to become more organized in their record-keeping and conscious of their responsibilities to the wider pool of CBO members within the local area. Some CBO leadership teams have instituted time slots for presenting digital stories to their own community members, for example at the CBO Annual General Body Meetings for setting the scene for an open review of long-term progress. These meetings are facilitated entirely by CBO members and external NGOs are not normally invited. Quite rightly, equipping the leadership team with tools with which they can measure and manage information has created conditions in which community members can be more demanding of them and push for a more accountable CBO.

Challenges, learning and risks

Can any outsider fully understand the ways in which community members track the growth of their CBO?

Regardless of whether a formal system of assessment is in place, people will typically form impressions of any institution in which they have a stake. CBO members are no different; they are likely to form impressions of how their CBO is progressing in the course of their daily work. There are multiple possible sources of evidence: the perception of their own success or that of their peers; the difficulties they encounter; their ability to meet timelines; the number of people attending meetings; the quality of their relationships with fellow CBO members; the camaraderie they experience at meetings; the strength they derive from the informal social networks and support structures they develop as a result of their membership; and many more. And whether or not the members would naturally, and in a systematic way, consider these different variables when judging the progression of the CBO – or whether they would even necessarily make 'assessments' or 'monitor' in ways that carry the weight associated with these terms – we should not lose sight of their ability to make inferences and judgements about the work of the CBO *without* the support of a framework. Indeed, community members' understanding, which might be both intuitively as well as empirically grounded, of how their work is progressing and how the CBO work is progressing, may even reflect a number of variables that cannot be contained by a template such as this, which is largely reliant on empirically observable data.

Given these considerations, a risk with developing an assessment template is that the introduction of a new or perhaps unfamiliar conceptual vocabulary around measurement colonizes an individual's comprehension of how they are doing, rendering their own territory of understanding around progression and assessment unfit for purpose. The work Praxis and partners engaged in with community groups testifies to this risk. A readiness to unlearn, to be flexible, and to adapt to differences according to context has been absolutely essential. For example, when the self-monitoring toolkit was taken to CBOs in Andhra Pradesh, it was initially introduced as part of a relatively low-intensity capacity building workshop. As the workshop unfolded, however, it became clear that a quite different approach would be needed: one that would enable a deeper and more comprehensive learning about self-monitoring processes and ease the revision of benchmarks in response to different contexts. On-going learning has also been key to external facilitation. Frequent workshops with CBOs were enormously generative in terms of helping external facilitators understand what approaches can work. For example, the session in Namakkal with the CBO there provided a template for thinking about how groups can use self-assessment data for action planning. It served as a useful resource for subsequent engagement with CBOs in other areas.

Openness to community perspectives – a willingness to enable *them* to lead – marked the development of the self-assessment tools and meant, necessarily, that the Praxis team was not entirely in control. Indeed, one aspect of the tools' development is that they took different final forms in different project locations. In some areas, certain indicators were added, while in other areas, certain indicators were prioritized. This dialectical engagement with community members, enabling them to co-direct development of the tools, often made the process more difficult and took a lot of time and effort, but it was a vital dynamic underpinning the movement towards a community-based MIS.

Ensuring the robustness of data is another challenge. When data needed to be generated for external consumption, there would sometimes be exaggeration. CBO members (like the rest of us, perhaps!) may like to 'put their best foot forward' when being judged by external stakeholders: on more than one occasion they scored themselves higher when they feared that they would be judged based on the scores and then the scores were taken down a notch from 'vibrant' to 'promising' when they knew the scores would be for their own consumption. This encourages us to see value in a culture of monitoring for *internal* consumption. A key aim has also been to try to make the self-monitoring framework relatable enough for CBO members that it serves to stimulate discussion on what is familiar. This discussion itself, apart from the actual recording of data, is an important vehicle for learning. Indeed, ultimately, self-assessment tools should be seen and used as instigators of critical reflection, not a replacement for it.

There were other positive spill-over effects of the utilization of the self-assessment tools. They prompted CBO members to recall a significant amount of information about what had been done over the last year, and encouraged them to see this not as a mere list of tasks completed, but as a resource for learning and action. Some community members said it has helped CBOs get a clear picture of what they should focus on and work towards in the next year – thus making it a good input for planning.

Other CBO members said that self-assessment tools have helped encourage documentation. In the first two years of the CMM process, CBOs would not have documentary evidence to support their claims. When the Praxis teams would ask for evidence, some CBO members would question why this was needed. The team explained that this was not just a study requirement, but rather something the CBO would need to submit to various authorities, to seek permission or at the time of making applications to demonstrate what the CBO had been doing. They saw the utility in this and began keeping their documents in order. One group of CBO members proudly mentioned that they were now able to maintain necessary paperwork for themselves without the support of any external agencies.

In some cases, the use of the self-assessment tools appears to have had a galvanizing effect. One CBO reported that earlier, the leadership team only knew tasks related to their role, for example in terms of addressing issues of crisis or advocacy. But self-assessment tools encouraged groups to come together and often jointly mull over issues. This helped them think collectively about key issues and build teamwork skills.

This brings us on to a development that is both encouraging and potentially troublesome. The increasing systematization of CBOs' work has led to a change in the way some CBO leadership teams have been perceived by NGOs. They are now seen by some as being organizational leaders rather than community leaders, which, whilst it reflects positively on the technical sophistication of CBOs' work, may raise questions about the extent to which they are seen as rooted in, and driven by, the community they represent. A concern for the future will be to find democratic ways of avoiding the consolidation of an elite class of CBO leaders within these communities.

Beyond the NGO? Self-measurement as an instrument of CBO independence

The movement towards self-measurement illustrates how CBO members have made a transition from generating data and giving it up for analysis by others, to generating it for use by themselves. NGOs have played a substantial role in this movement. Although the self-assessment tools were developed in consultation with community members, it would not have been possible without the dedicated work of NGO staff at different levels. Whilst the parameters and indicators contained within it resonate with community members, to a large extent they represent a simplification of the complex framework that COPI used, which was largely an NGO initiative. Furthermore, the action planning processes that CBOs have undertaken have drawn not just on the self-monitoring toolkit but also on the existing MIS. The toolkit has therefore not replaced an existing MIS, but, rather, complemented it. It was not designed to be a self-sufficient MIS, but rather, to be a prompt to community participation in the task of monitoring.

At the time of writing, lead NGOs in each target state continue to play a capacity-building role in relation to CBOs. However, the difference now is that some of them are reliant on community-generated data to be able to do this. What these processes promise, then, is a different kind of NGO–CBO dynamic. Self-assessment tools have put the power of monitoring in the hands of community members, with greater power to diagnose their own progress and make plans for the future. Enabling CBO leadership teams to assess themselves in a systematic way, to generate data on their own, to diagnose their level of development and make it intelligible for them *and* for facilitating NGOs has opened up new pathways.

Possibilities have also been created for the CBO to look at NGOs as a guide, rather than as a donor or leader. CBOs can relate directly to the donor, equipped with information and fundraising resources such as digital storytelling. Within this trajectory, the empowerment of the CBO is made possible through subverting the hegemony of external control of organized development processes. Overturning the paradigm of CBO dependency on an external NGO for monitoring, it actually generates potential for NGO dependence on the CBO; and even, ultimately, for the marginalization of the NGO as the CBO becomes increasingly self-reliant. Through this process, the role of the NGO gradually diminishes as the CBO equips itself with skills in the kind of monitoring, interpretation, planning and analysis that is traditionally the domain of the NGO, whilst still being comprised entirely of community members; though as mentioned above this trajectory of development is not without its risks.

In conclusion, the development of the self-assessment toolkit has introduced a culture of self-measurement into the ongoing work of CBOs. Self-assessment has been enabled. Data can be consumed and acted upon by the same people who produced it. Monitoring and evaluation has been de-projectized, and the question 'Who is the data for?' has a rather different answer. With CBOs able to gather information for themselves and disseminate it to internal and external stakeholders, a functioning community-driven monitoring system has a large significance on its own.

About the authors

Rohan Preece, Praxis. Rohan has worked with development sector organizations in different parts of the world and has experience in social research, teaching and monitoring and evaluation.

Stanley Joseph, Praxis. Stanley is a professional social worker who has specialized in community development, and has extensive experience working on issues of people living with HIV and marginalized communities.

Gayathri Sarangan, Praxis. Gayathri has almost two decades' experience working with a range of organizations globally.

Sowmyaa Bharadwaj, Praxis. Sowmyaa has over a decade's experience in the development sector as a facilitator and practitioner of participatory methods and approaches.

Endnote

1. This chapter is a compilation of information and analysis from a series of visit reports, papers and other similar documents, produced in the course of an 'Avahan – The India AIDS Initiative'-supported project facilitated by Praxis, called Measuring Community Mobilization in the Avahan Programme, led by Tom Thomas and Pradeep Narayanan. Details of CBOs facilitated by Tamil Nadu AIDS Initiative and Project Orchid that supported this process are available in Annex 1.

Bibliography

ACQUIRE (2006), 'Community Mobilization: Improving Reproductive Health Outcomes', ACQUIRE Technical Update, <https://www.k4health.org/toolkits/communitybasedfp/community-mobilization-improving-reproductive-health-outcomes>.

Avahan (2008), 'The India AIDS Initiative – The Business of HIV Prevention at Scale,' New Delhi: Bill & Melinda Gates Foundation.

Blankenship, K.M., West, B.S., Kershaw, T.S., and Biradavolu, M.R. (2008), 'Power, community mobilization, and condom use practices among female sex workers in Andhra Pradesh, India', *AIDS*, 22: 9–1.

Chandrasekaran, P., Dallabetta, G., Loo, V., Mills, S., Saidel, T., Adhikary R., et al (2008), 'Evaluation design for large-scale HIV prevention programmes: the case of Avahan, the India AIDS initiative' *AIDS*, 22: 11–5.

Chillag, K., Bartholow, K., Cordeiro, J., Swanson, S., Patterson, J., Stebbins, S., Sy, F. (2002), 'Factors affecting the delivery of HIV/AIDS prevention programs by community-based organizations', *AIDS Education and Prevention*, 14: 27–37.

Cornwall, A. (2008), 'Unpacking Participation: Models, Meanings and Practices, *Oxford University Press and Community Development Journal*, 43: 269–283.

Galavotti, C., Wheeler, T., Kuhlmann, A.S., Saggurti, N., Narayanan, P., Kiran, U., and Dallabetta, G. (2012), 'Navigating the swampy lowland: a framework for evaluating the effect of community mobilisation in female sex workers in Avahan, the India AIDS Initiative', *Journal of Epidemiology and Community Health*, 66: 9–15.

Gaventa, J. (2006), 'Finding the spaces for change: a power analysis' *IDS Bulletin*, 37: 23–33.

Gaventa, J., Petit, J., & Laura, C. (2011), 'Powerpack: Understanding power for social change <http://www.powercube.net/wp-content/uploads/2010/01/PowerPack_web_version.pdf> [Accessed 5 June 2014]

HIV/AIDS Alliance (2002), 'Policy Briefing No. 1: Supporting NGOs and CBOs responding to HIV/AIDS'.

Jacobs, A., Barnett, C., and Ponsford, R. (2010), 'Approaches to Monitoring: Feedback Systems, Participatory Monitoring and Evaluation and Logical Frameworks' *IDS Bulletin*, 41: 36–44.

Jana, S., Basu, I., Rotheram-Borus, M.J., & Newman, P. A. (2004), 'The Sonagachi Project: a sustainable community intervention program', *AIDS Education and Prevention*, 16: 405–414.

Narayanan, P., Moulasha, K., Wheeler, T., Baer, J., Bharadwaj, S., Ramanathan, TV, Thomas, T. (2012) 'Monitoring community mobilisation and organisational capacity among high risk groups in a large scale HIV prevention programme in India: selected findings using a Community Ownership and Preparedness Index' *Journal of Epidemiology and Community Health*, 2: 16–25.

Praxis (2009), 'Measuring Community Mobilisation Processes – A Monitoring Framework for Community-Based Groups Under the HIV/AIDS Programme in India' project report, Delhi: Praxis.

Praxis (2013), 'From Beneficiaries to Agents of Change: Self-Administrable Tools to Assess Community Preparedness for Vulnerability Reduction' project report, Delhi: Praxis.

Thomas, T., Narayanan, P., Wheeler, T., Kiran, U., Joseph, M.J. and Ramanathan, T.V. (2012), 'Design of a community ownership and preparedness index: using data to inform the capacity development of community based groups', *Journal of Epidemiology and Community Health*: 66: i26–i33.

Wheeler, T., Kiran, U., Jayaram, M., Dallabetta, G., (2012), 'Learning about scale, measurement and community mobilisation: Reflections on the implementation of the Avahan HIV/AIDS Initiative in India', *Journal of Epidemiology and Community Health*, 2: 16–25.

Annex 1: list of contributors

Representatives from community-based organizations: Deivani and Kalaimathi (Dharmapuri Maavatta Pengal Mempattu Sangam), Gandhimathi and Tamilkodi (Namakkal Maavatta Sabarmathi Pengal Mempattu Sangam), Pooja and Gopika (Salem Thirunangaigal Nala Sangam), Ooorvasi and Magarunisha (Madurai Social Welfare Development Society), Mary and Kala (Sri Lakshmi Pengal Munettra Sangam, Madurai), Sabitha and Sakthi (Salem Pengal Nala Sangam), Lakshmi (Gnanam Deepam Sevai Maiyam, Krishnagiri), Sudha and Panchavarnam (Theni Maavatta Pengal Samuga Porularatha Munettra Sangam),

Radha and Magalakhsmi (Erode Maavatta Pengal Suyasakthi Sangam, H Nanao Singh Counsellor (Care Foundation), S Motilal S (DPU-B More), Md Nashar (Dawn), Naorem Alex Singh (Helping Hand), Th. Hem and Th. Nabaketan (CERO - SASO), R K Sanjoy Singh and R K Godha (ESEWOSSA, Imphal East), Somiching (PASDO), Makar (SPU), Amon (Care Foundation), N Priyogopal (SASO East), Pangakpa (HFAF), S Bishojit (BAF), P Kenedy Singh (BAF), Wilson Shimrah and Kasing As (TMNL, Ukhrul), Timothy Hmar (Hope Foundation), G Mynthang (Hope Foundation), K Vithan (PASDO), Y Pryogopal (Brighter United), M Gandhar and N Sureshkumar (ECO, Kakching), Y Basanta Singh (SWACD), Thongamden (Rod), M Paul (SASO). Vanaroja and Manjula (Annai Theresa Makkal Sevai Mayam), Shilpa and Joe (Anbukarangal Samuga Nala Sangam), Pooja and Gopika (Salem Thirunangaigal Nala Sangam), Sathya and Sabitha (Salem Pengal Nalavazvu Sangam), Pushparani and Sumathi (Vellore Pengal Mempattu Sangam), Lakshmi and Laksmi (KrishnagiriGnana Deepam Sevai Mayyam), Deivayani and Kalai Mathi (Dharmapuri Maavatta Pengal Mempattu Sangam), Oorvasi and Megarunisha (Social Welfare Development Society), Sagaya Mary and Mariammal (Dindugal Pengal Munettra Sangam), Kala and Mary Angel (Sri Lakshmi Pengal Munettra Sangam), Rajeshkannan and Chittu (Vidivelli Thirunangaigal Nalavaazvu Sangam), Roseline and Mageswari (Sudaroli Pengal Munettra Sangam), Reeta Mary and Karoline (Jancey Rani Pengal Nala Sangam), Radhaand Magalakshmi (Erode Maavatta Samarpathi Pengal Mempattu Sangam), Sudha and Panchavarnam (Theni Maavatta Pengal Samuga Porulathara Munettra Sangam).

Support organizations: Bill and Melinda Gates Foundation, Project Orchid and Tamil Nadu AIDS Initiative.

CHAPTER 5

Lost policies: locating access to infrastructure and services in rural India

Tom Thomas, Moulasha Kader and Rohan Preece

Abstract

In Indian villages, social differences are often reflected in the configuration of habitations, with residents of similar backgrounds tending to live near each other. At the same time, scheduled castes, historically the most marginalized social group, typically live on the fringes of villages, farthest from crucial services.

As a five-state audit of infrastructural provision found in 2011, physical distance is not the only indicator of exclusion, and nor are scheduled castes the only group to experience a greater challenge in accessing government services. This chapter takes up some of the lessons of this study, which showed widespread state neglect of the interests of those who are often most reliant on public services. Without equitable involvement of the local community, infrastructure planners risk aggravating existing patterns of exclusion.

Community participation emerges as a non-negotiable accountability mechanism in contexts of embedded social inequity.

Keywords: equity, caste discrimination, access, infrastructure services, Indian policymakers, social audit, Dalits

Building India: policies, programmes and promises

By global standards, India has a poor record of investment in social services. In health, for example, public expenditure in 2012 was just 1.3% of gross domestic product (GDP) (World Bank 2014)[2], comparing unfavourably with most low-, middle- and high-income nations (cf., for example, Dreze and Sen 2013: 148–151). Social spending in India has come under even more pressure since the 1991 economic reforms, a period during which there has been increasing commodification of essential public goods such as basic health and education.

Still, policies have been pushed through – a great succession of them – aimed at doing justice to the vision of India heralded by a glorious constitution. Many have prioritized allocation of resources towards rural and socio-economically

http://dx.doi.org/10.3362/9781780448695.005

Table 5.1 Flagship Schemes introduced by the Government of India

Name of the scheme	Ministry	Relevant village level Infrastructure	Services provided	Crucial village-level service-providers
National Rural Health Mission	Ministry of Health	Primary health centre, sub-centre	Health services	Asha, ancillary nurse, midwife
Sarva Siksha Abhiyan	Ministry of Human Resources, Department of Education	Primary, secondary and high school	Education and midday meal	Teachers
Integrated Child Development Services	Ministry of Women and Child Development	Anganwadi, balwadi, mini-anganwadi (these are crèche and health centres for infants as part of a Government scheme	Supplementary nutrition, pre-school education, nutrition, health education, growth monitoring	Anganwadi worker, anganwadi helper
Targeted public distribution	Ministry of Food and Civil Supplies	Fair price shop (distribution) and Panchayat Bhawan (village council office) (identification, list revision)	Targeted Public Distribution Scheme (TPDS)	FPS dealer
Pradhanmantri Gram Sadak Yojana	Ministry of Rural Development	Road	–	Private contractor
NSAP/NREGA	Ministry of Rural Development	Post office (payment)	Payment of pensions, wages and other payment services	Postman, Postmaster

Table 5.1 Flagship Schemes introduced by the Government of India (Continued)

Indira Aawas Yojana	Ministry of Rural Development	*Pukka* houses (a house made with high quality material)	–	–
Rajiv Gandhi Grameen Vidyutikaran Yojana (RGGVY)	Ministry of Power Electricity	Connections to houses, street lights		
Rajiv Gandhi National Drinking Water Mission (RGNDWM)	Ministry of Rural Development	Hand pumps, open-dug wells, tap connection	Drinking water scheme	–
Telecommunications and internet	Ministry of Communication and Information Technology (department of communications)	Phone connection lines and houses having phone connection Internet Kiosks	–	–

Source: NIEA 2012

disadvantaged areas and communities. Called flagship programmes, they form one of two core strategy clusters for development in rural areas. The other, the Bharat Nirman (BN) Programme, included six infrastructural components: irrigation, drinking water, electrification, roads, housing, and rural telephones.

Infrastructure is the bricks and mortar of public services: a central component of sound delivery. The 11th five-year plan, for example, recognized rural infrastructure as crucial to achieving broad-based, inclusive growth. Most schemes, such as the National Rural Health Mission, Sarva Shiksha Abhiyan (The Education for All Movement), Integrated Child Development Services (ICDS), the National Rural Employment Guarantee Scheme (NREGS), and the Rajiv Gandhi National Drinking Water Mission (RGNDWM) require a guarantee of accessibility to certain kinds of built infrastructure at the village level.

The importance of providing basic civic amenities to the Indian population – which remains largely rural – has also been an explicit goal in many plan documents since independence. The central vision of the 11th five-year plan of 2007–12 had been to achieve inclusive growth, that is, a growth process which accrues benefits across diverse social groups and ensures equality of opportunity for all (11th five-year Plan, Vol.1., Chapter 1: 2). However, an assessment of the plan concluded that despite various measures undertaken by the government, effective implementation in India was lacking and the rate of improvement much slower than required (cf. for example, Burange et al., 2012).

Overall, the quality of public services differs markedly from context to context – from state to state, from village to village. On the whole, delivery is simply not good enough. Liberalization has not masked this shortfall. What we now frequently see in India are mansions built on sand: any trumpeting of world-class private health facilities, and cutting-edge higher education, seems imbalanced without an acknowledgement of the patchy (and more often weak) foundations on which these centres of excellence sit.

Equity and accountability

Systematic exclusion from and inequitable access to core public services in India has been documented in several studies (cf., for example, Deshpande, 2012, Baru et al., 2010, Govinda and Bandhyopadhyay, 2008). However, monitoring methods used to measure the reach of these services have often served to conflate universal infrastructural provision across a certain number of villages with universal access *to* these infrastructural services (cf., for example, in elementary education, DISE, 2012–13, SSA, 2006–07). Whilst the intention may not be to encourage reliance on these tools and resources when assessing overall progress, the implication is that the question of access is resolved once the bricks and mortar are in place. However, the presence of infrastructure in a village does not necessarily guarantee its equitable use by all households in a village.

Notably, government services are typically not the only choice facing people in cities but also in rural areas. Increasingly, vital public goods in India are becoming privatized and the role of a citizen vis-a-vis these goods is shifting from that of a rights-bearer to a consumer. In health, for example, the private sector has been the dominant provider for some time (Bhandari and Siddhartha, 2007) with governments since 1991 eager to usher it in. However, massive privatization of the scale we have seen in India poses enormous problems from an equity perspective, with great variance in quality, and the fundamental problem of affordability. Manifestly, public sector suppliers cannot simply be dismissed as outdated or inefficient: they are the last and often only resort for millions of Indian citizens who depend on them.

In this context, the question of accountability is raised. Good public services are a key enabler of justice for the most disadvantaged (cf. Dreze and Sen, 2013: 282), who often lack the means to access privately run institutions. Without being able to afford health insurance, or private transportation to take their children to and from school, or to obtain drinking water facilities where those that are provided are inadequate, the poor are more fundamentally dependent on the provisions of the state than the rich are in an era of privatization. Hence the accountability problem: the state is, *de facto* if not *de jure*, less accountable to the more affluent classes who can effectively 'opt out' and into the private sector to satisfy their ambitions for themselves and their children. Those who they are more accountable to, in practice, are people who have historically been less able to voice their demands, to press the state to deliver on its constitutional and legal obligations, or to choose private alternatives.

Private businesses operating in a competitive market have their own in-built accountability mechanisms that go some way to protect consumers; but – and this is an issue that has been discussed elsewhere – what systems of 'critical scrutiny' can be used to hold the public sector to account? (cf. Ibid., 2013: 84) This is of course an issue for the individual citizen, and also for civil society. Knowledge is an indispensable tool at the hands of these campaign groups when engaging and influencing the government, directly or indirectly through litigation. Whilst many civil society campaign groups have been able to mobilize informed public attention around equity issues and have played a vigilant role in critically engaging with government, in terms of access to infrastructure, civil society organizations have often had to make do with limited evidence with which to challenge the state.

Knowledge for accountability: the genesis of the National Infrastructure Equity Audit

It was in recognition of gaps in knowledge about access to infrastructure that the National Infrastructure Equity Audit (NIEA) emerged. An absence of information on infrastructure-based inequity had prevented civil society from making the state accountable for providing equitable access to crucial infrastructure for all citizens. Social Equity Watch, an inter-NGO forum on

Box 5.1 Social exclusion and social distance in India

In India, distinctions of gender, ethnicity, caste and religion coincide with markedly different levels of access to and enjoyment of public goods such as health and education. These variances are observable within households and communities, and in regional and national statistical trends (for example, NFHS, 2005–06; NSS, 2009–10 in Dubochet et al., 2013). Accompanying economic, historical, religious and socio-political narratives of exclusion enable identification of groups as more likely to be discriminated against and even excluded from social goods, for example on the basis of gender, caste, tribe and religion.

Gender and other social differences often intersect with and reinforce other drivers of exclusion, such as poverty, and geographic disadvantage: living in remote areas, or in parts of the country poorly served by government education policy and services. In India as in multiple other countries, discrimination is a key factor behind social exclusion, often leading to the relegation of one group to a position of weakness or subservience in relation to dominant groups. Social exclusion is often driven by discriminatory practices that inhibit individuals from accessing opportunities in health care, housing, basic needs, land ownership, social spaces, economic, cultural and political aspects of society, and constitutional and human rights. Statistically, in India – according to indicators such as education, health and nutrition – scheduled castes (*dalits*), Muslims and scheduled tribes (*adivasis*) find themselves disadvantaged with respect to other social groups. Those in the other backward class (OBC) category are not statistically as disadvantaged, though they are disadvantaged when compared with those in general caste categories. Also known as 'forward castes', 'general castes' is a broader descriptor that includes, though not exclusively, those who are 'upper caste' within the traditional caste hierarchy.

The term social distance, coined by the Bogardus in the 1930s and since widely used in sociology and other fields, refers to the extent to which different groups in a society are able to relate to each other and 'charts the character of social relations' (Bogardus, 1925). Marriage norms, precluding the union of two people from different tribes, castes or religions, may be the most foundational and fundamental distancing principle; but the notion of social distance – not, by the way, an easily measurable phenomenon but hugely complex, contestable, and inconsistent in its manifestation across different spheres – is nonetheless deeply applicable across many contexts in India.

Here, in cities, towns and villages, a considerable social distance typically marks relations between certain groups. Social groups often tend not to mix, and casteism can reduce ordinary human interaction to a polluting, defiling activity. Scheduled castes are severely discriminated against by higher caste communities, and typically relegated to the fringes of villages. There, their occupational practices can further reinforce exclusion from mainstream society due to perceptions of uncleanliness. This historic practice of untouchability is current in some parts of India and manifests itself in ways that often deprive individuals of dignity. Muslims are another group who often experience marginalization and isolation rooted in a politics of Hindu religious chauvinism. In some parts of the country, communal tensions have boiled over into violence, whilst in others suspicion and fear stalk the terrain, throttling cordial discourse and interaction. In others, such as parts of Odisha, Christians have been persecuted in their villages. Elsewhere, linguistic barriers and anxieties over discrimination can stand in the way of tribal people's easy access to services. Political parties have capitalized on and arguably contributed to such distancing practices with the development of caste-based and religion-based representation at regional and, most prominently, at the national level.

equity issues in India administered by Praxis, sought to take steps to address this limitation and strengthen the hand of civil society groups.

Social maps such as the one featured in Figure 5.1 revealed incidences of inequitable distribution of households with respect to key village services. As

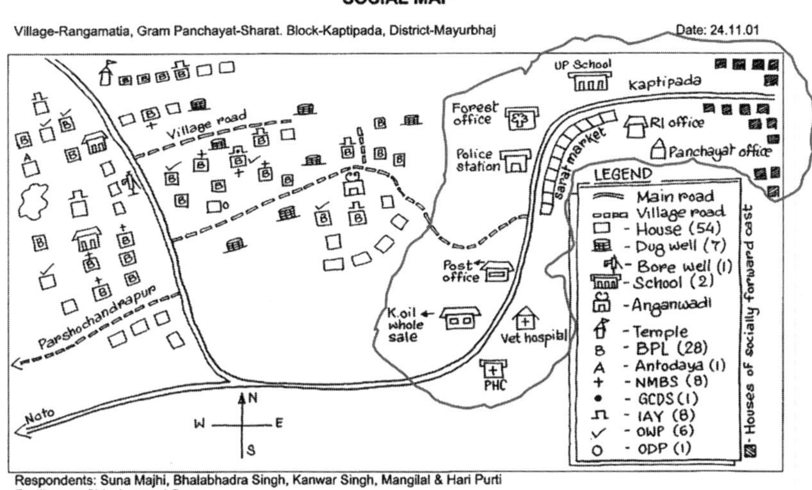

Figure 5.1. Social map illuminating proximity of key infrastructural services to forward caste households
Source: Praxis 2001

the map indicated, in this village, the houses of socially forward castes are located closest to the *panchayat* office, and the school. Maps such as these provided the impetus for the NIEA study.

In 2011 Social Equity Watch identified the need for a large-scale study to capture current infrastructure-and-service-based inequity at a representatively national level and identify disparities between social groups. The broad vision was to address issues of exclusion with regard to infrastructure and services. The key objectives were to capture access and control over resources across different segments of the population and to gather evidence on the equitability of infrastructure placement in villages. When situated within a broader understanding of social inequity, this study could prompt reflection of the contribution of infrastructural access inequity to the cycle of poverty and marginalization in India.

There were three main parts: an infrastructure audit, an equity audit, and an infrastructure access equity audit. The study looked into different infrastructures, met the intended beneficiaries, and found out whether they were accessing these services and why; attempted to understand the significance of location; and obtained some ideas about why certain pieces of infrastructure were improperly located.

The study was designed to enable differentiation of findings along commonly understood fault lines of social opportunity. Separate interactions were therefore held with scheduled castes, scheduled tribes, religious minorities (whether Muslim or Christian), other backward castes and general castes. The basic units of the study were rural villages. 124 villages in nine districts in the states of Andhra Pradesh (24), Bihar (25), Karnataka (25), Odisha (25) and Rajasthan (25), were covered. Two districts were selected in each state: one was a relatively backward district while the other was more developed. A total of twenty-five villages were reached. With the support of the local NGOs and grassroots groups the villages were identified at random, subject to the limitations of accessibility and transportation. While selecting villages attempts were made to ensure that the village councils (*gram panchayats*) were mixed caste, so as to represent the norm for *panchayats* in the district.

Infrastructure Audit

Access to government programmes are first and foremost predicated on these schemes actually being available at the local level. The fair price shop (a unit of the Public Distribution System) and primary schools were the two facilities available in the highest number of villages (121 out of 124). Similarly, the Integrated Child Development Scheme, safe drinking water, *panchayat bhawan* (village office), middle school, road connectivity and post office were available in 100 or more villages. The important facilities which were not available in more than 30 villages included health sub-centres, an electricity connection, community centres and higher secondary schools.

Among the sixteen infrastructural facilities identified, three (public health centre, agriculture office and police station) were always located outside the village at block headquarters, and two facilities, internet kiosks (only found in two villages) and village public telephone (VPT) were largely absent. Therefore only 11 kinds of infrastructure were analysed. Figure 5.2 indicates the number of villages in which certain infrastructure is located.

Table 5.2 Auditing process overview

Process	Key issues	Objectives
Infrastructure Audit	Presence of infrastructure Distance of infrastructure from habitations Status of buildings	To understand the presence of functional infrastructure, its distance from habitations, and the status of buildings in which services were provided
Equity Audit	Access of services from households of socially excluded groups	Presence of functional infrastructure and number of households from vulnerable groups accessing the infrastructural services
Infrastructure Equity Access Audit	Available for use Actual regularity of use Ease of use or access Attitude of service providers Quality of infrastructure	1. Rating the Infrastructure in a ten-point scale 2. Prioritizing the infrastructural services

The study highlighted the extent of gaps in the provision of infrastructure at the village level. Only 11% of the sample villages had all eleven functional infrastructure facilities, 15% of villages had less than five of the infrastructure facilities and a majority of the sample had none of the infrastructure facilities available in the village.

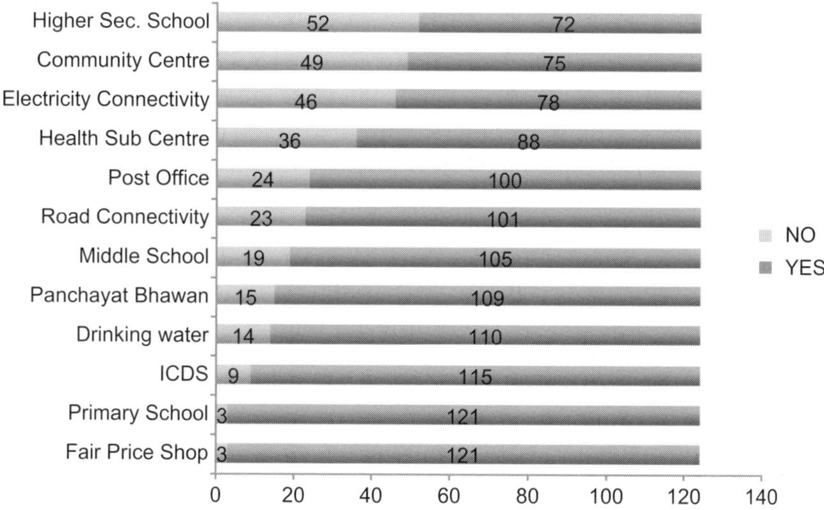

Figure 5.2 Frequency of distribution of certain kinds of infrastructure in sample villages

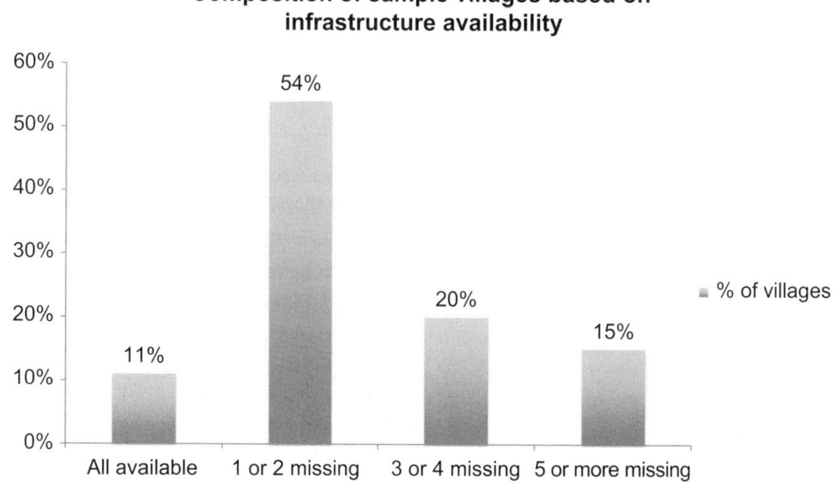

Figure 5.3 Composition of sample villages based on availability of infrastructure

Equity audit

The equity audit collected information on sixteen infrastructure facilities located inside the village. It looked at how infrastructure is distributed across social groups in a given village, as distance is one of the critical factors determining access to services. The equity audit identified that the majority of infrastructure facilities meant for scheduled castes, scheduled tribes and minorities are located in backward caste and general caste habitations. For example, concentration of four functional and important types of infrastructure (*panchayat bhavans* (75%), health sub-centres (61%), higher secondary schools (61%) and post offices (65%)) in general and backward caste habitations indicate how these more marginalized social groups often have to travel to access these services.

The study found that availability of functional infrastructure facilities in various habitations is clearly associated with the caste of inhabitants. For example, 57% of the sample villages had more than 50% of the available infrastructure concentrated in a few backward caste and general habitations. A complete lack of infrastructure in scheduled tribe and minority habitations was found in more than 10% of villages, with services only available in general and backward caste habitations. In some of these villages, the number of households from backward caste and other caste communities accessing the services was greater than the number of scheduled caste, scheduled tribe and minority households. However, from an equity angle it is undesirable that infrastructure should be located outside the habitations of the more disadvantaged groups. Table 5.4 gives an indication of the extent of inequity in the sample villages. The cumulative percentage figure indicates the number at that level of inequity or worse.

Information collected from 299 scheduled caste habitations, 378 scheduled tribe habitations and 50 minority community habitations indicated large-scale inadequacies in infrastructure provision in study areas. A substantial share of scheduled caste, scheduled tribe and minority habitations were left out of official coverage. Even in the case of facilities like primary schools and ICDS, where the coverage was relatively better than other facilities, the actual reach is still inadequate. Similarly, the progress of the flagship Bharat Nirman scheme for road and electricity components was found to be extremely poor with a large proportion of social habitations left uncovered and the scheme had remained a non-starter with respect to village public telephones and internet kiosk services.

The study also found that a substantial proportion of infrastructure facilities physically located in scheduled caste and scheduled tribe communities were located in rented houses and private land, betraying the impermanence and vulnerability of their circumstances. Additionally, even when habitations of scheduled caste, scheduled tribe and religious minorities are within accessible range of an infrastructure, control of the building itself and the services it provided was usually found to rest with those from backward caste and general caste groups.

Table 5.3 Distribution of infrastructure facilities across social habitations in sample villages

	Location of the functional infrastructure facility				
Functional infrastructure facilities	**Only in backward caste/general habitations**	**Spread across various castes' hamlet or in mixed habitations**	**Only in scheduled caste/ scheduled tribe or minority habitations**	**Only in scheduled caste habitations**	**Number of villages where the infrastructure is available**
Panchayat Office	75	3	22	8	109
Post office	65	11	24	9	100
Health sub-centre	61	14	25	7	88
Higher secondary School	61	7	32	11	72
Fair Price shops	46	38	16	3	121
Middle school	44	35	21	7	105
Community centre	35	52	13	9	75
Primary school	22	67	11	3	121
ICDS (including Mini AWC)	21	70	9	3	115
Good road connectivity	18	75	7	0	101
Electricity connectivity	10	81	9	1	78
Drinking Water	10	88	2	1	110

Table 5.4 Extent of inequity of infrastructural provision in the sample villages

Inequity	Definition	Number of villages	Percentage	Cumulative percentage
Critical	Villages where all available facilities are only located in backward caste/general habitations	24	19%	19%
Extreme	Villages where 75% and more (less than 100%) of the available infrastructure facilities are only located in backward caste/general habitations	13	11%	30%
Severe	Villages where 25%–50% of the available infrastructure facilities are only located in backward caste/general habitations	33	27%	57%
Of concern	Villages where 25%–50% of the available infrastructure facilities are only located in backward caste/general habitations	30	24%	81%
Moderate	Certain infrastructure facilities are located only in backward caste/general habitations	24	19%	100%
		124 villages	**100%**	

Infrastructure Access Equity Audit

Separate focus group discussions (FGDs) and infrastructure rating exercises were carried out in each social habitation in a village. In total FGDs were conducted in 121 scheduled caste habitations, 100 scheduled tribe habitations, 99 backward caste habitations, and 82 general caste habitations. Community members rated infrastructural services and also reflected on their engagement with them, using the following indicators: (i) importance, (ii) availability, (iii) ease of access, (iv) regularity of use, and (v) attitude of service providers.

Along each indicator, participants gave a score of between 1–4 (poor), 5–7 (moderate) and 8–10 (good). To ensure appropriate affirmative policy action, community members were then asked to rank each infrastructure and corresponding service in terms of its importance for their habitation.

Ratings based on aggregated results along the different indicators demonstrated clear variations by social group. Ratings by different social groups showed larger variations in the case of certain infrastructural facilities such as the PDS, ICDS and health sub-centre, with ratings of scheduled castes, scheduled tribes and minorities generally lower than those from BC and general caste communities. When ratings for ease of access, regularity of use and attitude of service providers were aggregated and sorted for social group, minorities were found to fare the worst, followed by scheduled castes, scheduled tribes, backward castes, and general castes.

Table 5.5 Access ratings of eight services by different caste and religious groups

	SC	ST	Minorities	BC	General	SC	ST	Minorities	BC	General
	Public distribution system					**Health sub-centre**				
Poor	42	32	30	11	11	54	30	65	44	20
Moderate	32	46	44	37	54	38	58	22	33	58
Good	26	23	26	52	35	9	30	13	22	22
	Primary school					**Post office**				
Poor	24	11	31	16	9	29	27	45	22	15
Moderate	44	53	31	34	62	53	39	24	33	36
Good	32	36	38	49	29	17	34	31	44	49
	Middle school					**Community centre**				
Poor	20	24	39	20	18	54	57	69	48	28
Moderate	46	44	25	40	63	35	19	24	27	49
Good	34	31	36	40	18	11	24	7	25	23
	High school					**ICDS**				
Poor	29	29	48	38	17	34	22	45	16	15
Moderate	47	51	39	32	55	44	51	41	44	45
Good	27	20	13	30	28	23	27	14	40	40

Fair play? Attitudes of service providers

Zooming in on the data on perceived attitudes of service providers illuminates a key dimension of service delivery (see Table 5.6). The perceived attitude of the service provider is likely to be linked to quality of interaction between the rights bearer and the provider.

Scheduled castes, scheduled tribes and minorities' composite ratings of attitudes of service providers to the key public services featured in Table 5.7 are consistently lower than those of backward castes and general castes. The situation is particular alarming with respect to minorities, who, for six of the eight public services, gave a 'poor' rating more frequently than any other social group. The contrast is even clearer in the distribution of 'good' ratings. For five of the eight public services, general castes give this rating more than any other social group, and for the other three services it is backward castes who were most positive about the attitude of service providers.

The satisfaction of various social groups was also generally higher when accessing services within their own habitations (Table 5.7). Ratings by scheduled castes, scheduled tribes and minorities fell when these groups accessed infrastructure in socially distant, upper-caste habitations. However the reverse is not equally true. When upper-caste groups access services in areas belonging

Table 5.6 Group-wise ranking of infrastructure based on attitude of service provider

	Rating (%)	SC	ST	Minorities	BC	General
PDS	Poor	43	38	27	17	17
	Moderate	32	36	36	28	28
	Good	26	26	36	55	55
Primary school	Poor	32	26	33	20	14
	Moderate	37	33	24	32	45
	Good	31	41	42	49	42
Middle school	Poor	35	26	38	26	16
	Moderate	32	36	25	34	49
	Good	32	38	38	40	35
Post office	Poor	40	34	47	37	23
	Moderate	46	44	20	32	34
	Good	14	22	33	31	43
Panchayath Bhavan	Poor	34	20	36	23	13
	Moderate	46	43	30	42	36
	Good	20	37	33	35	52
Sub-centre	Poor	63	54	60	42	27
	Moderate	29	39	24	36	38
	Good	7	7	16	22	35
ICDS	Poor	35	25	39	23	11
	Moderate	44	49	30	40	44
	Good	21	25	30	37	45
Higher secondary school	Poor	38	20	44	33	21
	Moderate	42	54	36	42	40
	Good	20	26	20	25	40
Community centre	Poor	52	59	73	64	27
	Moderate	30	16	17	18	31
	Good	17	24	10	18	41

to scheduled castes, scheduled tribes or religious minorities there is a lower rating, but their experience does not appear to be *as* substantially different as when facilities are located in their own habitations (see Annex 2).

Challenges and limitations

The approach of the NIEA was to work with civil society organizations and give them a tool to work with, rather than a tool for communities to use. This is obviously one step away from a community-driven system, although the potential exists for it to be adapted for community use. As it is, community members were part of the consultative process of the infrastructure access equity audit.

Another limitation is that it was not possible to disaggregate, within the constraints of this study, by particular social group; scheduled castes, scheduled tribes and those from minority religions (Christians and Muslims in our sample) were taken as a single category. This means that figures may obscure varying outcomes for scheduled castes, scheduled tribes and different religious minorities at the village level. Recent studies on social exclusion have tended to focus on the exclusion of Muslims (cf. Sachar et al., 2006).

Subverting for good

NIEA systematically looked at infrastructure-related inequities with the objective of identifying structural barriers that prevent equitable access to government services. Using large-scale field data it scientifically challenged the credibility of government claims on the reach of flagship programmes. It made clear details not visible in official data sources – recognizing the sheer presence of infrastructure is inadequate without some equitable access *to* this infrastructure – particularly from the perspective of the poorest and most excluded. Just as growth data cannot be seen in isolation without probing the inequality behind it, infrastructural and social services data cannot be seen without exploring hidden inequities.

The audit focused on systemic biases in infrastructural provision, arrangements for the delivery of key services and their impact on communities who depend on them. The investigation into infrastructural location showed marked patterns of inequity in favour of more privileged social groups: general and backward castes. It showed that *dalits*, tribal and religious minorities of India face multiple deprivations and discrimination with regard to access to infrastructure. Critical public services are consistently located in upper-caste locations and there are still numerous scheduled tribe and scheduled caste habitations officially left uncovered. The people in these habitations have to travel longer distances than prescribed in official norms.

Refusing to treat the village as a homogenous entity in the way that it is normally presented by policymakers, the study – unusually – took account of inter-social group power dynamics. It showed not just that the infrastructure was located nearer the habitations of these more privileged communities; more often than not, the staff running these facilities also hailed from these communities. Focus group consultations also showed that people from religious minorities, SC and ST backgrounds rate the services these infrastructure facilities provide less highly than more privileged social groups. The study also found that more disadvantaged social groups – and especially religious minorities – experience a greater drop in the quality of the service provider's attitude when they try to access services outside of their own habitations than more socially privileged castes do (see Table 5.7).

In wider public discourse, distances involved in accessing facilities from another social habitation are often trivialized and homogenized as geographical distance. Whilst geographical distance may play its part, in the rural Indian context there are other factors that need to be taken into account. Although socio-economically excluded groups are more dependent on some of these services, the study suggested that they find it harder to access them. Furthermore, when infrastructure is located in the area of an upper caste group, this appears to be more of a barrier to access than it is for upper-caste community members when the infrastructure is located in a habitation belonging to one of the excluded groups. It is possible that the social power of general and backward caste groups places them in a better position from which to access service providers from other habitations.

It is likely that social distance compounds geographical distance due to difficulties (feared or realized) involved in negotiating the route to a destination. In village contexts in India, 'as the crow flies' is far from adequate as a true measure of how much effort is required, and how much risk needs to be taken, to reach essential services. Where geographical distance to a service in a village favours a more powerful group, such as an upper-caste community, those who live further away, and who have to manage a trip through an upper caste area to reach the destination point, are further disadvantaged. The route – every step – can be a challenge for someone from a disadvantaged background. For example, for a girl child from a *dalit* community, going, for example, to school, it can be daunting to travel through upper caste communities. It is not surprising, given such circumstances, that numerous schemes to provide bicycles for girls have been set up in India. Social distance thus adds to geographical distance to contribute to social exclusion. This combined disadvantage can, in some circumstances, take the form of exclusion from regular, easy access to services. Merely situating infrastructural facilities in general or backward caste habitations can, in effect, fence off less privileged groups from regular access to them.

Thus it is particularly concerning when, as the infrastructure audit revealed, there are concentrations of multiple infrastructural facilities in certain higher caste habitations. And even more so in the case of infrastructure under the Bharat Nirman scheme – such as roads and electricity, infrastructure that cannot effectively be 'shared' – which is unavailable outside general and backward caste habitations in more than 10% of villages.

This state of affairs calls for some critical discussion. The array of targeted policies, reservations and safeguards introduced since independence has undeniably played an essential role in challenging some of the country's most deep-rooted patterns of discrimination and exclusion. However, implementation of visionary schemes continues to hit considerable ground-level barriers.

It would appear that flagship schemes and other programmes assume the existence of certain local level factors, which are in fact missing, such as a context of equity and equal rights for different communities. The idea that introducing certain infrastructure in a village will secure the equal access of all social groups in that village to a particular service is predicated on the possibility of equality of access to services in the village. But if that possibility is remote or, indeed, out of the question, then the achievement of the scheme has effectively been made contingent on a set of circumstances that it itself has no scope to tackle. Evidently, location matters, but currently, infrastructural schemes do not enforce equitable locational norms. The trends observable in the NIEA data go further than suggesting that the configuration of habitations do not matter for equity of access in relation to services; they actually imply the existence of factors that pull services into the habitations of more privileged communities.

The audit showed that policies cannot be implemented in a power-neutral way: local power structures can subvert any policy, vested interests can use programmes for their own ends; a recent study into infrastructure suggested that a considerable amount of funds is diverted to political rent seeking (see Khemani, 2010). And, at the point of delivery, the attitude of many government staff at the local level can also mar citizens' experience of services.

Infrastructure that is harder to access for some groups than it is for others is self-evidently failing infrastructure. As policy – at the level of a promise – a scheme may represent an abstract form of justice. But its delivery as *entitlement to justice* is indeed vulnerable to multiple forms of corruption and manipulation, dependent as it is on many layers of human involvement, and subject to tackling whatever barriers to equity exist at the local level. The empowering potential of policies cannot be reaped without understanding these issues and mechanisms are needed to quash any local-level barriers to implementation.

The framing of policy itself also warrants some scrutiny. The language of the flagship programmes is typically goal-oriented, not barrier-focused (see Chapter 7). They are therefore somewhat depoliticized and lacking in analytical teeth, eschewing barriers of social exclusion and corruption. A lesson from the study is that securing social justice is not just about empowering the poor, but also about providing good services for the poor; it is not just about strengthening the demand-side, but also about getting the supply-side right. However, achieving this requires tackling forces that are deeply opposed to any kind of equitable vision for India.

Conclusions

NIEA emerged out of a value-based 'social equity audit' approach which looked at development from the lens of the most marginalized. Significantly for a large-scale policy audit, it was led by local civil society groups. The role and support of partner organizations, civil society organizations and community volunteers was crucial in this study, and the partner organizations contributed to study expenses as well.

It is a tool to influence policymakers and decision-makers to be sensitive to hitherto under-discussed dimensions of inequity. It can arm community groups and civil society organizations with information they need, to expose injustice in public service delivery. The methodology used in the NIEA study has the potential to hold the state to account on reaching out to the most marginalized social groups. It can also, as an ongoing monitoring tool, address the intermediate need of reviewing the progress made in terms of infrastructure-based inclusion. In the long term, it may also help to uncover some of the deeper structural barriers embedded in the fabric of post-feudal social relations in contexts of agrarian transition, especially in parts of north India. Such relations are characterized by a new kind of exploitative patron-client typology in which powerful groups are now running the services and the disadvantaged groups are the ones knocking on the door of these services.

Clearly, a bold option for the poor and the marginalized is required if investment in infrastructural services is going to generate equitable returns. What is most critically needed is to involve all social groups, but especially the most marginalized, in decision-making processes about infrastructural allocation. They need to be asked not just what infrastructure they want, but also where they want this infrastructure to be located (see Chapter 2 and Chapter 4 for examples of where community consultation has been used effectively within aided development work). Typically, policy implementation has been unchecked by such equity tools.

The study proved that social inclusion does not 'just happen'. The task ahead is to monitor the location of new infrastructure, so that the existing equity gap can be closed over the years. The fact that the equity gap is less for certain services such as ICDS – where some government guidelines exist for encouraging equitable distribution of infrastructure – than for other infrastructure, suggests that scope exists for equitable distribution of resources through proactive measures. This is crucial for scarce resources such as drinking water and will in the coming years also be important for certain newer infrastructure such as internet kiosks.

Equitable infrastructural services have to be carefully planned, comprehensively designed and sensitively executed. Inclusion needs to be core to development planning and service delivery, not an optional add-on. If infrastructure is developed without proper mechanisms to ensure that the voices and interests of different social groups within the community are heard and acted upon, development schemes will actually serve to entrench inequity rather than end it. To address this, consultation with community members, or community involvement in village planning, is vital to ensure that the interests of marginalized people are not sidelined.

About the authors

Tom Thomas, Praxis. Tom has over 20 years' experience in the development sector and has led Praxis on several tasks that have provided critical inputs into development policy and thinking on social development, in India and in several countries across South Asia.

Moulasha Kader, Praxis. Moulasha is a demographer and researcher by training. He has more than 15 years' experience working with national and international development agencies.

Rohan Preece, Praxis. Rohan has worked with development sector organizations in different parts of India and the UK and has experience in social research, teaching and monitoring and evaluation.

Endnotes

1. This chapter is a compilation of information and analysis from the National Infrastructure Equity Audit (NIEA) report produced by Praxis at the culmination of a study by the same name. The study was led by Tom Thomas and M. Kumaran from Praxis, and the secretariat of Social Equity Watch (SEW), a network of organizations working in the development sector with a keen interest in issues of social equity. A detailed list of contributors and supporters is in Annex 1.
2. This figure indicates a slight increase from 2011, when it was 1.2% of GDP, and 2010, when it was 1.0% of GDP; but is still very much at the low end of the global scale of public spending on health. See World Bank Health Expenditure, public (% of GDP) available at <http://data.worldbank.org/indicator/SH.XPD.PUBL.ZS>.

References

Baru, R., Acharya, A., Acharya, S., Shiva Kumar, A.K., and Nagaraj, K., (2010), 'Inequities in Access to Health Services in India: Caste, Class and Region', *Economic and Political Weekly Volume*, 45:38 pp. 49–58.

Bogardus, E.S. (1925) 'Measuring Social Distance', *Journal of Applied Sociology* 9: 299–308.

Brenneman, A., Kerf, M. (2002) *Infrastructure and Poverty Linkages – A Literature Review*, Washington, DC: The World Bank <http://www.oit.org/wcmsp5/groups/public/@ed_emp/@emp_policy/@invest/documents/publication/wcms_asist_8281.pdf> [last accessed on 6 June 2014].

Burange, L.G., Karnik, N.N., and Ranadive, R.R. (2012) 'India's Exclusive Growth and Assessment, Articles and Case Studies: Inclusive & Sustainable Growth Conference', *International Journal of Academic Conference Proceedings*, 1:2 <http://www.ijacp.org/ojs/index.php/ISG> [last accessed on 4 June 2014].

Deshpande, A. (2013) 'Exclusion and Inclusive Growth', United Nations Development Program, Delhi.

Dreze, J., and Sen, A., (2013) *An Uncertain Glory: India and its Contradictions*, London: Penguin – Allen Lane.

Dubochet, L. (2013), 'Making Post-2015 Matter for Socially Excluded Groups in India', Oxfam, Oxfam India Working Papers Series.

Govinda, R. and Bandhyopadhyay, M., (2008) 'Access to Elementary Education in India – Country Analytical Review', *Consortium for Research on Educational Access, Transitions and Equity (CREATE).*

Nambissan, G.B., (2009) 'Exclusion and Discrimination in Schools: Experiences of Dalit Children', *Working Paper Series*, New Delhi: Indian Institute of Dalit Studies and UNICEF, <http://dalitstudies.org.in/wp/wps0101.pdf> [Accessed 5 June 2014].

National Family Health Survey, 2005–06, Indian Institute of Population Studies, <http://www.rchiips.org/nfhs/> [Accessed on 5 June 2014].

Planning Commission (2007), 11th Five Year Plan 2007–2012, Volume 1: Inclusive Growth, http://planningcommission.nic.in/plans/planrel/fiveyr/welcome.html (Accessed on 4 June 2014).

Planning Commission (2011) 'Faster, Sustainable and More Inclusive Growth', *Approach Paper to the 12th Five Year Plan*, Government of India, Government of India Planning Commission.

Sachar et al. (2006) *Report on Social, Economic and Educational Status of the Muslim Community of India*, Prime Minister's High Level Committee, Cabinet Secretariat, Government of India.

Sedwal, M and Kamat. S, (2008) 'Education and Social Equity – With A Special Focus on Scheduled Tribes and Scheduled Castes in Education', *CREATE: University of Sussex*, Research monograph Number 19.

SSA (2006–07,) 'National Evaluation of Civil Works Under SSA in 11 States – Synthesis Report', Sarva Shiksha Abhiyan, Ministry of Human Resource Development, Government of India.

UNESCO (2009) *Education for All Global Monitoring Report 2010: Reaching the Marginalised*, <http://unesdoc.unesco.org/images/0018/001866/186606E.pdf> [Accessed 4 June 2014].

World Bank (2014) Health expenditure, public (% of GDP), Available at: <http://data.worldbank.org/indicator/SH.XPD.PUBL.ZS> [Accessed 4 June 2014].

Annex 1: list of contributors

Participating Organizations: Agragamee, Orissa; Centre for Social Equity and Inclusion, Bihar; Gram Jagat, Bihar; Maruganga Society, Rajasthan; National Campaign for Dalit Human Rights (NCDHR), Delhi and Bihar; Prajwala Sangham, Andhra Pradesh; Sanchaynela, Bangalore; Unnati, Rajasthan; Vasundhara Sewa Samiti, Rajasthan.

Design and Methodology: Praxis – Institute for Participatory Practices, New Delhi; Daniel Edwin; Manuel Alphonse; Paul Diwakar.

Annex 2

The study results show that the satisfaction of a social group is higher when they access services from their own habitation. The rating declines when the social groups access infrastructure from 'upper' caste groups, which is socially distant from these marginalized social groups. However the reverse is not equally true. When the 'upper' caste groups access services from SC/ST or minority groups there is a lower rating, but these are not as substantially different from the ratings they give to facilities in their habitations. However for certain services like AWC, and to some extent in schools, where midday meals are provided, the ratings by general caste groups for infrastructure located in SC habitations were poor. However their ratings for ease of access, availability, and attitude of service providers resulted in moderate or good ratings for infrastructure in SC and ST habitations. Perhaps the social power with the general and backward caste groups places them in a better position to make the service providers from other habitations accountable. This information is presented in the tables below.

Table 5.7 Group-wise rating of service at different types of village infrastructure, according to location of infrastructure

Interviewed groups	Rating	Habitation where the fair price shop is located				Habitation where the primary school is located			
		SC	ST	BC	GEN	SC	ST	BC	GEN
SC	Poor (%)	0	13	56	50	0	50	17	12.5
	Moderate	25	25	33	50	100	0	67	50
	Good (%)	75	63	11	0	0	50	17	37.5
ST	Poor (%)	0	22	71	29	NA	0	NA	0
	Moderate	0	44	14	71	NA	33	NA	60
	Good (%)	100	33	14	0	NA	67	NA	40
BC	Poor (%)	25	0	11	25	33	0	0	25
	Moderate	0	25	53	25	67	0	43	25
	Good (%)	75	75	37	50	0	100	57	50
Interviewed groups	**Rating**	**Habitation where the middle school is located**				**Habitation where the senior secondary school is located**			
		SC	**ST**	**BC**	**GEN**	**SC**	**ST**	**BC**	**GEN**
SC	Poor (%)	17	22	0	31	13	8	0	60
	Moderate	50	56	55	46	50	62	50	20
	Good (%)	33	22	45	23	38	31	50	20
ST	Poor (%)	0	11	44	22	60	15	0	57
	Moderate	0	78	11	56	40	62	43	29
	Good (%)	100	11	44	22	0	23	57	14
BC	Poor (%)	25	20	15	50	0	33	27	57
	Moderate	75	30	31	25	33	33	9	14
	Good (%)	0	50	54	25	67	33	64	29
GEN	Poor (%)	0	NA	33	22	0	0	25	43
	Moderate	100	NA	33	67	67	100	38	29
	Good (%)	0	NA	33	11	33	0	38	29

(Continued)

Table 5.7 Group-wise rating of service at different types of village infrastructure, according to location of infrastructure (continued)

Interviewed groups	Rating	Habitation where the AWC is located				Habitation where the sub-centre is located			
		SC	ST	BC	GEN	SC	ST	BC	GEN
SC	Poor (%)	0	0	25	14	75	14	40	56
	Moderate	100	80	75	86	25	71	40	44
	Good (%)	0	20	0	0	0	14	20	0
ST	Poor (%)	NA	0	NA	20	50	25	20	25
	Moderate	NA	75	NA	80	50	63	40	75
	Good (%)	NA	25	NA	0	0	13	40	0
BC	Poor (%)	0	0	0	0	67	33	45	57
	Moderate	0	0	50	0	33	50	18	29
	Good (%)	100	100	50	100	0	17	36	14
GEN	Poor (%)	100	NA	0	0	0	NA	40	23
	Moderate	0	NA	0	25	100	NA	40	69
	Good (%)	0	NA	100	75	0	NA	20	8
Interviewed groups	**Rating**	**Habitation where the community centre is located**				**Habitation where the post office is located**			
		SC	**ST**	**BC**	**GEN**	**SC**	**ST**	**BC**	**GEN**
SC	Poor (%)	0	100	67	20	29	18	24	19
	Moderate	80	0	33	80	29	64	55	69
	Good (%)	20	0	0	0	43	18	21	13
ST	Poor (%)	50	100	NA	0	25	27	14	50
	Moderate	0	0	NA	0	50	55	36	20
	Good (%)	50	0	NA	100	25	18	50	30
BC	Poor (%)	67	100	50	50	33	27	4	40
	Moderate	33	0	50	0	0	27	50	10
	Good (%)	0	0	0	50	67	45	46	50
GEN	Poor (%)	0	NA	67	25	25	NA	17	7
	Moderate	0	NA	33	50	50	NA	56	27
	Good (%)	100	NA	0	25	25	NA	28	67

Note: Not Adequate (NA) in certain cells refers to an inadequate sample size for inference purposes

CHAPTER 6

A new deluge? People and aid in the aftermath of disaster

Moulasha Kader, Ajai Kuruvila, and Shireen Kurian

Abstract

The days that followed the 2004 tsunami witnessed an unprecedented generation and mobilization of aid. In Tamil Nadu, the deluge of aid pushed NGOs and the Government to act in haste without considering ground realities and local perspectives that held communities and their livelihoods together. Amidst all this efforts were made to highlight the primacy of ownership of the coast by people who, for generations, earned their livelihoods from fishing and by other artisanal communities who had sustained their livelihoods from the sea. Testifying to the robustness of these local communities and the distinctiveness of their world views, this chapter suggests that community participation in post-disaster planning is non-negotiable, and can be undertaken effectively.

Keywords: tsunami, relief and rehabilitation, fishing communities, coastal communities, village-level plan

Background

The tsunami that struck the east coast of India on 26 December 2004 caused tidal waves that were 7–10 metres in height, penetrated 1.5 km inland and left in their wake a massive trail of destruction. It devastated coastal communities, killing thousands, wiping out the livelihoods of tens of thousands of households, and destroying houses, boats, fishing gear, agricultural lands and salt pans. Tamil Nadu was the worst affected Indian state, with the official death toll close to 8,000.

Although the fishing community was the worst hit, the livelihoods of other coastal communities were also equally affected by this disaster. The response to the tsunami was unprecedented. In India, as elsewhere, the government, donor organizations, various NGOs, religious institutions, corporate entities and individuals poured in relief material and exhibited timely concern and care. The district administrations were provided with sufficient resources by directive of the state leadership including personnel, technical and emergency support to ensure that the relief phase was a comprehensive success. The district administrations enlisted the help of organizations such as South India

http://dx.doi.org/10.3362/9781780448695.006

Federation of Fisherman Societies (SIFFS) and Social Need Educational and Human Awareness (SNEHA), who had a presence in the coastal villages over many years and were engaged in fisheries-related livelihoods and social uplift.

Moving into the recovery and rehabilitation phase required a concrete understanding of the socio-economic, cultural and political contexts of the coast. Fisheries-related livelihoods remain the primary source of income and sustenance for the majority of the communities on the coast. Although one can come across a few agriculturists and traders within the fishing community, by and large fishing remains the primary livelihood choice of the community. Fishing has its high and low periods and the months of March, April, and August are the best in terms of size of catch. The fish catch reduces between October and December as the sea is rough and very few households are able to venture out to sea. Migration is common during this lean phase and fishermen generally migrate to areas with comparatively gentler waves. Caste plays a predominant role in the fishing community that was most affected by the tsunami.

The fisher community that was affected most by the tsunami, largely used to sail in traditional fishing boats called *kattumarams*. With time, due to aggressive fishing strategies to maximize the fish catch, fish stocks within the continental shelf started dwindling and some community members started using fishing boats with outboard engines to go longer distances into the sea. Fibreglass boats with engines, also referred to as *maruti* boats, were also used. These boats tend to be expensive and typically have high operating costs. *Maruti* boats were able to venture into deeper waters than *kattumarams*, and so their catch consisted of larger fish varieties that fetched better prices at market.

In all this, however, complex processes over time enabled some to become boat owners, net owners, and outboard motor owners. A cooperative infrastructure brought the coastal community together into fisheries-related livelihoods. The fishing community had evolved its own equitable ways of breaking the vessel's catch into shares that were distributed as per the participation of each person, both by way of skill and kind (by way of ownership of boat, nets and motor). In these relationships, the ones who own fishing gear or the boat often take upon themselves greater risks than the one who is participating in the fishing operation without gear. Each time the boat goes out to sea, the catch would not necessarily break even when the costs associated with gear, fuel and other incidental costs were taken into account. During such times, those who have an ownership stake in the gear or boat suffer most.

The caste dimension comes into play because the *dalit* commuity, closely associated with one of the two dominant groups, live on the fringes of the coastal habitations. They are involved in providing the labour and enterprise needed to move the post-harvest operations from the domain of the dominant community to the market. They are engaged in preparing, loading and moving the catch out of the coast. They are further hired as wage labourers in the larger fishing vessels (trawlers) that operate off the coast in deep seas. The nets that these vessels use are not suitable to maintain the sensitive balance that exists between fish catch and its sustainable propagation.

The coastal communities were located in a very fragile relationship with the marine fish resources and the coast itself. The coast, being the tail-end of the terrestrial ecosystem, was being subjected to a lot of stress, and this was affecting the fisheries-related marine resources. This situation often put fishermen in direct conflict with other interests that were growing the area, such as the hospitality industry. Industries found the coast a convenient place to be located as they could save on the management of industrial effluent by dumping it into the sea. Tourism as well as related interests were eyeing the coast for better prospects. The state itself had come into the picture through the introduction of Coastal Regulatory zones in the Environment (Protection) Act of 1986. The state, though recognizing fishermen as guardians of the coast, did little to challenge the growth of other private interests in sensitive parts of the coast, instead siding with them in promoting different commercial ventures on the coast.

This pushed the fishing communities into direct conflict with these interests. There were few regulatory norms governing the coast and the fisheries sector could do little to prevent these interests from appropriating the coast and traditionally coast-dependent communities. Gradually the traditional fishing practices were displaced by larger interests that hoped to maximize on marine fisheries-related resources for the export and retail market outside the coast. With these came predatory fishing practices, including trawler fishing using nets, and large mechanized vessels that quickly eroded the marine resources of the continental shelf and then moved further into deep-sea fishing. The balance between adequate supply of fish for consumption, the market, and a healthy marine environment was already being tested in the pre-tsunami period. The post-tsunami relief efforts added to this equation the excess supply of non-traditional motorized fishing boats which far outweighed the carrying capacity of the coast. Ironically, this happened during a time when the fishing community was giving serious thought to diversifying livelihoods amongst at least a small proportion of the community so that there would be reduced stress on dwindling marine resources.

The fishermen's villages in the region retained much of the characteristics of a village republic, with the traditional *panchayat* (*meenavar panchayat* or fisherman's council) at the helm of affairs. The institution has modernized to a significant extent, with its own systems of revenue generation, dispute resolution mechanisms and adjudication procedures, public relations and interface with the outside world. In several respects, the traditional *panchayat* had evolved as a meaningful form of democracy. The deliberations and decision-making process were more akin to direct democracy, where almost every major decision is taken in a larger consultative process, involving all the men in the community. As much as the *panchayat* played a vital role in developing norms mainly pertaining to fishing, its role extended to almost every aspect of the fishermen's lives.

Yet, while the *panchayat* had maintained its level of power because of its incredible level of accountability to its people, the institution had not been very inclusive of vulnerable and disadvantaged sections such as women. They had further not been equitable in the sharing of common resources with socially backward groups who participate in the sustainment of fisheries-related livelihoods. Women were completely excluded from all decision-making processes of the body. Although the *panchayat* had some important democratic characteristics, there was no formal place for women to express opinions, let alone participate. This level of unquestioned authority was paralysing for certain vulnerable groups, which were left with no place to turn in the aftermath of the tsunami. It was common to find single women who had been excluded from the relief net of the state and civil society, as community norms justified this exclusion based on the patriarchal idea that they did not have a family to support and so did not merit the recognition due to those who had. Having a family enabled participating in a strategic economic function that upheld the community identity.

The post-tsunami scenario threw open the door to many well meaning interventionists for whom the disaster had opened up a window of opportunity, and the possibility of social re-engineering, even if at the cost of side-stepping the unique institution of the traditional *panchayat.* What we observed, then, were overzealous agencies of relief, rehabilitation and reconstruction breaking down and dismantling long-established community institutions. This threatened to alter the social fabric of these districts, disrupting the power equations prevalent within this relatively homogenous community.

Social re-engineering in the name of development

Given the magnitude and international scale of the tsunami, there was an unprecedented level of aid money available from across the globe. The post-disaster situation, regretfully, required several agencies to spend the money disbursed to them quickly, irrespective of ground-level complexities. The indiscriminate use of money and the tendency to spend on visible things was thus built into the international emergency aid framework. For example, NGOs had, in several reported instances, been reduced to telling the donors that 'x' number of communities or people were covered or 'n' number of things were distributed within record time.

In the process, the intricacies of the political economy of the coastal communities, especially the fishing community, seemed to have been lost on several agencies involved in relief, rehabilitation and reconstruction efforts. Agencies with no previous experience of engaging with the coastal communities ended up superimposing their agrarian analysis onto the fishing community. In the scramble to provide relief and rehabilitation to affected communities, international NGOs and aid agencies overlooked the obvious by misunderstanding that the political economy of the fishing community is vastly different from that of the agrarian political economy.

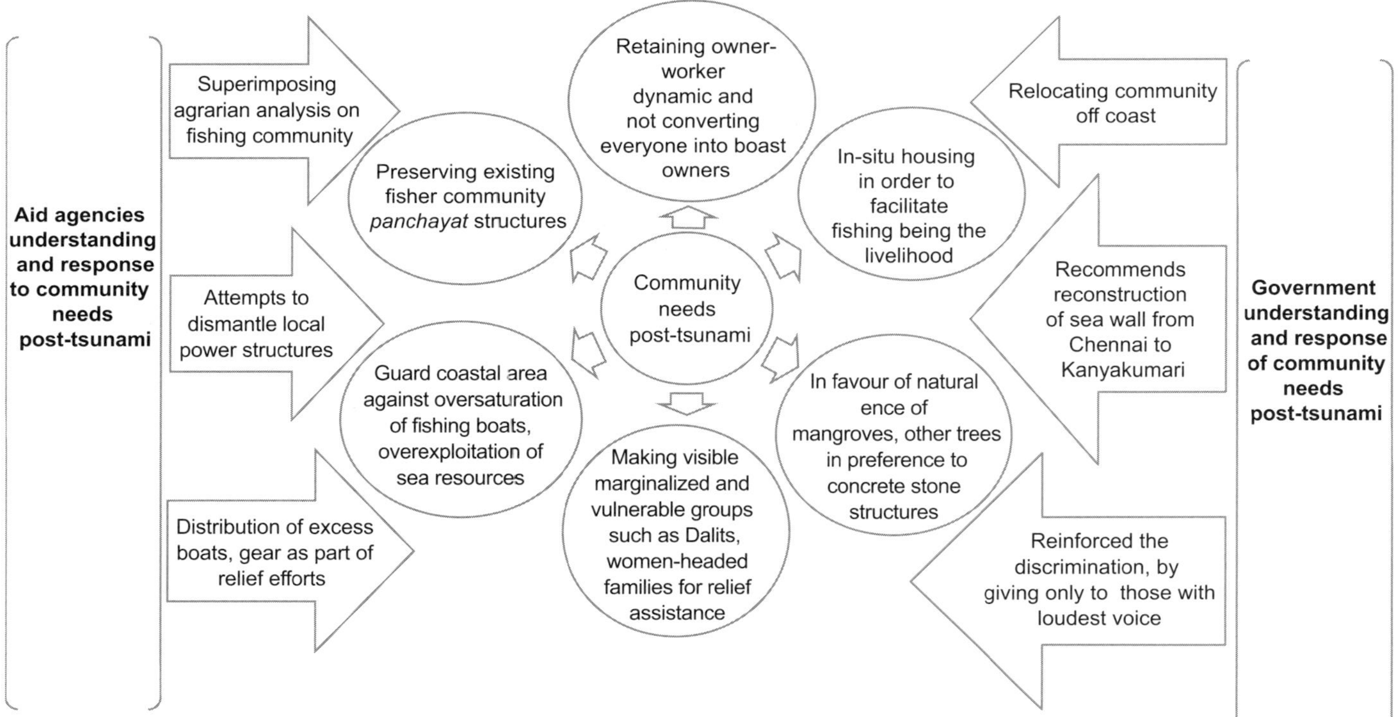

Figure 6.1 Mind map of how aid agencies and government squeezed community interests in the name of development

The fishing community, which was the worst affected, had hundreds of years of storied traditions, with unique social, political, and economic dynamics, that fell outside the worldview of these agencies. Often, these intricacies are not easily understood by the outsider, leading to a rather crude quest for social re-engineering. The enthusiasm often springs from the mindset that development agencies are mandated to use disasters to re-engineer the social fabric in favour of the disadvantaged.

This became apparent in the post-tsunami scenario, as the tsunami presented an opportunity for government, and aid and relief agencies to do some social equity engineering, and lift the crew members to the boat-owning class, by providing them with equipment and gear. Boats were given out under group ownership schemes, with the avowed objective of turning boatless labourers into boat owners, all the while assuming that this was similar to turning a landless labourer into one of the land-owning class. It became clear that in a post-disaster situation, when it was critical that the government, donor and NGO community strategized on how to approach livelihood rehabilitation, they had to avoid looking at the fishing community through an agrarian lens.

One thing that most interventions did not take into account was that unlike in agrarian contexts where the farmers and labourers interact with private property, in fisheries-related livelihoods, the community interacts with a common property – the sea. Thus, perceiving the owner-worker dynamic in the fishing community as similar to the well-defined class-based relationships in the agrarian context was a mistake, as the distinction between owner and worker is not between classes, but between strata within the same class. In addition, unlike the agrarian economy where the labourers are wage-earners, the fisherman is a shareholder in a business. Surprisingly, while social engineering was attempted in the fishing sector under the garb of tsunami rehabilitation these agencies shied away from any such attempts in the agricultural milieu of Nagapattinam.

A large number of NGOs and development support agencies distributed motorized fibreglass boats free of cost to tsunami-affected fishermen. While the spirit underlying the act may have been praiseworthy, there was a need to guard the coast against an oversaturation of fishing boats in view of the declining catch for small and marginal fishermen. Even afterwards, in the ensuing debate on mechanized boats and trawlers, it became clear that fishing off coastlines was evidently a zero-sum game, and no incremental catch was possible without denting the catch of fellow fishermen operating in the area. A large number of trawlers used nets of very small mesh-size, which not only caught small fishes but also wiped out fish fingerlings from the deep trenches of sea. There was a strong need to regulate this to avoid endangering marine fisheries resources in the long run.

In the aftermath of the tsunami, as fishermen awaited the new boats and nets to return to the sea, the formerly thriving fish market was completely paralysed.

Box 6.1 Panchayat struggles

Nambiar Nagar, as the head of village for all the 64 villages of Pattinavar community, enjoyed a prestigious position. No major temple festival or function began before the arrival of the *panchayat* members of Nambiar Nagar (a village). In the aftermath of the tsunami, however, a bitter struggle for supremacy erupted between the *panchayats* of Nambiar Nagar and Akkaraipettai. Akkaraipettai proclaimed itself as the head village of the Pattinavar community on the grounds that it has a higher population and wealth.

With its proximity to the sea, this fishing community was directly hit by the tsunami. The traditional *panchayats* were at the forefront of all relief and rehabilitation efforts being undertaken in their respective villages. The *panchayat* members worked to locate and identify the dead and make arrangements for last rites. The *panchayat* was the nerve centre on whom officials of various government departments depended, be it the district collectorate or the fisheries department, to identify details of damage and loss of life. They were also the contact point for external agencies that were engaged in distribution of relief and planning for the rehabilitation of the tsunami-affected. The key role played by the *panchayat* after the tsunami clearly indicated the acceptability and respect the traditional governance system had amongst the community members. However, the mammoth damage and unprecedented flow of funds and relief material resulted in turmoil and dissatisfaction with the functioning of many *panchayats* in several tsunami-affected villages. Instances of corruption and exclusion, especially of women-headed families were recorded in several villages, with a number of corruption charges levelled against some *panchayat* members.

The sudden upheaval resulted in Nambiar Nagar's *panchayat* being dissolved, in a major blow to the traditional system. The trawler labourers of the village were dissatisfied with the *panchayat's* decision not to exaggerate the losses of engine *kattumarams* and fibreglass boats despite the fact that it had the opportunity to do so. Instead, the *panchayat* only showed the labourers as owners of small vessels. As a result, the trawler labourers formed a labour union to protect their interests – a major departure from the traditions of the Pattinavar community. It indicated a loss of faith in the *panchayat's* ability to represent the interests of all sections of the community. While the members of the labour union saw the formation of the union as an attempt to take up the legitimate concerns of labourers, the *panchayat* and their supporters perceived it as a revolt against the traditional institution. The *panchayat* members stepped down from their posts as they felt it would be difficult for them to function effectively given the polarization of the village. The *panchayat* thus stood dissolved.

The perception that rehabilitation of the fishing sector was a simple straightforward issue of replacing fishing gear was challenged. One of the lessons post-tsunami was that indiscriminate distribution of boats, motors and nets, with the intention of improving the livelihoods of fishermen, would lead to severe economic repercussions. This distribution did not factor in that these engines involved an increased financial burden, because of their increased running costs (fuel, repairs, etc.): an expenditure that many fishermen (those who were not previously boat owners) were not used to bearing.

Thus, while the community attempted to maximize its sasset base in the context of external agencies' willingness to spend indiscriminately, the fisheries-related cooperative infrastructure broke down. This resulted in widespread ambiguity and conflict among participating fleet members who would go into the sea. In turn this had an impact on the traditional *panchayats* and their ability to address livelihood-related upheaval and resulting conflict.

The contribution of aid agencies to the dismantling and reinvention of power structures and disruption of power dynamics within the *panchayat* structure had a telling blow on the community's efforts to rebuild their lives. The callous disregard shown by some relief agencies to the traditional governance structure of the coastal communities was an acute problem. It was therefore important for aid agencies to move beyond the stereotype when assessing the role and relevance of traditional institutions of self-governance. The immense role that the *panchayat* and the collective consciousness of the fishing community played in bouncing back from the tragedy needed to be deciphered and its true worth acknowledged. Instead, organizations assumed that they could engage with a fishing village on their own terms, without properly consulting the traditional *panchayat*. There had been instances of attempts at demonizing the traditional *panchayat* as '*katta panchayat*' (meaning a corrupt *panchayat* where decisions were taken based on caste and financial power). In more than one instance this degenerated into conscious re-engineering attempts to dismantle traditional *panchayats*, work directly with families, and even form alternate groupings that subvert the authority of the *panchayats*. Bypassing leaders in the community, and making assumptions about the relevance and responsiveness of the traditional governance structure is risky when formulating relief and rehabilitation initiatives. Aside from inappropriate short-term relief efforts, this misjudgement was often on display when discussing with the institution of the traditional *panchayat* in long-term rehabilitation plans.

The reality could not be skirted around: emergency relief and rehabilitation had assumed the proportions of a full-fledged sector or industry. What it underscored was the need for interventions to take on board the question of downward accountability to communities and not just upward accountability to donors. There was clearly a compelling case for a thorough reassessment of the framework of accountability associated with emergency money.

The role of government

Following the tsunami, ill-conceived government plans under the guise of implementing safety measures came under much criticism. These plans for indiscriminate construction of sea walls were a case in point. Going by experience, attempts of this nature were usually only meant to fill the pockets of the contractor lobby and could have irrevocably altered the marine environment while offering little protection against natural disasters. They had therefore to be approached with caution. Due to proactive lobbying by the community, environmentalists, agricultural scientists and civil society, the critical importance of natural protection measures such as sand dunes and mangroves was emphasized. The native as well as scientific wisdom of such protection measures was highlighted, ensuring that mangrove plantation took place in areas along the coast.

Government departments and hundreds of aid agencies were confronted by an overwhelmingly complex situation and a lack of coordination – and policies – to guide the response. It was of utmost necessity that the disaster and the aftermath take into consideration the history of the coastal communities, the community voice in process of rehabilitation, the inequitable distribution of power (decision-making and access to resources be it political and/or economic) along with societal dynamics. Beyond livelihood restoration, the need of the hour was interventions, with a participatory, equitable, flexible, decentralized and transparent approach.

The traditional *panchayat* continued to serve as the key communicator with other fishing communities through Nagapattinam district and Tamil Nadu. The *panchayat* was the main representative of the village to the outside, particularly when it involved any interface with government officials. In spite of the state's active role in supplying villages with certain services, such as housing, the socio-political organization of the community centered around the traditional *panchayat*. Given that issues of conflict resolution were entirely managed by the *panchayat*, and the state had a minimal role to play, villages such as Chinnangudi and Tharangambadi (Nagapattinam) consciously avoided the sort of active involvement of the state, and adopted their own mechanisms to handle internal conflicts and financial obstacles.

This process was supported by organizations such as South India Federation of Fisherman Societies (SIFFS) and Social Need Educational and Human Awareness (SNEHA), who facilitated extensive consultative processes with communities and elicited community perspectives that were circulated among the aid and state machinery. The efforts of such fisherman organizations to sensitize aid perspectives and subvert aid agencies' efforts to socially re-engineer coastal communities without understanding their contexts enabled organizations such as Praxis to facilitate participatory processes that could engage the communities, map their livelihood-related issues, and increase their bargaining power in the context of sound perspectives and village-level plans. Praxis, then, in collaboration with SIFFS and SNEHA, further used these perspectives as primary starting points in their efforts to move from the mapping of the tsunami-affected habitations to facilitating the documenting of aspirations and change plans that the community brought together as village-level change plans.

Tools for knowledge

While Praxis recognized the need to facilitate the community's participation in the rehabilitation process, it strongly believed that community involvement in these planning processes was non-negotiable and crucial to the empowerment of communities. It was critical that the actions taken towards rehabilitation were directly responsive to the affected community's pressing needs, and actively incorporated the invaluable wisdom and expertise of those affected. Praxis therefore undertook intensive village-level planning and social mapping exercises in tsunami-affected villages across Nagapattinam (Tamil Nadu) and Karaikal (Pondicherry). Praxis chose to engage in these two districts because Nagapattinam and Karaikal were the worst affected areas on the Indian mainland. In the race to initiate rehabilitation, sufficient efforts had not been made to understand ground realities. The devastating disaster had forever changed the lives of fishermen, farmers, traders, and other fishing and agriculture dependent communities residing along the Coromandel coast.

The village-level people's plans specifically focused on involving the affected communities in the planning process, and actively captured their realities, aspirations, and challenges. The plans served as powerful statements, directly from the communities, and have been utilized as planning and reference documents by all investors, government and non-government.

Praxis's efforts were in close collaboration with SIFFS and SNEHA, and the NGO Coordination and Resource Centre (which, leading from the recovery phase, was a collaborative effort of SIFFS, SNEHA and the UNDP). The village-level people's plans provided a profile of the village, its political economy and the post-tsunami realities, aspirations and challenges of the affected communities. In addition, community-led pre-tsunami social maps were created to establish a public document detailing the property ownership that existed before the tsunami. In order to gain a comprehensive understanding of each village's dynamics, and the challenges and aspirations of different community groups, Praxis therefore facilitated the following processes and meetings in villages across Nagapattinam and Karaikal:

- Introductory meeting with traditional *panchayat*;
- Social map: a large group of community members map the status of the village, and the properties of the community before the tsunami;
- Participatory census: detailed household information collected on different indicators;
- Discussion with elders and *panchayat* members to understand local history;
- Discussions with fishermen and female vendors to understand fish market dynamics;
- Focus group discussions on a range of issues with men, women, young men, young women, boys, girls, widows and women-headed households, disabled, elderly, dalits and religious minorities.

Through these village-level planning processes it was possible to gain a great deal of insight into initiatives that the communities were interested in pursuing, while also gauging other dynamics that organizations would have to contend with as they implemented programmes across these districts. Throughout the entire process, Praxis utilized participatory tools such as venn diagramming, card sorting, mobility mapping, and livelihood analysis to facilitate discussions with community members. The analysis was able to establish a comprehensive understanding of individual village dynamics (including the history, socio-economic profile and governance structure), and detail the post-tsunami aspirations of different community groups, with a special focus on vulnerable groups.

Box 6.2 Using social maps to challenge government and assert rights to the coast

For generations the fishing community had been in possession of the coastal land. Given the fishing community's historical presence in the area, many of its members had not previously had papers certifying ownership, since there had never been a need to acquire documents for land they had inhabited for generations. In the chaos following the tsunami, it was very clear to community members that they had to retain their ancestral lands. They insisted that the government's attempts to push the entire coastal community inland was disastrous and would be detrimental to their livelihoods. The government's efforts to open up beachfronts for acquisition by various vested interests, including the prawn-farm lobby and the tourism industry, was unacceptable. The fishing community's position that they would only move from the coast if their beachside dwellings were retained was therefore vigorously championed.

However, the threat of politicians and private companies manipulating a disaster situation to gain control of the precious land that had rightfully been out of their reach for years, loomed large. Due to pressure by government, many of the fishermen were coerced into signing a paper testifying that they were willing to move off their land if new housing was provided elsewhere. Through discussions with *panchayat* members facilitated by Praxis, the community members were quite clear about how they wanted to approach the controversial issue of resettlement. As they saw it, they had an absolute right to the coastal land that had been with their community for generations. It was an inseparable aspect of their lives and livelihood. On the other hand, after the events of the tsunami they also deemed it necessary to build secure houses for their families at a safe distance from the coast. Therefore, it was the aspiration of many of the communities to retain possession of their present land, and, in addition, build new housing for all villagers at a distance of 1 km from the coast. There was a lack of understanding by the government that it was necessary for the fishermen to retain their existing land to facilitate their fishing activities and that it was unfeasible for them to transport their boats and nets very early every morning to the coast and prepare to go out to sea. Therefore, it was essential that the community owned the coastal land to store the equipment. At the same time, it was critical for their families to be living at a safe distance from the sea.

It is in this context that Praxis facilitated the creation of community-led pre-tsunami social maps, to establish a public document detailing the property ownership that existed before the tsunami. This helped the communities to gain ownership details that related to the pre-tsunami times and gave them leverage to demand ownership rights over their coastal habitations.

Community members came together to map the status of the village, and the properties of the community before the tsunami. A participatory census was conducted in each of these villages where detailed household information was collected on different indicators. In many of the villages, the fishermen consulted during the process expressed their willingness to be relocated beyond the Coastal Regulatory Zone. However, they did not intend to relinquish the location of their pre-tsunami settlement on the coast. This needed to be kept in mind while planning any resettlement. The fishermen's insistence on retaining their pre-tsunami habitation stemmed from several occupational conveniences, e.g. the ease of sighting the movement of fish (*mappu pakkirathu*) and the convenience of storing fishing equipment close to the sea. In light of deliberate government efforts to dispossess tsunami victims from their coastal land, it was critical to record the pre-tsunami locations of houses, fixed assets, and other resources of the community. Praxis sought to accomplish this through facilitating participatory social mapping exercises across affected villages. These maps created by the communities were an authoritative record of the communities' property status before the tsunami, elevating the status of local knowledge during disaster rehabilitation.

Many of the *panchayats* established a unified position amongst the whole village. Their overall stance towards resettlement was that they wanted both pieces of land. Even the female fish vendors were in favour of resettling on the new land while retaining their previous land. This was despite the hardship they would have had to undergo while commuting the extra distance to transport fish. The main reason being that, for the women, their primary concern was the safety of their children, and they believed that living at a safe distance from the sea was the best way to ensure that. In discussing the conditions for the construction of new houses, some villagers were also quite clear about their terms for building the new settlement. Most importantly, they did not want any middlemen or contractors involved in the construction of the houses. The community felt that they themselves could contribute to the reconstruction process by contributing their own labour. Certain villages like Chinnangudi had first-hand experience with the poor quality of colony housing that the government had built in the past. Therefore, the community was quite clear that the process of rebuilding houses was something that they could manage on their own, as long as the government or relevant agency could provide the necessary funds and materials. By allowing the community to self-manage the reconstruction process and build the houses as per local needs, individual families had a choice of putting in additional money to their house. This unified position among the whole community increased their negotiating power with outsiders as the reconstruction process got underway.

As Praxis conducted its village-level planning exercise in villages across Nagapattinam and Karaikal, it became clear how eager the communities were to contribute. Prior to the tsunami, the fishing community embodied traits of empowerment. For example, they rarely sought assistance from outsiders and were known for their incredible self-reliance. Therefore, despite the trauma and complexity of the tsunami, these communities were not merely interested in being passive recipients of relief and rehabilitation efforts, but instead wanted to get involved and take responsibility for relief action. They wanted to be proactive in decision-making processes to ensure that their perspectives were heard and acted upon in this process. Many communities were not expecting the government to do everything, and were finding creative ways to take their own initiative. Whether it be in Chinnangudi village where the community wanted to contribute their labour to assist in the construction of permanent houses, or in Vizhunthamaladi, where the villagers were willing to purchase land for housing themselves, affected communities sought different avenues to get involved.

In the discussions that ensued with the *panchayat* members, fishermen, elders, women vendors and the focus group discussions with vulnerable community members (that included young men and women, as well as vulnerable groups such as persons with disabilities, dalits and religious minorities) one of the findings that emerged was the disproportionate share of relief assistance that reached vulnerable communities due to the political economy influenced by the caste system and gender-related discrimination. Further, due to the understandable focus on the fishing community, who were literally in the mouth of the tragedy, the agricultural community whose livelihoods were ravaged due to the immense inundation of their lands by the large waves was ignored. This happened as the death toll was a primary point of consideration for the delivery of relief among these communities sharing the coast. This consideration was extended into the recovery and rehabilitation phase. Among the affected agricultural habitations, though the death toll itself was minimal, the effect on their livelihoods was almost complete as their lands were left completely inundated by the saline water that entered their fields. As a result there were gross disparities in compensation for crop loss and land reclamation in comparison to how aid was reaching the affected fisheries-related communities that in themselves had greater resilience than the affected agricultural livelihoods.

The village-level plans were a result of hundreds of person days spent by the communities, researchers, village volunteers, and Praxis team members across 28 villages in Nagapattinam and Karaikal districts; a product of an intense community engagement with the girls, boys, women, and men of the affected villages.

The planning process was successful in capturing the community's realities, aspirations, and challenges, since the plans specifically focused on involving

Box 6.3 No time to listen?

According to local fishermen, there was an increase in number of fishermen and a substantial increase in the number of fishing vessels during the two decades leading up to the tsunami in Tharangambadi *panchayat*. Till the onset of the eighties, the village had fewer than 100 fishing vessels, predominantly comprising manually operated *kattumarans*. However, the decades of the eighties and the nineties brought about a jump in the number of mechanised vessels (trawlers and motorised fibreglass boats). The number of trawlers burgeoned to 60 by the onset of the nineties, but reduced to 30 by 2004. This was attributed to a steep hike in the price of diesel over the two decades up to 2004 and a decline in the fish density off the Tharangambadi shore. The 1990s witnessed a rampant increase in the number of motorised fibreglass boats. While there were onlyfour such boats in Tharangambadi in 1994, their number had shot up to around 200 by 2004. Such was the frenzy to own the motorised fibreglass boats that many *kattumaram* owners discarded their wooden vessels and switched over to the fibreglass boats. As a result, the number of operational *kattumarams* in Tharangambadi was estimated to have halved between 2000 and 2004. The collective pleas and reasoning of the fishermen that trawlers should not have been compensated on equal terms for their tsunami-related losses fell on deaf ears.

Our learning was that community wisdom and collective agreement is a critical component in determining livelihood rehabilitation in light of all these extraneous factors. Carefully planned distributions of boats, motors and nets were essential for maintaining the health of the fishery and ensuring profitability in fishing operations. In generations to come, fishing would no longer be a secure and prosperous profession if the sea was oversaturated with fishing equipment in a hurried rush to rehabilitate.

the affected communities. The maps enabled the community to present information in a better and more structured way.

Although Praxis was not specifically an implementing agency, as a support organization its objective was to translate the aspirations of the affected communities into actionable plans for organizations. As conceptualized by, with, and for the community, these plans served as powerful statements that were utilized as planning and reference documents by investors, government and NGOs. These findings served as a bargaining tool, as communities were better prepared to negotiate with the government and other relevant stakeholders on the terms of the rehabilitation process.

Exposing discrimination: the genesis of the Social Equity Audit

While carrying out the mapping and socio-economic analysis with the local community, that was even more devastating than the natural disaster, the discriminatory practices and deep-rooted biases that determined the nature and scope of relief and rehabilitation emerged. The theory that common adversity brought about solidarity was thoroughly debunked, with many of the affected refusing to be under the same roof with dalits or to drink water with them, even on the first day of the disaster.

It was evident post-tsunami that in many cases the government and NGOs in effect reinforced the kind of structural norms that cause discrimination, by ignoring the most vulnerable and least organized communities and only heeding the demands of those with the loudest voice and the strongest influence. In the Nagapattinam and Karaikal contexts, these most vulnerable communities were the dalit and tribal communities, as well as women, people with disabilities and children. As these structural norms have been unchallenged for many generations, the discrimination merely played out its natural course. While much of the exclusion related to relief distribution was subtle, it highlighted some of the deeply entrenched discrimination that prevails in the coastal communities. The external agencies lacked the skills to to challenge these dynamics of exclusion.

There was an urgent need to address these dynamics of social exclusion and marginalization of dalits, tribals, minorities, women-headed families, and other vulnerable social groups in relief and rehabilitation measures in the wake of the tsunami. Accountability mechanisms had then to be devised that enabled the inclusion of the entire coastal community. Challenging as it was, it was carried forward by a dedicated group of concerned development workers ranging from grassroots organizations to donors. Several months of deliberations, formulations and trials testified to the feasibility of collective and highly participatory processes. This led to the development of a framework and set of tools that help to hold a mirror up to forms and levels of exclusion that might exist in the work that is done, known as the Social Equity Audit. Having tried and tested this tool in the context of emergencies, efforts have been made since to make it a tool applicable in other contexts as well.[2]

Conclusions

Following the tsunami, and confronted by a complex and unpredictable situation of overwhelming dimensions, several aid agencies and government departments were unable to guide the response owing to a lack of coordination and policies. While these agencies in all probability specialize in disaster response, given their experience and expertise, it is often easy to overlook the perspectives of the affected communities, as no two disaster situations are similar. The need to facilitate community involvement was particularly pressing in the tsunami situation, considering how few organizations had any knowledge of the coastal community dynamics – and the relief efforts largely went against the grain of the community's interests. Often, the capacity of communities to become central strategists in the post-disaster planning process is, for many, difficult to fathom. The village-level people's planning illuminated the kinds of roles communities can play as strategists in the planning and rebuilding process. Crucial perspectives that make or mar effective rehabilitation are available only through inclusive planning processes that accord primacy to the views of the affected community.

With the phase of rescue and immediate relief over, the most urgent task at hand was to engage and consult with the community members, involve and include them in all phases of disaster recovery – for short-, medium- and long-term relief and, more crucially, in long-term rehabilitation efforts. Creating mechanisms for community leaderships in relief and rehabilitation processes undoubtedly ensured that the efforts were conducive to community dynamics and fulfilled genuine needs within the community. A collaborative effort with a community that already had a voice only enhanced the use of community knowledge and expertise to ensure that the relief and rehabilitation efforts were responsive to the unique needs of the affected communities.

Through Praxis's post-tsunami work, it became clear that community participation in planning relief and rehabilitation is a non-negotiable aspect that needs to be incorporated into all post-disaster planning initiatives. The positive results and outcomes outweighed the challenges that may arise when taking part in such planning exercises in post-disaster circumstances. These plans and analysis testified to the fact that community members that willingly get involved can be irreplaceable strategists in the planning process. Considering the preceding approaches that excluded them and marginalized their core concerns, our experiences suggest that community-centered planning in post-disaster scenarios is not only feasible, but necessary.

About the authors

Moulasha Kader, Praxis. Moulasha is a demographer and researcher by training. He has more than 15 years of experience working with national and international development agencies.

Ajai Kuruvila, Praxis. Ajai has led a process of participatory post disaster recovery with the Community Facilitation Unit of the NGO Coordination and Resource Centre (A UNDP supported process in Nagapattinam).

Shireen Kurian, Praxis. Shireen is a journalism and media activist with an interest in gender issues, development media, law, civic issues and human rights.

Endnotes

1. The chapter is based largely on the articles in 'Accountability Overdue: learnings from participatory engagement with the tsunami affected', published by Praxis in 2007. Praxis, under the guidance of Tom Thomas, facilitated a series of processes with coastal communities in the wake of the tsunami and was supported by the South India Federation of Fisherman Societies, Social Need Educational and Human, Awareness, and NGO coordination and Resource Centre. Acknowledgements are detailed in Annex 1
2. More details about the Social Equity Audit tool are available online: <www.socialequitywatch.org/social-equity-audit.html> [Accessed 11 June 2014]

References

National Centre for Advocacy Studies, (2007), 'An Introduction to the Social Equity Audit'.

Praxis (2007) 'Accountability Overdue: Learnings from Participatory Engagement with the Tsunami Affected' Delhi.

Praxis (2007) 'Village Level People's Plans: Realities, Aspirations, Challenges, Post Tsunami Community Planning' Delhi.

Annex 1: Acknowledgements

Praxis would like to thank the community members across Nagapattinam and Karaikal who spent time with us. This is the product of an intense community engagement with the girls, boys, women, and men of the affected villages. The communities' openness to share their perspectives made this possible. Everyone from the young children to the 'panchayatyars' welcomed us with such warmth and openness, into the intimate spaces of their lives at a time of great difficulty.

These learnings would not have been possible without the hard work of all the researchers and village volunteers who worked tirelessly with the Praxis team. The co-operation of South India Federation of Fishermen Societies (SIFFS), Social Need Educational and Human Awareness (SNEHA) and NGO Coordination and Resource Center (NCRC) requires special acknowledgement, as they played a crucial role in local facilitation. These exercises greatly benefited from the guidance of Ephrem Soosai, V. Vivekanandan, Vijay Kuppu of SIFFS; Jesu Ratnam of SNEHA; and Ram Mohan, Ajay Kuruvilla, Vinay Raj, Annie George of NCRC.

CHAPTER 7

Subverting for good: sex workers and stigma

Sowmyaa Bharadwaj, Shalini Mishra and Aruna Mohan Raj

Abstract

In normative project frameworks, community-based organizations (CBOs) are typically viewed as 'vehicles' for targeted intervention programmes. In the HIV/AIDS sector, as in other areas of work, NGOs tend to control CBOs, wittingly or unwittingly, through the use of outcome-related indicators based on a pre-defined template of project expectations.

This chapter analyses the process through which community members – including female sex workers and transgendered persons – reshaped a monitoring framework to reflect and prioritize issues that mattered most to them. This brought about a significant change in the way in which stigma was understood by external project stakeholders. From being seen merely as a symptom of HIV, it became clear during the course of engagement with members that stigma was in fact a driver of other difficulties these communities face. For members of these CBOs, the key learning was that negotiating and overcoming stigma is a critical part of a journey towards empowerment.

Keywords: stigma, discrimination, identity, empowerment, HIV/AIDS, sex workers, community-based organizations

Introduction

HIV prevention programmes have often targeted as beneficiaries communities of transgendered people, men who have sex with men, and sex workers, with multiple identities and vulnerabilities. Interventions have typically been designed to highlight and address symptomatic issues that require target communities to be sensitized to this limiting set of project goals in the interest of project success. This could involve the facilitation of community-based organization (CBO) formation, followed by the gradual withdrawal of the facilitating partner as the CBO becomes capable of working independently. However, this could be problematic if a predefined framework binds project activities. While CBOs might only be construed as vehicles for effective targeted intervention (TI) management, if an organization is committed to community

http://dx.doi.org/10.3362/9781780448695.007

members' voices becoming more prominent in CBO management, issues core to the community will need to start getting prioritized. A challenge for those wedded to HIV prevention, including NGOs, is therefore to facilitate the creation of CBOs that work independently but do so with broadly the same project goals in mind. This may not always be easy.

The Avahan India AIDS Initiative of the Bill and Melinda Gates Foundation (see Chapter 4) was an HIV/AIDS prevention programme operating in 82 districts across six states of India. Launched in 2003, it engaged with persons at greater risk of HIV infection, including female sex workers (FSWs) and transgendered people (TGs). A key initial strategy within Avahan was the TI programme, including components such as running sexually transmitted infection (STI) clinics, creating drop-in centres (DICs), condom promotion, and behaviour change communication, among others. While behavioural and medical interventions remained central, over time, community mobilization was foregrounded within the programme.

The NGO-led TI programme began by involving community members in a number of their activities. At the outset, community members participated as peer educators and mobilized fellow members to enrol in project activities. Gradually they started occupying positions of greater responsibility within the project, such as outreach workers, crisis coordinators and even project managers. In addition to these roles, the programme had created mechanisms through forming a number of committees such as DIC committees and crisis response committees that provided vital spaces for community members to participate in programme activities.

Over time, spaces and avenues were created for community voices to be raised, which often led to a reprioritization of issues to the extent that the focus on HIV became secondary to community issues. Community interactions highlighted that livelihood and issues of personal crisis were more important than an HIV-centric approach. For community members, one of the most 'valued' components of the programme was the growth of drop-in centres as 'safe spaces' for discussion of any and every problem they faced, without fear of being 'stigmatized'. These spaces, even in project-driven set-ups, became spaces 'owned' by community leaders. They also gave birth to a new consciousness within the community: the desire, as well as the need, to have their organization working on the many issues dear to them.

In a community-led approach, problems encountered by members in their day-to-day lives, from discrimination and verbal abuse, to violence and emergent crises, to exclusion and denial of entitlements, emerged as raisons d'êtres for the CBOs. The community understood these problems as structural barriers to accessing HIV prevention services, and they identified the root cause of these problems as stigma. This was not necessarily stigma regarding their HIV status, but around the perceived immorality of sex workers' activities. Stigma, along with the various ways in which it manifested itself, (the problems that were being discussed), therefore came to be seen as a 'root cause' of even the problem of HIV. The powerlessness of the community in relation to clients and other stakeholders was understood as the defining feature of their lack of status in society and of their vulnerability to HIV.

Over time, CBOs started creating crisis response teams and advocacy teams to address these issues, and evolved processes and practices to address problems of the community in a systematic way. Activities of community members started going beyond conventional TI activities and included a number of issues related to community rights and entitlements. However, while the purpose and scope of activities of CBOs was rapidly changing, the monitoring and information system (MIS) was not keeping pace. The TI indicators measured very little of the processes actually unfolding on the ground, having been designed with a different set of priorities in mind. The situation required a challenging – and, in many ways, a subversion – of the existing TI in favour of a monitoring system that reflected community priorities. Although CBOs had been formed under the larger umbrella of HIV prevention, it had become very clear that HIV was not the only issue affecting their daily lives and status, nor was it viewed as the most important one. The need to evolve indicators that better reflected the totality of the problems faced by the community was quite clear.

Redrawing indicators: working with female sex workers

Spaces made available through Avahan's monitoring of community mobilization were used to initiate a dialogue on stigma faced by the community. Communities reflected upon the stigma they face in their lives, attempted to define it and offered illustrative examples of how they experienced it. There was no imposition of an academic or external understanding of stigma – community groups' perceptions of stigma revolving around real life experiences were explored and given primacy. What could have been a purely data-gathering exercise was modelled very differently, to give space to build community understanding and perspectives while identifying indicators relevant to these communities.

Group discussions ensured that community members' understanding of stigma was furthered through a cross-cultural and cross-sectional approach in which female sex workers, transgendered people and men who have sex with men explained, contextualized, and illustrated stigma differently. Community members analysed both causes and effects of stigma, and identified perpetrators and stakeholders in an attempt to understand better the nature of the stigma each of them they faced, and explored linkages and relationships with stakeholders (see Figure 7.1). In the process a course of collective action and engagement with larger society on the issue of stigma was charted.

To develop indicators that measured the progress made by CBOs in terms of access to rights, entitlements and stigma reduction, the first important step was to understand what the community perceived as 'stigma' and how it related 'stigma' to its problems. A problem tree analysis was undertaken with

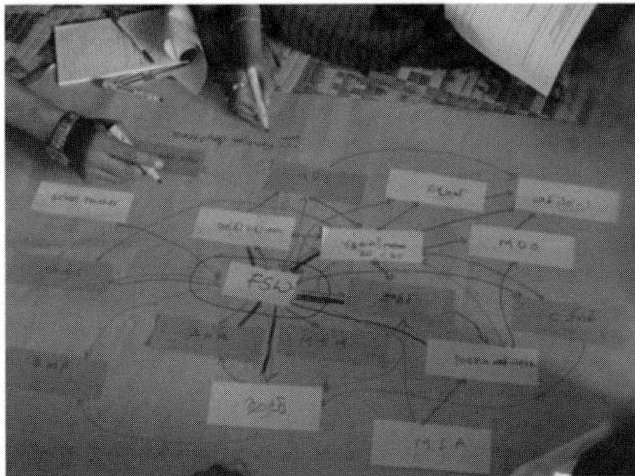

Figure 7.1 Causal loop analysis (participatory tool) facilitated with sex workers

participating community groups of FSWs, TGs and MSMs. Through drawings of the root and branches of a tree, participants identified the key and linked causes, and the main as well as secondary effects of the problem.

A stakeholder analysis followed. Different categories of stakeholders and the nature of harassment faced from each category was discussed with community members and listed. Each group of stakeholders was then categorized according

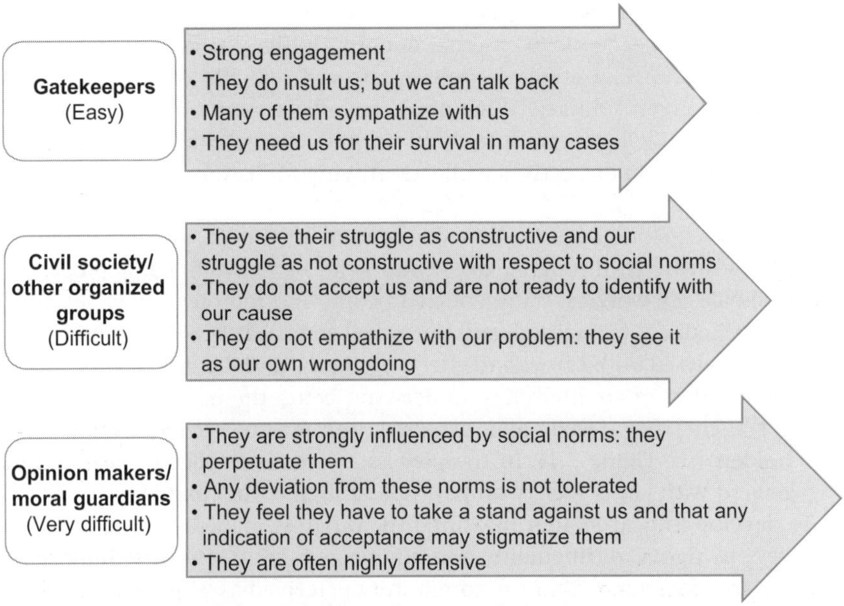

Gatekeepers (Easy)
- Strong engagement
- They do insult us; but we can talk back
- Many of them sympathize with us
- They need us for their survival in many cases

Civil society/ other organized groups (Difficult)
- They see their struggle as constructive and our struggle as not constructive with respect to social norms
- They do not accept us and are not ready to identify with our cause
- They do not empathize with our problem: they see it as our own wrongdoing

Opinion makers/ moral guardians (Very difficult)
- They are strongly influenced by social norms: they perpetuate them
- Any deviation from these norms is not tolerated
- They feel they have to take a stand against us and that any indication of acceptance may stigmatize them
- They are often highly offensive

Figure 7.2 Stakeholder analysis

to the ease with which the sex workers were able to engage with them. Gatekeepers – those who control clients' access to sex workers – were categorized as 'easy', indicating that sex workers had no difficulty working with them. Civil society and other organized groups were categorized as 'difficult', and opinion makers or moral guardians were perceived as 'very difficult' to engage with.

There was then further exploration of sex workers' perceptions of other people in their social and professional worlds, listed under the three categories mentioned above.

An interesting aspect of how the community understood stigma was the fact that the practice of ignoring was sometimes felt more severely than physical assault. For members of CBOs, it was easier to engage with gatekeepers (*goondas* [thugs], lodge owners, pimps and other stakeholders with whom they needed to develop business-only relationships), even though they have to deal with the risk and reality of physical violence at their hands. However achieving a social standing is often a far more difficult proposition than running a smooth business or even getting social security, as this requires building relationships with some people who are typically most deeply antagonistic such as faith leaders, people in their own neighbourhood community, and even NGO groups.

	Stakeholder	**Why are they important to you?**	**How do they harm you?**	**Do they openly harm you or indirectly?**	**Do you feel that they exclude you or discriminate against you because you are a sex worker?**	**How easily can you engage with them?**
Category A: Gatekeepers						
1	Goondas	Smooth Business	Physically	Openly	No	Easy
2	Lodge owners/ Shopkeeper	Smooth Business	Physical, Insults	Openly	No	Easy
3	Pimps/ brothel owners/ drug peddlers	Smooth Business	Physical, Insults	Openly	No	Easy
Category B: Civil Society/Other organized groups						
1	Workers Union/Trade Union	Social security	Insults	Openly	Yes	Difficult
2	Dalit groups/ Women's groups/NGOs	Social security	Ignore	Not to our faces	Yes	Difficult
3	Political parties/ Politicians	Social standing/ social security	Ignore	Not to our faces	No	Easy
Category C: Opinion Makers/ Moral Guardians						
1	Faith leaders	Social standing	Insult	Openly	Yes	Very Difficult
2	Neighbourhood community	Social standing	Verbal abuse, Insult, Ignore	Not to our faces	Yes	Very Difficult
3	Media	Social security	Insult, Ignore	Openly	Yes	Difficult

Figure 7.3 Analysis of ease of engagement with stakeholders for stigmatized members of communities

Box 7.1 Stories of stigma

Participatory exercises with sex workers and sexual minorities brought to the surface stigma attached to these identities and discrimination that results from this. It also disclosed how these two identities had become associated with a range of other identities that each, in their own way, build further stigma.

In this process sex workers and transgender communities are socially tarnished, and their behaviour labelled as deviant and threatening public morality. The stigma surrounding a transgendered identity clearly emerged when participants spoke about how even partners refused to see them as anything beyond sex objects and their own families as objects of ridicule. Society apart, even the medical fraternity has put up barriers: 'When I go to hospitals for treatment the doctors and nurses never come near me. They maintain distance. So I keep a smiling face and try to be friendly with them. Then I explain to them that we (transgendered people) are also human beings.' Transgendered participants described the police as the worst abusers of all.

Many transgendered people are assumed to be sex workers, and this assumption becomes another basis for discrimination. Sex workers themselves are often criminalized, and discriminated against for being dalits. Some are stereotyped as being 'family-breakers', 'tradition-breakers' or assumed to be HIV-infected. 'Despite repeated assertion of my rights as an Indian citizen, it took me two years to get a ration card', said one sex worker. Knowing she was a sex worker, the local staff deliberately delayed her application. The discrimination did not end there. 'When I used to go to the ration shop, they always used to make me wait longer than others. It was the same with voting; they would always allow others in line to go first.'

Stigma was described by one participant as 'the way in which society has defined social norms that refuse to accommodate problems faced by sex workers and sexual minorities'. One participant said that it was as if wider society was making the statement that exclusionary forms of behaviour were warranted because of their perceived violation of norms. 'For us, this is stigma,' she added.

Source: Praxis – Voice for Change (2013)

Table 7.1 Terms used to describe the communities

Sex workers	Transgendered people
Traffickers, snatchers, thieves, criminals, slum, poor, shabbily dressed, dalit, lower-caste, HIV infection or risk, pleasure-seekers, Bengalis, Bangladeshis, breakers of social norms, family-breakers	Begging, sex work,dressing provocatively, effeminate, dalit, lower-caste, low-income, Sex reassignment surgery, HIV-positive status

Based on information collected through discussions with community groups, a series of indicators reflecting people's capacity to claim rights, entitlements and address stigma were finalized. These included the following:

a) Community group's collective understanding of issues of stigma and discrimination;
b) Community group's demonstrated collective action and engagement with wider society on issues of stigma;
c) Community group's ability to engage with the state on issues of rights and entitlements;
d) Community group's ability to make themselves visible themselves to wider society and show capacity to assert their interests;
e) Community leadership's ability to mobilize the group, whenever required, to assert their identity or in support of their demands.

The Praxis team realized that it was important to measure the progress of CBOs in terms of their capacity to address discrimination, and gained some insights into how the notion of stigma as a problem impacts the CBO's vision, mission and objectives. The extended investigations and discussions on stigma therefore formed the basis for the revision of the self-monitoring framework (see Chapter 4) to incorporate two new parameters. A separate parameter on rights and entitlements was also incorporated into the monitoring framework. Another parameter on engagement on issues of stigma in relation to wider society – including gatekeepers, solidarity groups and opinion makers – was also incorporated. These parameters sat alongside six others covering leadership, governance, decision-making, resource mobilization, networking, and project management.

Pushing the barriers: exploring stigmatization

The concept of stigma permeated a number of parameters in keeping with the community groups' identification of stigma as the root cause of their problems. Leadership quality in this framework is measured in terms of the CBO's ability to support the community in addressing crises. Other measures of leadership quality include their ability to mobilize members and non-members, in particular on issues of significance to the community and especially where discriminatory policies are concerned.

Networking with solidarity groups became an important indicator within the networking parameter. The CBO's ability to develop a grand alliance on poverty and discrimination with other marginalized communities was an important indicator. This helped communities sharpen their understanding of their stigmatization through interaction with other groups also experiencing discrimination. The parameter on rights was defined both in terms of generic rights as well as in terms of specific entitlements for the community.

Progress in terms of engagement with wider society on stigma was related to the ability of community groups to assert their identities as female sex workers, men who have sex with men, or transgendered people, and to address stigma-related issues. To identify a group's standing on this, there was a decision to focus on how they relate to various stakeholders mentioned in Figure 7.2. Towards this, community members would write down names or symbols representing various sets of hostile stakeholders that they encounter (referred to hereafter as 'perpetrators') as well as potentially constructive stakeholders who can support the CBO's work.

To summarize the nature of their engagement with these people, they then placed these in an appropriate space on a matrix such as the one shown in Figure 7.4, below, trying to locate the best combination (with row and column options) for that specific stakeholder or perpetrator.

So, in the context of a female sex worker's, CBO, it is possible for the CBO to be visible to pimps, opinion makers or NGOs as a collective with a specific objective and, at the same time, for there to be no interaction between them. The information collected from such a matrix was summarized and analysed, as reflected in Figure 7.5, below.

Once it was established how many stakeholders lay in the weak, average and strong categories, the CBO was then put on a six-band scale of community strength ranging from basic to vibrant.

		CBO visible because of promoter group	CBO visible because of individual community member	CBO visible as a collective with a specific objective
No engagement	WEAK	WEAK	WEAK	WEAK
Started interacting	WEAK	WEAK	AVERAGE	AVERAGE
Regular one-sided interaction	WEAK	WEAK	AVERAGE	AVERAGE
Regular reciprocal interaction	WEAK	AVERAGE	STRONG	STRONG
Developed trust	WEAK	AVERAGE	STRONG	STRONG

Figure 7.4 Mapping engagement with stakeholders

BASIC	FOUNDATION	PROMISING I	PROMISING II	VIBRANT I	VIBRANT II
If all stakeholders were in a 'weak' cell	If at least one stakeholder was in an 'average' cell	If at least one stakeholder was in a 'strong' cell	If two or three were in a 'strong' cell	If four to seven were in a'strong' cell	If eight and above were in a 'strong' cell

Figure 7.5 Scale of progression of engagement with stakeholders

Conclusion

With community voices gaining centre stage within HIV prevention programmes, the focus of programme activities has shifted away from HIV prevention to mainstream community issues. Thus both NGOs and community groups have met each other halfway. Whereas HIV was previously understood to be the driving issue, and others issues such as stigma, discrimination and denial of entitlements were seen as effects of HIV, the process of reprioritization has brought stigma related to the identity of sex workers and sexual minorities to the forefront. HIV, along with issues like discrimination, denial of entitlements and violation of rights, has come to be seen as a manifestation of stigma. The process of community-led understanding has resulted in identity-related stigma superseding or subverting HIV-related stigma as the root of the problem, thus effecting a paradigm shift in approaches to problem solving.

It is notable that the challenge of measuring stigma, discrimination and associated issues was taken up in the monitoring framework, the evolution of which was reflective of the evolving understanding of community issues in the context of the HIV/AIDS prevention programme. A participatory process of developing a monitoring framework that was more responsive to the community's experience and priorities facilitated this. This represented a step towards greater grassroots accountability.

Indeed, the very process of evolving indicators involved the participation of community leaders from different CBOs across Avahan. Participatory processes ensured that the paradigm shift in understanding community issues was reached by mainstreaming their voices and giving primacy to their accounts. What was unleashed, was a subversive process in favour of issues that are close to the community – especially those relating to addressing the stigma associated with being sex workers. Involvement of community members not only ensured that indicators moved from being purely health-based and HIV-related to being more reflective of the totality of the everyday experience of stigma, discrimination and denial. Community members' perspectives on the relative significance of each indicator in the larger community mobilization framework were also taken into account (Thomas et al., 2012).

Discussions around stigma also paved the way for significant reflection on the nature and reach of a community's power. In a conventional project-driven system, approaches seldom venture into discussions around micro- and macro-level power structures and equations unless there is a direct mandate to do so, and almost never engage with the community's ability to understand and challenge them.

The participatory processes illuminated power relations for the CBOs. They helped to bring about recognition that power structures operate in a very real manner and affect the lives of community members. A power relationship matrix with the community helped them to understand how different stakeholders engage with them and recognize that there is an undertone of discrimination based on a moral paradigm. This empowered community members in multiple ways.

Most conventional programmes visualize empowerment of the community strictly in terms of community health indicators such as health-seeking behaviour or use of condoms. In this case, empowerment was visualized in terms of the transition from a state of powerlessness to one of empowerment; not strictly along health-based indicators, but along the axis of community groups' capacities to address stigma, and assert their identity and rights.

About the authors

Sowmyaa Bharadwaj, Praxis. Sowmyaa has over a decade's experience in the development sector as a facilitator and practitioner of participatory methods and approaches.

Shalini Mishra, Praxis. Shalini has over two decades' experience on a range of issues, especially gender and power relations.

Aruna Mohan Raj, Praxis. Aruna's core expertise in development issues stems from a strong background in child rights and child protection.

Endnote

1. This chapter is a compilation of information and analysis generated from a series of interactions while designing and facilitating tools in the course of the project supported by Avahan - The India AIDS Initiative, facilitated by Praxis, called Measuring Community Mobilization in the Avahan Programme. A detailed list of contributors is available in Annex 1

Bibliography

Avahan (2010), 'Common Minimum Programme for HIV prevention in India', Delhi: Bill & Melinda Gates Foundation.

Avahan (2008), 'The India AIDS Initiative – The Business of HIV Prevention at Scale', Delhi: Bill & Melinda Gates Foundation.

Ayres, W., Quinn, T., & Stovall, D. (eds) (2008), *The Handbook of Social Justice in Education*, Routledge.

Bill and Melinda Gates Foundation (2010), 'Breaking through Barriers – Avahan's Scale-Up of HIV Prevention among High-Risk MSM and Transgenders in India', New Delhi: Bill & Melinda Gates Foundation.

Biradavalou, M.R. et al. (2006), 'Can sex workers regulate police? Learning from an HIV prevention project for sex workers in southern India', *Social Science Med,* 68: 1541–47, <http://www.ncbi.nlm.nih.gov/pubmed/19261364> [Accessed 3 June 2014].

Biradavalou, M.R. Blankenship, K.M., Jena, A., Dhungana, N. (2012), 'Structural stigma, sex work and HIV: contradictions and lessons learnt from a community-led structural intervention in southern India', *Journal of*

Epidemiology and Community Health, 66: 95–992, <http://www.ncbi.nlm.nih.gov/pubmed/22705653> [Accessed 3 June 2014].

Chandrasekaran, P., Dallabetta, G., Loo, V., Mills, S., Saidel, T., Adhikary, R., et al. (2008), 'Evaluation design for large-scale HIV prevention programmes: the case of Avahan, the India AIDS initiative', *AIDS,* 22:1–15.

Cooke, B. and Kothari, U., (eds) (2001) *Participation: the New Tyranny?* London: Zed Books.

Gaventa, J., (2006), 'Finding the Spaces for Change: A Power Analysis', *IDS Bulletin,* 37: No. 6. pp. 23–33.

Hay, K., and Kumar Range, S. (eds) (2014), *Making Evaluation Matter – Writing from South Asia*, IDRC, Sage.

HIV/AIDS Alliance (2002), 'Policy Briefing No. 1: Supporting NGOs & CBOs responding to HIV/AIDS' HIV/AIDS Alliance.

HIV AIDS Alliance (2006), 'All Together Now': communithy mobilisation for HIV/AIDS' <http://www.aidsalliance.org/assets/000/000/369/228-All-together-now_original.pdf?1405520021> [last accessed 4 February 2014].

Jana, S., Basu, I., Rotheram-Borus, M.J. and Newman, P.A., (2004), 'The Sonagachi Project: a sustainable community intervention program', *AIDS Education and Prevention*; 16:405–14.

NACO (2007), National Aids Control Organisation, Government of India, 'Targeted Interventions Under NACP' 2:1, New Delhi.

Narayanan, P. et al. (2012), 'Monitoring community mobilisation and organisational capacity among high risk groups in a large scale HIV prevention programme in India: selected findings using a Community Ownership and Preparedness Index' *Journal of Epidemiology and Community Health* 2:2, 16–25.

Naryanan, P. (2012), 'Embedding social transformative approach within Monitoring and Evaluation: Reflecting on Gender Equality and Human Rights in Evaluation,' UN Women and Sri Lanka Evaluation Association.

National AIDS Control Programme, Government of India, *Targeted Interventions under National AIDS Control Programme – Core High Risk Groups,* 3:1.

Patton, M.Q. (1997), *Utilization-Focused Evaluation,* 3rd ed, Thousand Oaks, CA: Sage Publications.

Praxis (2009), 'Measuring Community Mobilisation Processes – A Monitoring Framework for Community-Based Groups Under the HIV/AIDS Programme in India', Praxis, Delhi.

Praxis (2013), 'Voice of Change: Collective Action for Safe Spaces by Sex Workers and Sexual Minorities' Praxis, Delhi.

Teddlie, C. and Tashakkori, A. (2009), *Foundations of mixed-methods research: integrating quantitative and qualitative approaches in the social and behavioral sciences,* Sage Publications.

Thomas, T., Narayanan, P., Wheeler, T., Kiran, U., Joseph, M.J. and Ramanathan, T.V. (2012), 'Design of a community ownership and preparedness index: using data to inform the capacity development of community based groups', *Journal of Epidemiology and Community Health* 66: i26–i33.

UNAIDS (2007), 'Technical Update, Community Mobilization and AIDS'.

Wheeler, T., Kiran, U., Jayaram, M., Dallabetta, G., (2012) 'Learning about scale, measurement and community mobilization: Reflections on the implementation of the Avahan HIV/AIDS Initiative in India', *J Epidemiology and Community Health* 2:2 pp 16-25.

World Bank (2009), *Making Smart Policy: Using Impact Evaluation for Policy Making; Case Studies on Evaluations*. Working Paper, World Bank.

World Health Organization (2007), '2007 Policy Briefing, No. 1: Supporting NGOs', National AIDS Program Management, Module 4.

Annex 1: list of contributors

Praxis acknowledges the valuable contributions of The Tamil Nadu AIDS Initiative (TAI) administered by Voluntary Health Services (VHS), V-CAN, a state-level network of sex workers and sexual minorities in Tamil Nadu, participants of the participatory video process, Real Time, Institute for Development Studies, Participate, Avahan and all the sex workers and members of sexual minorities who shared their experiences, to help produce this document. Participants from the following organizations shared their stories: Anbukarangal Samuga Nala Sangam, Annai Theresa Makkal Sevai Mayam, Dharampuri Maavatta Pengal Mempattu Sangam, Dindugal Pengal Munettra Sangam, Erode Mavatta Pengal Suyasakthi Sangam, Gnana Deepam Sevai Maiyam, Jhansi Rani Pengal Nala Sangam, Social Welfare Development Society, Namakkal Maavatta Sabarmathi Pengal Mempattu Sangam, Salem Pengal Nala sangam, Salem Thirunangaigal Nala Sangam, Sri lakshmi Pengal Munettra Sangam, Sudaroli Pengal Munettra Sangam, Thenni Mavatta Pengal Samuga Porularatha Munettra Sangam, Vellore Pengal Mempattu Sangam, Vidivelli Thirunangaigal Nalavaazvu Sangam.

In addition, the participants of the participatory video process include: Inba, Jeeva, Kaavya, Mohan, Nisha, Roja, Swathy and Thenmozhi.

CHAPTER 8

Making people count: from beneficiaries to evaluators

Anindo Banerjee, Rohan Preece and M. J. Joseph

Abstract

This chapter features a 2004 community-led evaluation of a multi-state UNDP-Government of India project called the Community-Based Pro-poor Initiatives Programme (CBPPI). *Twenty six project beneficiaries, mostly female self-help group members, were trained to lead a rigorous evaluation process. They were given various responsibilities, including developing the indicators against which the CBPPI sub-programmes would all be investigated, facilitating the use of tools in villages, and presenting the findings. They used participatory techniques to involve local community members and drew on their experience to deliver pertinent insights from a perspective of solidarity. Challenging conventional wisdom on evaluations, this process prioritized field knowledge over academic knowledge, flattening established hierarchies and channeling resources towards the development of community capabilities. Though not without its limitations, it afforded rich opportunities for learning for the various stakeholders concerned.*

Keywords: community-led evaluation, participatory tools, beneficiary as evaluator, experience, development programmes

Introduction

Today, community-centredness has become an almost indispensable requirement for development programmes – in rhetoric if not always in practice. Rights-based approaches now dominate project discourse, going beyond the language of service delivery to advocate for community-based institutions and community-driven change. In the context of such initiatives, significant community participation is seen as vital.

As far back as the 1970s, some agencies recognized that the areas of monitoring and evaluation should also be participatory. Although most organizations remained wedded to more traditional methods, there were islands of innovation through the 1980s, not least in India. Various reasons have been articulated for these innovations, including the contribution that beneficiaries can make (when involved in evaluations) to understanding ways in which development can unfold and the need for locally meaningful evaluation findings (Estrella and Gaventa, 1998: 4).

http://dx.doi.org/10.3362/9781780448695.008

However, while most programmes have become more visibly concerned with community empowerment[2], evaluations have more often still been top-down in their approach. A recent review of the evaluation practices of US international non-governmental organizations (INGOs) is instructive in this respect, highlighting the lack of consideration often given to accountability to community members:

> The findings on evaluation purpose, dissemination of results, and formal feedback mechanisms suggest that international non-governmental organisations typically develop stronger formal accountability measures for donors and staff-members than for beneficiaries...In the findings, beneficiaries were much less likely than funders or staff to be considered as a stakeholder group when framing evaluation purposes, and correspondingly less likely to be considered as recipients of evaluation results. (Kang et al., 2012)

Guba and Lincoln (1989) have charted the progression of evaluation practice from 'first' to 'fourth' generation, through measurement, to description, to judgement, and finally to 'negotiation'. In the first three generations, evaluation is largely the domain of outsiders. Yet, as Kang et al.'s study suggests, even in 2012, much evaluation practice was limited, at best, to 'participation by consultation' or, more commonly, to 'passive participation' (Pretty, 1995 in Cornwall, 2008: 272) or even to no participation, with community members sometimes not consulted at all during the evaluative process (Kang et al., 2012).

Within the middle ground on which many evaluations are conducted, they remain the preserve of an educated elite typically drawn from different socio-economic backgrounds and even in the case of INGOs very different geographies to the beneficiaries. Here the beneficiaries largely remain objects of the evaluative process, even in cases where they have been quite active participants in development programmes.

Why is this so? Constraints and exigencies of time and resources may be decisive: an external evaluation may be seen by external agencies as a tidier, lower-risk, more efficient option. Perceptions about what is required for the discipline of evaluation may also be a factor: maintaining 'scientific' robustness through controlling for bias and developing quantitatively measurable indicators are tasks for which externally located experts are often deemed most suitable. Evaluation is also often viewed as a higher-order cognitive activity requiring a certain level of training – evidenced, for instance, in the widely used Bloom's taxonomy framework, which associates the capacity to evaluate with relative achievement in formal education.

These perceptions may betray some deeply held biases and preconceptions about different kinds of knowledge, privileging – for example – that which has been formally rather than experientially learnt. In planning evaluations, we would argue, attention needs to be given to the proper role of community beneficiaries in these processes, the opportunities for expression of agency and voice that are due to them, and the value of their understanding and perspectives.[3]

The present chapter focuses on part of an evaluation of a large-scale, multi-state programme. The reader should note that we do not claim it to be a comprehensive exposition of a participatory approach. Indeed, the community evaluation did not sit alone but rather alongside more conventional approaches, and we are unable to report in detail how community participants took up the lessons of the evaluation in their work or its immediate impact upon institutional practices. What we do hope to do, however, is to show clearly the potential that community beneficiaries have for the task of evaluation; to sketch out a way in which a community-led evaluation can be implemented; and to reflect on the significance of an endeavour of this nature.

Background: Community-Based Pro-poor Initiatives Programme

In 1998, the Government of India launched the Ninth Five-Year Plan (1998–2002), according participatory planning a place of strategic importance within the broader agenda of rapid economic growth with a (purported) commitment to equity. Soon afterwards, the United Nations Development Programme (UNDP) initiated a wide-ranging US$10.7 million programme, implemented through 17 sub-programmes across 11 states. The range of interventions facilitated was exceptionally diverse. Contextualized in response to local realities, they included natural resource management, work with self-help groups (SHGs), education and child rights, technical skills training, mobilizing access of entitlements, and the strengthening of *gram sabhas* (village council sessions) and *gram panchayats* (village councils).

Overall, the programme set out to:

- Support social mobilization efforts to build and strengthen Panchayati Raj Institutions (PRIs) (which are the systems of local self government in India) and people's organizations representing the interests of poorer groups such as scheduled castes and scheduled tribes, and women's organizations.
- Facilitate the creation of family and community assets and encourage demand-driven social services.
- Establish alliances and partnerships amongst various interest groups so as to mainstream lessons of pilot initiatives into macro policy and programmes.
- Advocate for pro-poor policies to enable the fulfilment of these objectives.

The programme was led by UNDP, working closely with the Department of Rural Development and the National Institute of Rural Development, Hyderabad. As the Community-Based Pro-Poor Initiatives (CBPPI) programme drew to an end in 2003, it was decided to arrange for a final evaluation to take place at three levels: an externally organized evaluation of all sub-programmes by external consultants, a community-led evaluation of all sub-programmes by a team of representatives of the communities, and a programmatic overview based on these two evaluations.

The second component of the evaluation was a departure from the mainstream. Only secured thanks to internal advocacy from one of Praxis's alumni, it provided an opportunity for those who had been the beneficiaries to enjoy some direction of the evaluative process. The terms of reference document helps situate the objectives of what became known as a community-led evaluation.

> Community-based Pro-poor initiatives is a pioneer programme both for the Government of India and UNDP. This is the first time that UNDP and the Ministry of Rural Development funded NGOs directly in the field – and the very first time that projects are being implemented at the community level. It is a programme designed with the help of the economically and socially backward communities to improve their quality of life.
>
> True to its spirit, the communities themselves should evaluate such a community-led programme. As it is a programme with seventeen sub-programmes (thirteen of them being implemented by NGOs), the Ministry of Rural Development and UNDP would be interested in getting feedback on the programme as a whole and not on individual sub-programmes. Communities evaluating the sub-programmes they are involved in would not give this holistic picture. A group of persons representative of the various communities involved in the programme can visit all the sub-programmes, interact with the communities, help them evaluate their own sub-programme and present the collective view to the Ministry of Rural Development and UNDP. This could be a learning process both for the Ministry of Rural Development and UNDP and the communities/evaluators themselves. The community team could brief the Ministry of Rural Development and UNDP about the process and the findings. This could help in the design of future programmes/projects.
>
> (UNDP (2003), 'Terms of Reference, Community-Led Evaluation of UNDP Programmes', shared with Praxis by UNDP in 2003)

With a slight evolution in the methods suggested here – 'the group' of persons did not visit all the sub-programmes but rather the different sub-programmes were visited by different teams – the evaluation got under way in 2004. A total of 26 representatives were selected to participate from amongst the diverse beneficiary communities, comprising 22 women and 4 men.

At a preparatory meeting, some of the partners expressed concern about whether the community representatives would be able to travel on their own and manage being away from home for a whole month. It was suggested that a member of staff from one of the partner agencies should travel with the evaluators for the whole month due to concerns that women would not be safe travelling alone. However, the group of 26 community representatives flagged this as jeopardizing the integrity of the evaluation. Ultimately, it was decided to arrange for one person to travel with the evaluators to their first destinations, and then meet them at their final destinations to travel back with them to Delhi for the final meeting (Menon, 2005).

Certain limitations related to the context of the programme as a whole made it difficult to attribute impact and to make fair comparisons between sub-programmes. In some cases, for example, the sub-programme had been implemented in environments where the organization had already been working for many years and so had been designed to be consistent with pre-existing work. An additional constraint was the lack of baseline data and of a mid-term review. These limitations helped to justify giving the evaluation a forward-looking and essentially qualitative emphasis. Attempts were made to gather perspectives from a range of different groups and from different organizations within target communities. To try to avoid possible conflicts of interest, community representatives did not evaluate in their 'home' locations but visited other sites on a non-reciprocal basis: this meant, for example, that a situation where representatives from Tamil Nadu visited Orissa *and* representatives from Orissa visited Tamil Nadu was avoided.

Evaluation from experience

Community representatives were invited from all the project areas. Partner NGOs and communities were consulted, and asked to nominate two representatives. It was not possible to get data on the social group of the representatives, but an attempt was made to achieve diversity in terms of ages, which ranged between 22 and 60. As a first step, the group attended a pre-evaluation workshop in Jodhpur in western Rajasthan. There, they were divided into four evaluation teams of six to eight members.

Figure 8.1 outlines the process of the evaluation from the perspective of the community representatives. The upward-moving arrow indicates some of the key activities that the community was involved in after formally joining the evaluation process in Jodhpur. The three interlocking shapes at the base represent the engine of the community's participation in this evaluation: their experience. Through leveraging their unique experience in different ways, the community was propelled to facilitate and lead the evaluation.

As indicated in Figure 8.1, the evaluation involved community members in a range of different activities:

Learning

As with any other collaborative study, there was a need to build coherence among team members, and to standardize key aspects of what was to be studied and how it was to be studied. A workshop in Jodhpur was therefore organized to bring all participants onto the same page.

During this process there was also some discussion on participatory evaluation methods. The community representatives reflected on and understood the importance of listening and their changed role as listeners while local community beneficiaries took centre stage. Use of participatory methods and analysis helped them to make that shift. The workshop was designed to develop skills in evaluation, arrive at a list of key indicators that the beneficiary communities could use, and identify a suitable set of methods for the

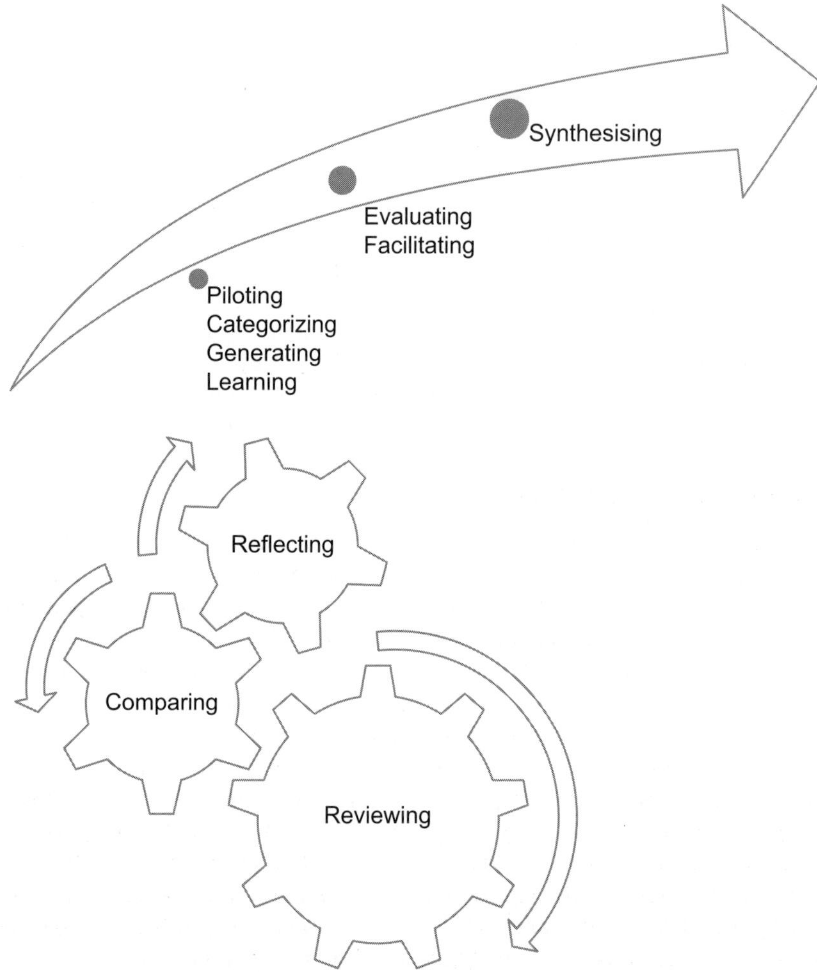

Figure 8.1 The process of the evaluation from the perspective of the community representatives

evaluation process. All tools to be used in the evaluation were introduced, explained and practised during the workshop.

The process of identifying indicators had its own amusing moments. To start discussions on the subject, the concept of evaluation was introduced with a simple analogy – the act of buying potatoes. There wasn't a single individual in the team of community representatives who had never been involved in purchase of potatoes, and they were asked about possible criteria that could be used to distinguish good potatoes from bad ones. Several interesting responses emerged. Someone said that a good potato is white in colour, while others

Box 8.1 The engine of experience

Having themselves been beneficiaries of the CBPPI programme, the community representatives had a ready frame of reference to which they could turn to make sense of their observations. Their personal experiences of the project in their home locations, of its limitations and of the opportunities it offered people; of the ways in which it can be effectively – or not so effectively – institutionalized within communities, gave them a unique vantage point from which to critically engage with the evidence they encountered. Retrospective learning was a driver and enabler of active learning throughout the evaluation journey.

The evaluation was therefore designed around the community representatives and their capabilities. They drew on their experience to suggest indicators for evaluating the project, and to form judgments about the work going on. Most importantly, though, their own experience as project beneficiaries enabled them to relate and connect – in a way that ordinary evaluators would be unable to do – to the specific experiences, stories, issues and observations of the community members whom they met at different locations.

thought that a good potato is tight in composition, doesn't have wrinkles on its surface, doesn't smell bad, or carry rotten cavities. The analogy was extended to the possibility of distinguishing a good programme from a bad one, a thought that gave people something to smile about., (cf. Banerjee, 2009).

Generating

Between them, the group generated 77 unique indicators. Sharing some of their own expectations and areas of greatest concern, this large set of indicators reflected how community representatives understood the programme implemented in their native localities. It represented a decisive contribution from community insiders to the design of the evaluation framework. A sample of the indicators suggested by one of the groups of community representatives is shown in Figure 8.2, below (for a full list of the 77 indicators selected by community representatives, see Annex 2).

Categorizing indicators

Not unexpectedly, perhaps, there were some unusual indicators. For example, some of the community representatives wanted to know whether the CBPPI programme was tackling social issues such as out-of-school children, dowry and child marriage. Others were interested in finding out about the extent of caste-based discrimination and of other possible forms of discrimination *within* project processes; and others wanted to examine the contribution the programme made to enabling women to express themselves at village meetings. One group stressed that the programme's ability to reach the poorest of the poor families should be scrutinized, and decided to put beneficiary identification under the microscope. The 77 indicators were subsequently classified by a smaller team of four community representatives into seven

Box 8.2 Indicators suggested by one of the groups of community representatives in Jodhpur

- Identification of the poorest (based on looks, clothes, family size, caste, etc.);
- Social status of the poorest (eg. whether caste-based discrimination exists, whether included or not);
- Whether loans are being disbursed or not, and the purposes and priorities thereof;
- Process of assessing need for a loan;
- Number of times loans were taken and returned by a person;
- Whether leadership in groups rotates or not;
- Process of drawing money from the bank – who goes to the bank?;
- Written records of the group;
- Status of women (in terms of decision-making role, living standard, education, wage entitlement, etc.);
- Role of the community worker in mobilizing people to join and remain in the groups (for example, persisting in persuading people, advocating for saving, etc.);
- Impact of the project on economic condition, education and decision-making processes;
- Role of women in making specific decisions relating to the number of children, family planning methods, etc.;
- Whether women own assets (eg. land and house) in their name or not;
- Responses of husbands on women joining the groups, or taking decisions;
- Performance of the project in relation to community's vision of change;
- Community's vision of future and well-being;
- The process of conflict resolution within the group;
- Whether the group takes up social issues prevalent in the local area;

thematic categories (using a colour-coding method aimed at identifying similar indicators listed on charts) with some help from the support facilitators. This sorting into a smaller subset of categories was done to ensure that indicators used in the evaluation were relevant to the varied project contexts. Indicators 1 and 2 reflect the community beneficiaries, emphasized interests in issues of women's empowerment and in social inclusion – interests that were re-emphasized during the course of the evaluation (see below).

Broadly summarized, the final seven categories were:

1. Inclusion of the poorest;
2. Enhancement in the status of women;
3. Quality of the collectives (of poor) formed under the programme;
4. Quality of work done or services delivered under the programme;
5. Engagement of the project with pressing local problems and issues;
6. Quality of linkages formed with government agencies, institutions of local self-governance and other local institutions;
7. Sustainability (prospects of continuation of the processes after withdrawal by the implementing organization).

Piloting the tools

To gather data along these community-generated indicators, the Praxis facilitators recommended a bundle of participatory reflection and action PRA tools generally used in similar studies. These were adapted by community representatives during the preparatory workshop. Following the workshop, the community representatives broke into smaller groups and visited a few villages of the nearest organization implementing the CBPPI programme, to pilot their approach to the evaluation exercise and test out a number of tools. This helped in sharpening their grasp of some of the methods discussed earlier.

Choosing tools that would help them understand the realities required by the indicators, the community representatives used them in original and creative ways during the evaluation process itself. One of those adapted was the well-being analysis tool. After categorization of various households of a community into locally defined strata of wellbeing, emerging clusters were used to identify beneficiaries of various interventions and judge their relative level of wellbeing. This enabled some examination of the degree of equity in the choice of beneficiaries.

Facilitating

Box 8.3 Snapshot 1

At one of the evaluation sites, the women in the group were refused entry into the air-conditioned coach of a train by a coach attendant who thought that they were entering the wrong compartment. He promptly ushered them to the unreserved compartment of the train at another station. A vendor selling tea inside the air-conditioned compartment thought the same and hesitated for a while before serving them tea. Such instances, according to the women of the group, happened because they were wearing ordinary clothes and did not look like seasoned travellers travelling by the more comfortable coaches.

Whilst the framework for evaluation was facilitated jointly by Praxis and the community representatives, the community representatives took the lead in the field. Each of the four groups of community representatives, accompanied by a support facilitator from Praxis, visited three different sub-programmes. A purposive approach had been taken to selecting the sample of villages; chosen villages all had different kinds of sub-programme activities, to enable interaction with a diverse array of project stakeholders.

The community representatives facilitated PRA processes in the different locations. Typically, this involved setting up the framework of that particular interaction, anchoring discussions, and summarizing learnings at the end. Local community members participating in the exercises would bring in their experience-based data and observations, analyse them, and validate the findings. They generally related much better to the community representatives than the way they might have been expected to relate to non-community evaluators, being 'peers' in terms of their stake in the CBPPI project.

The participatory processes facilitated in the various locations afforded multiple opportunities for local community beneficiaries to participate in the evaluation process. These were not restricted to a consultative mode of engagement, in which they were simply allowed to voice their perspectives. Using the PRA tools that they had been trained to use in the Jodhpur workshop, community representatives were able to involve the local beneficiaries in making meaning out of the data.

The tools were specifically chosen to address the sought-for indicators agreed upon during the preparatory workshop. Each tool provided a means of generating data along one or more indicators, as shown in Figure 8.2.

The evaluation teams tried as far as possible to capture data without any distortions by retaining a copy of the visual footprints and outputs of each process with the permission of the participating community members; original outputs were left with the local community members participating in the evaluation. Community representatives also took pictures of the process outputs and collected samples of local materials used in the evaluation, which were later reassembled to enable comparisons across various units of the national level programme.

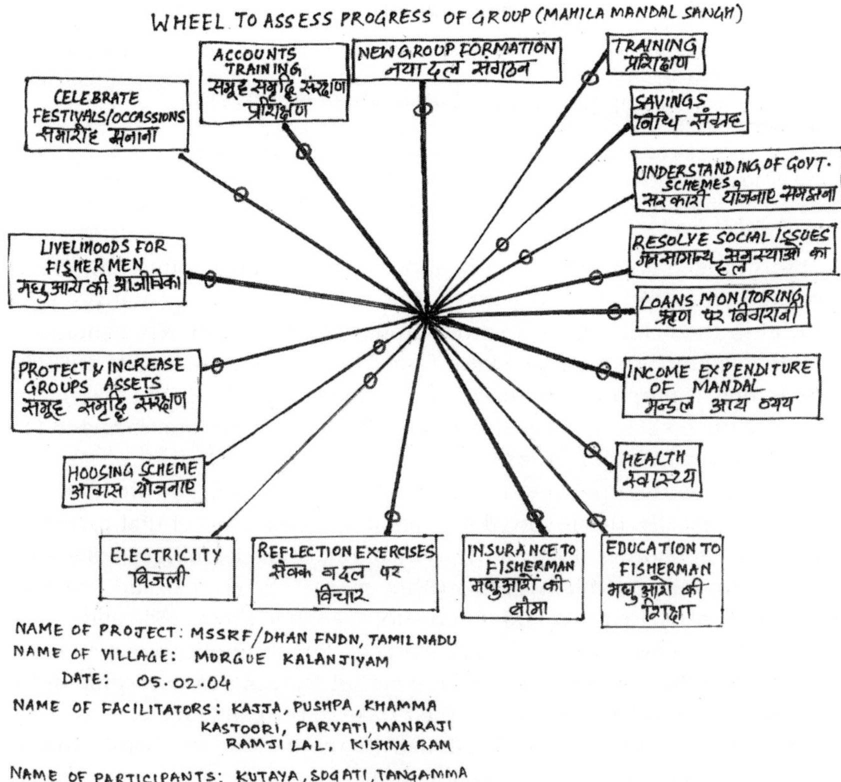

Figure 8.2 Cobweb analysis of one of the teams of community representatives

Table 8.1 Participatory tools used during the evaluation process

Tool	Use by community evaluators and participants	Indicator category
Social maps	• Participants generated criteria for identifying poor households. • Participants used these criteria to identify the poorest households. • Participants judged whether physical assets realized through the project are accessible to these households.	Inclusion of the poorest
Well-being assessments	• Participants verified whether the poorest households had, or had not, been included in the SHGs. • Participants checked whether or not these households had received project benefits.	Inclusion of the poorest
Cobweb analysis	• Participants analysed the quality of the groups and collectives formed under the project • Participants analysed the degree of empowerment of women beneficiaries of the project. • Participants analysed the quality of structures and services available through the project.	• Enhancement in the status of women; • Quality of the collectives (of poor) formed under the programme; • Quality of work done or services delivered under the programme.
Before and Now analyses	• Participants used an open-ended range of parameters to map changes attributable to the work of the project.	• Enhancement in the status of women; • Engagement of the project with pressing local problems and issues; • Quality of linkages formed with government agencies, institutions of local self-governance and other local institutions.
Case studies	• Participants focused on one individual beneficiary and tracked changes in the life of that person, especially in terms of changes in levels of poverty.	Multiple indicator categories
Card sorting	• Participants used a card-sorting process to identify key problems in the community.	Engagement of the project with pressing local problems and issues
Gender roles and decision-making matrix	• Participants tracked changes in one individual beneficiary in terms of gender-roles and decision-making.	Enhancement in the status of women
Project performance rating	• Participants rated the performance of the project on key parameters, such as inclusion of the poorest, and enhancement in the status of women.	Multiple indicator categories

The support facilitators from Praxis were only expected to help out in handling logistics of the visits, playing a secretarial role to document processes and outcomes (as visually as possible), making checklists, translating (whilst a considerable number knew the national language, Hindi, nine did not), and reading documents. Key traits looked for in the support facilitators included a friendly attitude and the ability to keep the process community-led. They were expected to refrain from imposing their own opinions or judgments about the work of the organizations under evaluation.

Evaluating

The community teams praised a number of implementing organizations for their interventions. Their observations were replete with acclamations that spoke of wonderful efforts in regenerating natural resources, successful campaigns forcing government institutions to act, popular innovations in imparting elementary education, effective operations to free poor people from the misery of bonded labour, numerous livelihood-support interventions helping the poor during lean seasons, efficient collectives managing huge amounts of self-pooled resources, and ingenuous local initiatives seeking to deal with social evils.

Criticism, often constructive, was also forthcoming. The team visiting Gujarat found that the size of SHGs in some of the project sites was simply too large to be manageable. One evaluation team visiting Rajasthan found that women's groups formed under the sub-programme were not following certain rules and regulations properly. Chitri Mali, one of the members of that evaluating team, maintained that collecting information through a village survey is one of the prime functions a women's collective has, particularly as it sets up the collective's engagement in development issues a community faces. Such a survey, she said, could yield a host of valuable details, including, for example: the number of functional taps, number of school-going children, the population of the village, immunizations, *anganwadi* (childcare centres providing nutrition and pre-school activities), number of landless people, liquor sales, whether or not the *pradhan* (*panchayat* president) is helpful, and problems facing the poorest people in the community. These issues could then be brought into discussion at meetings of the federation and dealt with at block and district levels.

Meanwhile, the limited nature of the linkages that community groups had formed with local and government institutions led some community representatives to question the sustainability of development activities (by way of illustration, in the Cobweb analysis shown in Figure 8.2, the team visiting Tamil Nadu scored the SHG relatively poorly on its 'understanding of government schemes' and 'housing schemes' and relatively well along a range of other indicators). In one area, the pernicious effects of conditioned loaning – which led to some villagers losing their land – were attributed to an inappropriate programme strategy. In a large number of programme sites, livelihood promotion activities were deemed barely viable due to lack of suitable markets.

Community representatives brought an authentic concern for inclusion to the evaluation process. In one sub-programme site in Rajasthan, the team found that the local SHG's stance that members should pay INR50 was preventing poorer women from joining. This was problematic: many of these were in greatest need of available livelihood interventions.

Another group remarked on instances of gender inequity in income despite interventions to the contrary. Indeed, the status of women and girls proved to be a major concern of the community evaluators.

Women in all the four teams tried different approaches to investigate gender relations, with methods ranging from random household visits to self-help group members, to participatory group meetings to discussions with men and elderly people. The visit to the sub-programme in Kurnool provided the group a good benchmark of how intensive engagement in process-oriented microfinance activities was instrumental in enhancing the self-confidence and financial independence of women. Similar conclusions were drawn after visiting communities in Uttaranchal, where the women's groups had strongly engaged with political processes at the level of local institutions of governance. While micro-finance and livelihood activities were found to be at different stages in various sub-programmes, the impact of the sub-programme processes on the status of women was still felt to be below expectations.

The community representatives felt very strongly that, barring some exceptions, the workload and drudgery of women has not reduced in communities covered by most sub-programmes. In addition to household responsibilities, women are additionally required to participate in group processes, besides being required to work outside the household boundaries. At the other extreme were the sub-programmes in Uttar Pradesh and Rajasthan, where veiled women were still subjected to highly patriarchal and subjugating traditions despite some of their collective initiatives to secure basic services and livelihood opportunities. However, the fact that a women's collective could act as a pressure group was clearly evident through the experiences of most sub-programmes, including those located in feudal and patriarchal social settings like Alwar in Rajasthan (operational area of Tarun Bharat Sangh, an ecological research and land development movement to provide people with clean water.)

Another team, visiting Uttar Pradesh, was disturbed to see that some young girls in a village had not been able to continue studying beyond class 8 (age 13 or 14). The eight-mile distance between home and school was the problem. Community representatives identified this as an issue that the NGO should take up, and urged them to either organize a vehicle or start a girl's hostel so that those children were not deprived of a secondary school education.

Similarly, the community representatives were also keen to assess the inclusion of the poorest sections of communities in the sub-programme processes and benefits. Some of the well-being assessments facilitated by the groups in various communities yielded significant revelations about the relevance of the sub-programmes to the lives of the poor. On the whole, the programme was rated high on this parameter, but the groups also brought to the fore some critical programme-design issues that had a bearing on the inclusion of the poorest. In one of the sub-programme sites of GVVS, the *swashakti* (self-help) group found that the insistence of the local SHG for a monthly deposit of fifty rupees prevented some poor families from joining the group, though several beneficiaries of *tankas* (a circular structure for conserving rainwater widely constructed in the arid regions of Rajasthan) and livelihood support belonged to the poorest segment of the community. Even in some of the most dynamic SHGs of women, such as those in Kurnool, Nuapara, or Gulf of Mannar, many of the poorest families were not associated with the processes at all due to their inability to deposit savings. One group noticed how, in several villages, marginal landholdings of the poorest in the community had missed out on the benefits of a rainwater harvesting facility due to being located too far away.

Synthesizing and speaking out

Box 8.4. Unpacking expertise

As soon as the group arrived at its destination, one of the project representatives from the NGO who had come to receive them made fun of some of the group members, saying what an anti-climax it was for them to receive 'experts' who were nothing but ordinary villagers! The remark hurt several of the group members. However, it did not take the group very long to recover their pride. The moment they concluded their presentation at the UNDP office about a month later, the same person who had made the unpleasant remark was found overwhelmed with the range and depth of findings relating to his project.

More commonly, where community members collect data, analysis is taken up by external people. Here, after the community representatives had completed fieldwork, they arrived in the UNDP office in Delhi for a closing workshop. And it was the community representatives themselves that led a process of sifting through and synthesizing the data, identifying the most pertinent issues facing communities across different sub-programmes. Key findings and observations from the evaluation were organized around the seven thematic categories earlier identified by the groups to categorize their indicators.

Each group had an opportunity to present its key insights. While the group members took turns in presenting analytical diagrams and tables drawn on chart papers, the support facilitators translated their observations to the audience, which included influential members of staff within UNDP and the Joint Secretary from the Ministry of Rural Development. The following key learnings were identified:

- On the whole, collectivization of the poor into groups has helped them to realize their rights and their entitlements.

- With a few exceptions, it was felt that the drudgery of women's work had not been dealt with in the context of most sub-programmes, despite promising indicators of progress in other domains of women's empowerment.
- It is imperative to ensure that norms and rules around membership that are set by a SHG are not exclusive – for example, demanding a level of financial commitment that the poorest in a community cannot afford to meet.
- Going forward, NGOs would still be likely have a role to play to protect the interests of the poorest groups in a community.
- There is significant scope to improve the coordination of sub-programmes with government institutions in order to ensure proper provision of fundamental services.

Constraints, challenges and institutional learning

The pioneering nature of the evaluation exercise did not always lend itself to a smooth process. Translation, though managed, was a major logistical challenge. Another frequently cited issue was the interference of NGO staff. It was difficult at times to convince certain NGO staff that the group wanted to hear the voices of the communities directly and not their interpretations and explanations. Separate interactions had been planned for these purposes.

Handling the busy schedule and being away from home for an entire month was also difficult. The evaluation schedule, which targeted 13 of the 16

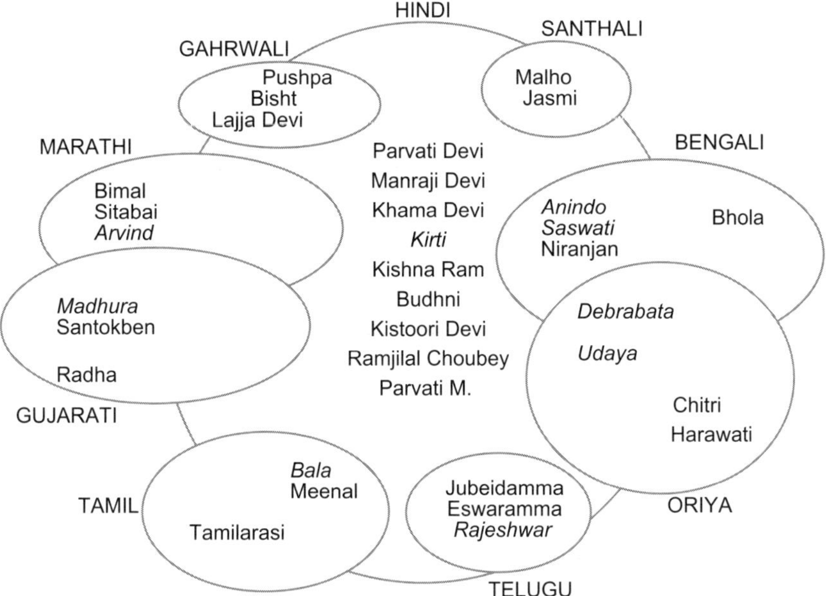

Figure 8.3 Known Indian languages of community representatives *(Praxis support facilitators in italics)*

sub-programmes in just one month, also ran the risk, at times, of privileging quantity of coverage over quality and depth of insight. An alternative approach would have been to set up more focused and longer assessments of fewer sub-programmes.

Whilst this community-led process was part of the overall evaluation, it did not stand alone. Alongside this, a more conventional evaluation process took place, and a programmatic overview drew the two together. Certainly, if local community members had been involved in the conception of evaluation indicators at the time of project planning, they could have been involved in the evaluations much more organically. Whilst it might still have been possible to make the entire evaluation community-led using indicators conceptualized entirely retrospectively, on the grounds that community members are the most important stakeholders, this was not attempted in this case.

The outputs of the community evaluation[4], together with a more conventional evaluation process (still participatory to a large extent, but facilitated by 'professional evaluators'), both fed into a summative evaluation. As an end-of-project evaluation, there was not scope for the learning gained to feed into the CBPPI project cycle. However, within UNDP, the community-led evaluation prompted significant reflection, specifically on the need to provide more space to community inputs to other aspects of programming such as planning, proposals, and NGO appraisal. In fact, in a subsequent UNDP project on natural resource management, discussions with the community formed the basis of involvement with NGOs, enabling them to set the agenda for the rest of the project

Conclusions

Beneficiaries of development programmes are not generally enabled to participate in formal evaluation processes of such programmes. Interaction often largely takes place between the funding agency and the NGO, whose staff are seen to 'represent' the views of the community. If the community participates at all, it is in a primarily consultative mode: they are asked questions and their views sought, but they do not play a determining role in the evaluation process itself.

Here, community members were at the heart of the process. They played a decisive role in creating the evaluation framework, from suggesting 77 indicators, to grouping these into seven categories. It was *community members themselves* (both representatives and local beneficiaries) and not field staff of NGOs, who were the core generators of the data for the evaluation. Nor were processes of data interpretation and analysis on the ground left to outsiders: the community members were directly involved in them. Furthermore, it was community members who facilitated the evaluation: setting the agendas for the sessions, asking the questions, filling out the charts, seeking clarifications.

As a participatory process within the tradition of participatory monitoring and evaluation, the evaluation challenged the practice of making evaluations the preserve of 'qualified' outsiders who are 'technical specialists'. In the design and running of the evaluation, credit was given to field knowledge, popular knowledge, and primary knowledge as opposed to bookish, academic, and secondary knowledge. By inviting community members into a space that has traditionally belonged to donors and development professionals, it put the community representatives into a position whereby they were able to contribute directly to development discourse. They were given platforms from which to interrogate change at different levels of civil society (such as community-based organizations or NGOs) and government (eg Panchayati Raj Institutions, Block Development Offices (BDOs), or Collectors' Offices (the chief administrative and revenue officer of a district) to view familiar institutions and systems from a critical distance, and then to share their findings. Bringing NGOs (and, to some extent, government bodies) into the evaluation space provided community representatives with opportunities to make judgements on those charged with providing a service to them; and, ultimately, to be heard by decision-makers in Delhi.

Within this community-led evaluation paradigm, the community played a facilitator and instigator role vis-à-vis the evaluation process and the stakeholders engaged within it. Two groups from within the community played roles: community beneficiaries, who interacted with the evaluating team, and community representatives, who led the evaluation team. Here, the community members were enabled to critically evaluate the same programme that had been set up to serve them. The beneficiaries were invited not just to be consulted, but also to do the consulting.

The community-led evaluation lends credibility to the view that if institutions are to be community-owned, then so can the means of judging the interventions designed to support these institutions. As unusual as it may have been, to enable community representatives to play this role is – in a number of important ways – entirely consistent with project aims. Conventional evaluations subvert the aims of development projects insofar as they drain resources (time, money and knowledge) away from the poor and towards development professionals. A community-led evaluation process such as the one discussed here is much more consistent with the thrust and priorities of the project as a whole, since resources are directed towards the intended beneficiaries. Yet the commitment to community participation that this approach demands is itself a subversion of many standard evaluation processes, since here it is beneficiaries who evaluate how well the donor's funds have been spent *on the beneficiaries*.

That the community representatives experienced a sense of achievement from the exercise was quite evident. As the process came to an end, they took the opportunity to make a statement, and by the end of the evaluation process, the community representatives seemed sad to say goodbye. It is not unreasonable to suggest that most enjoyed the process. As has been noted:

> To an extent easily overlooked, people enjoy and learn from the process of analysis and sharing of knowledge, values and priorities, and feel good at discovering what they can show and express, and having their own views heard. A typical observation has been that, 'People participating

> in the groups seemed to enjoy the discussions and exercises and most stayed for the entire duration (Adato and Nyasimi, 2002 in Chambers, 2008: 120).

The evaluation also served some quite practical purposes for the community representatives. With many of them members of SHGs themselves, the exercise was a forum for reflection and learning, with the team able to meet people in different contexts who were trying to achieve comparable goals. It provided SHG members with an opportunity to draw lessons and apply them to their own contexts.

Box 8.5 Recollections from Rameswaram

Pushpa Bisht, an SHG member from Uttaranchal and one of the 26 community representatives, reflected on how members of the SHG she visited in Rameswaram, Tamil Nadu, were able to generate income that made a difference to their families – enabling them to send their children to school. She also recalled how one SHG member shared her problems with other SHG members, who now took the help of the cluster (a group of villages) to resolve their difficulties

Visiting parts of the country where SHGs are particularly well established, such as Tamil Nadu and Andhra Pradesh, was a good learning experience. She was able to learn about methods of working in a pressure group, strategies for communicating and linking with other departments in other places, and new perspectives on how to address issues. She saw, for example, how problems might not be solvable by a single person but that considerably more can be achieved when larger numbers are mobilized.

Being put in the position of an evaluator proved to be a confidence-builder, but it also served as an experience in reflective learning for Pushpa as she considered her own work and context in the light of what she saw in these new terrains.

Box 8.6 Daring to evaluate

Haravati Maihi and Chitri Mali, community representatives from Orissa, found that the evaluation process, which took them to Rajasthan, Uttaranchal and Uttar Pradesh, helped them to understand a number of social issues better. They learnt ways of using inclusive, participatory methods to resolve matters in their communities. Haravati drew on her experience to take a lead role in implementing a watershed project in her village, and Chitri found that it was an enabler of her work in enrolling drop-out children at school.

As newly literate women, they were not comfortable with much more than writing their signature and in reading some letters in Odia (the local language in Odisha state). However, thanks to the pictorial tools they employed in the evaluation they were now better able to identify the poorest of the poor, and use social maps to identify and aggregate local problems. They said that the process provided them with an enabling environment in which they could dare to evaluate. They felt that, whilst the process of CBPPI developed their capacity to work with the community, after being involved in the community evaluation they had more confidence to take the initiative within the community through a participatory approach.

In some cases, NGOs being evaluated also benefited from learning about participatory approaches such as resource mapping and social mapping. One partner NGO reported that, more than ten years later, they still use some of these methods in their work to tackle distress migration.

Overall, the community-led evaluation process demonstrated the viability of an alternative way of doing and understanding evaluation. Indeed, to some observers, the community members had seemed like natural evaluators. In reality, though, they were schooled; but just not in the conventional way that evaluators are schooled. Evaluation may seem complicated to outsiders who haven't been through the training of experience. But when you yourself have helped to grow and nurture them, who better than you to tell potatoes apart?

About the authors

Anindo Banerjee, Praxis. Anindo has over a decade's experience in international social development, particularly in conducting participatory assessments, policy analysis and capacity building processes.

Rohan Preece, Praxis. Rohan has worked with development sector organizations in different parts of the world and has experience in social research, teaching, and monitoring and evaluation.

M. J. Joseph, Praxis. Joseph has over two decades' experience in social work research and practice, with a major part of the experience in development research across various themes.

Endnotes

1. This chapter is based on a report called Terminal Evaluation of GoI-UNDP 'Community-based Pro-poor Initiatives' (CBPPI) Programme by Praxis, which was commissioned by UNDP. A detailed list of contributors is available in Annex 1.
2. Robert Chambers has argued that, despite the inroads it has made, participatory work has remained on the borders of much development practice (Chambers, in Holland, 2012) and this would seem to apply to an even greater extent to evaluation practice.
3. The scope for community involvement has already been well theorized and reflected upon. Participatory Impact Assessment (PIA), for example, has been defined as:

   A process of evaluation of the impacts of development interventions which is carried out under the full or joint control of local communities in partnership with professional practitioners ... In PIA, community representatives participate in the definition of impact indicators, the collection of data, the analysis of data, the communication of findings, and, especially, in the post-assessment actions designed to improve the impact of development interventions in the locality' (Jackson, 1995 in Estrella and Gaventa, 1998).
4. The full Community Evaluation report compiled by Praxis is available online, at <http://erc.undp.org/evaluationadmin/downloaddocument.html?-docid=4416>.

References

Anderson, S.G. and Finnegan, D., (2012), 'The Evaluation Practices of US International NGOs,' *Development in Practice* 22: 3 17–333, <http://www.tandfonline.com/doi/abs/10.1080/09614524.2012.664621> [Accessed 5 July 2014].

Banerjee, A., with Mishra, K., Pandit, M., Bhattacharya, S. and Bhuniya, D. (2004) 'Through the eyes without lenses! Handbook based on community-led evaluation of UNDP-funded Community-based Pro-poor Initiatives Programme in India'.

Banerjee, A., 'Voices of Verity' in Random Strokes [blog], (Posted September 16, 2009). <http://anindobanerjee.blogspot.in/2009/09/last-word-community-led-evaluation-of.html> [Accessed 5 July 2014].

Chambers, R. (2007) 'Who Counts? The Quiet Revolution of Participation and Numbers', *IDS Working Paper,* 296.

Cornwall, A., (2008) 'Unpacking 'Participation': models, meanings and practices,' *Community Development Journal,* 43 (3): 269–283.

Estrella, M., and Gaventa, J., (1998) 'Who Counts Reality? Participatory Monitoring and Evaluation: A Literature review'; *IDS Working Paper,* 70.

Fernandes, W., and Tandon, R. (1982) 'Participatory Research as a Process of Liberation', *Sociological Bulletin,* 31, 2: 254–258.

Hickey, S., and Mohan, G. (2005), 'Relocating participation within a radical politics of development,' *Development and Change,* 36 (2): 237–262.

Kang, J., Anderson, S.G. and Finnegan, D., (2012), 'The evaluation practices of US International NGOs,' *Development in Practice,* 22:3, 317–333.

Menon, G. (2005), 'Consolidated Report of Terminal Evaluation of the Programme, submitted to UNDP-Government of India', Praxis, Delhi.

Praxis (2004), 'Community-led evaluation of CBPPI sub-programmes in India', Delhi.

Sen, A. (1999), *Development as Freedom,* Oxford: Oxford University Press. <http://planningcommission.nic.in/plans/planrel/fiveyr/9th/vol1/v1c1-2.htm>

Annex 1: list of contributors

The authors and editors would like to acknowledge Shashi Sudhir for her support in developing this chapter. Thanks are also due to Pushpa Bisht and colleagues at RLEK, Abani Mohan Panagrahi, Chitri Mali and Haravati Majhi and others connected with Lokadrusti for their contributions to the chapter.

The community representatives who carried out the evaluation include: Mrs Nanduba Hamirji, Mrs Radha Bahen Garva, Mrs Santokben Barot, Mrs Mainaben, Thakur, Mrs. Sitabai Walkoli, Mrs. Bimal Agiwali, Mrs Budhani Sao, Ms Parvati Mahant, Mrs Chitri Mali, Mrs Haravati, Mr.Niranjan Sabar, Mr. Bholanath Sabar, Mrs T. Meenal, Mrs. A. Tamilarasi, Mrs. Jubedabi K., Mrs. K. Eswaramma, Ms. Jasmi Murmu, Ms. Malho Murmu, Mrs Lajja Devi, Ms. Pushpa Bisht, Mrs Kistoori Devi, Mrs. Khama Devi, Mrs. Parvati Devi, Mrs. Manraji Devi, Mr. Ramji Lal Choubey and Mr. Kishna Ram.

The support facilitators are: Ms. Kirti Mishra, Ms. Madhura Pandit, Ms. Saswati Bhattachrya, Mr. Debabrata Bhuniya, Mr. Rajeshwar D., Mr. Girish

Chandra Mishra, Mr. Udaya Panda, Mr. Arvind Rane, Mr. P.K. Balasubramaniam, Mr. Sundar, Mr. Anindo Banerjee, Mr. Tom Thomas.

Annex 2

The scope of evaluation (as suggested by the four groups of community representatives)

Output from Group 1

Participants: Haravati, Chitri Mali, Budhni Sao, Kamla, Sudha, Parvati, Rajo
Supported by: Debabrata

- Whether women are fully participating in the *gram sabhas*
- Whether women's voices/suggestions are heard in the *gram sabha*
- Whether the Below Poverty Line poor are being allotted a house under *Indira Awaas* (a national rural housing project) in the *gram sabhas*
- Whether the landless are being allotted land
- Were the poor given money to repair land?
- Improvement in living standards
- Awareness amongst women
- What benefits did they get from the project?
- Whether they can hold discussions openly and freely with women from outside the village
- Whether they have health-related awareness?
- Improvement in education status of girls
- Decline in instances of child marriages
- Regularity of meetings and savings; how many were given loans?
- Attendance of women in the meetings; whether there is provision for penalties for the absentee women or not; if yes, how many have been penalized?
- Participation of women in protecting forests and afforestation activities
- Whether women's groups are aware of development activities in the village
- Mutual co-ordination between *panchayats* and women's groups
- Whether one can tactfully place one's point of view before the *panchayat?*
- How much work did the group get, and what work was undertaken?

Output from Group 2

Participants: Kistoori, Ramji Lal, Parvati, Manraji, Lajja, Pushpa, Kishna Ram
Supported by: Kirti

- *Tankas* are located near whose house?
- Number of poor girls in the school
- Do women get equal wages with men?
- Improvement in economic well-being of poor women

- Whether the poorest have got BPL cards
- Whether rations are conveniently available in the fair price shops
- Whether there is casteism in the group; whether people have equal rights to sit together and speak
- Participation of women in government employment schemes
- Selection of eligible beneficiaries by women's groups
- Participation of poor women in the watershed management projects
- Improvement in the situation relating to dowry and child marriages
- Appropriateness of the systems followed in the school run by the organization
- Improvement in health services, for example relating to immunization and family planning. Does the Auillary Nurse Midwife (ANM) undertake visits from house to house?
- Whether women attend *gram sabha* meetings or not
- Whether bonded labourers have been freed from the clutches of money-lenders

Output from Group 3

Participants: Tamilarasi, Meenal, Jubeida, Eswaramma
Supported by: Saswati

- Identification of the poorest (based on looks, clothes, family size, or caste)
- Social status of the poorest (e.g. whether caste-based discrimination exists, whether included in group of poor)
- Whether loans are being disbursed or not and if so, the purposes and priorities of these loans
- Process of assessing need for a loan
- Number of times loans were taken or returned by a person
- Whether leadership in the groups rotates
- Process of drawing money from the bank – who goes to the bank?
- Written records of the group
- Status of women (in terms of decision-making role, living standard, education, or wage entitlements)
- Role of the community worker in mobilizing people to join and remain in the groups (e.g. in persisting in persuading people, in advocating for saving)
- Impact of the project on economic conditions, education and decision-making processes of intended beneficiaries
- Role of women in making specific decisions relating to number of children or family planning methods
- Whether women's own assets (e.g. land and house) are in their name
- Whether loan-transactions are based on any plan; who takes part in making such plans?
- Whether the group has purchased new instruments
- Responses of husbands to women joining the groups, or taking decisions

- Performance of the project vis-à-vis the community's vision of change
- Community's vision of future and well-being
- The process of conflict resolution within the group
- Whether the group takes up social issues prevalent in the local area
- Responses of neighbours vis-à-vis individual case studies (for cross-examination)
- Comparison between work of different groups / clusters
- Is there a process of redistribution of community resources?
- Measures to deal with non-repayment of loans
- Duration of loans and rate of interest
- Assessment of marketing strategies of the clusters – for example, are the rates fixed, and who goes to the market and where?
- Other initiatives taken by the cluster, e.g. in providing drinking water facilities or houses
- For agricultural interventions – regularity in provision of fertilizers or pesticides; how health hazards are met and alternative approaches
- What is the cluster's role in addressing women's health issues?
- Political awareness – do people know about ward members?
- What is the relationship of cluster members with other prominent people in society?
- How many people are covered under the cluster? Who is responsible for this?
- Is the cluster registered? Do members know about it?
- How are bookkeeping and auditing done for the cluster? Who is involved?
- Did the work of the cluster generate individual employment or group employment? Were women's groups given employment or was work executed through contractors?
- Has the cluster been successful in arresting migration? How many people have been helped?
- How many clusters are formed in an area? Do special clusters for adolescents, pregnant women, or children exist?
- How many exposure visits or trainings were completed?

Outputs from Group 4

Participants: Santokben, Nanduba, Radhaben, Mainaben, Bimal, Sitabai
Supported by: Madhura

- Accumulation of savings for women
- Freedom from the mortgaging arrangements of moneylenders
- Awareness amongst women about health issues, and the confidence to talk about their own health

- Awareness amongst women about different forms of gender-based injustices and their rights
- Awareness amongst women about insurance arrangements and ways of utilizing insurance benefits during emergencies

(Source: Community-Led Evaluation of CBPPI Sub-Programmes in India, Praxis 2004)

CHAPTER 9

Re-imagining development: marginalized people and the post-2015 agenda

Pradeep Narayanan, Sowmyaa Bharadwaj, and Anusha Chandrasekharan

Abstract

[1]Global policymaking has traditionally been a space dominated by representatives of nation states. At times, it has also been a place in which non-governmental spokespersons representing different issues have come together to frame policies purporting to address the concerns of people living in poverty. More recently, these global spaces have even played host to luminaries who choose to speak out on different issues concerning the poor and excluded. But rarely has it been a space in which marginalized people can make themselves heard directly.

Certain participatory processes have provided poorer people with opportunities to directly voice their concerns within globalpolicy making processes. Going beyond representation, these efforts have seen the poor and marginalized groups participate in policy discussions. As a counterpoint to the High-Level Panel set up by the United Nations in 2012, Ground-Level Panels[2] were established in four countries in the global South. This chapter focuses on the methods of this initiative and its contribution to providing community members with a space to articulate their views within the highly plural, deeply unequal, and enduringly complex context of India. It shows how the panel highlighted power relations that are the underlying causes of poverty, and gives weight to the argument that such processes should be institutionalized to bring the voices of marginalized people to the fore in a more systematic and regular way.

Keywords: millennium development goals, global development debate, community participation, post-2015, marginalized, goal-setting

Introduction: framing development agendas

The presence of multiple and differently constructed power relationships is a significant challenge in global policymaking. Spoken or unspoken rules of engagement determine relationships within, among and between both developed and developing countries, which are coloured by domestic politics and a changing global political economy. In the context of rapid globalization, different interest groups in the form of large donor agencies have increasingly come to occupy significant spaces for policymaking and have used them to

http://dx.doi.org/10.3362/9781780448695.009

align with their strategic interests, often backing initiatives in support of the poor. Many corporate entities are already using these spaces to further their interests. Hard-nosed diplomacy, evident most clearly in the politics of international aid, plays out in many ways to shape global policies and define key questions – *What's in? What's out? Who's in?* and *Who's out?*

In the international policy arena, there has historically been a chasm between local and global agents of change. In the policymaking activities of international bodies such as the United Nations, the World Bank and the World Trade Organization, negotiations are largely between nation states, their representatives and the United Nations bureaucracy. While it is understood that global directives may have local triggers as well as impacts, discussion of such directives remains mostly the preserve of 'elites': policymakers, government functionaries, academics and sector experts. At the level of global policy debate, space for inclusion of the very people whom development frameworks purport to serve is limited, for example because of a perceived lack of ability and knowledge.

At the national level, civil society organizations have created and in some cases even taken over spaces for policymaking and advocacy (Ghaus-Pacha, 2005). Over and above their traditional 'third sector' role of bridging the gap between the state and the market, non-governmental organizations (NGOs) are increasingly seen as articulating the voices of the people. These developments are at once exciting and potentially problematic. The possibilities for civil society engagement with the poor and marginalized have perhaps never been so vast and vibrant. Yet with these developments new kinds of power relationships have also evolved. Embedded structures of inequality, including implicit or explicit biases towards certain forms of knowledge and modes of expression, tend to limit opportunities for the participation of certain groups in these processes. Civil society actors have typically taken up the task of representation, buttressed by studies aimed at achieving a better understanding of the conditions and experiences of people living in poverty.

Over the past two decades, the United Nations has brought together the international community under the aegis of Agenda 21, which set out in 1992 a strategy for achieving sustainable development and, more recently, the Millennium Declaration and Millennium Development Goals (Geoghegan, 2013). The latter were designed to boost and strategize poverty reduction work across the world, and were adopted by all UN member states in 2000. The declaration committed nations to a new global partnership to reduce extreme poverty by setting out a series of time-bound targets, with a deadline of 2015. It prioritized eight focus themes for the work of donors and governments worldwide, and calculated targets for national governments and regions according to the countries' existing levels of poverty and the volume of aid they received.

The Millennium Development Goals and related campaigns have been criticized for a perceived lack of analytical rigour and justification behind the chosen objectives (Deneulin and Lila Shahani, 2009), as well as for lacking strong indicators for inequality within countries, despite significant disparities in many developing nations (Kabeer, 2010). There have also been criticisms of the nature of roll out of plans, financing, scale-up of development programmes, methods of implementation, and evaluation, and these limitations have in turn been cited as reasons for slow progress on various goals. In addition, several core issues that keep certain groups in poverty were not incorporated in the goals. Most significant to this study is the lack of space for people's direct participation in the framing of goals and indicators. The way in which the goals were formulated has been widely criticized (Amin, 2006), from being construed as lacking 'consultation in the conception stage' (UN System Task Team, 2011) to being seen as nothing but attempts to legitimize the interests of dominant people.

This chapter features a case study that provides a different perspective vis-à-vis some of the trends cited above. In doing so, it also reveals a deep social justice approach to resolving issues of poverty and inequality. The analysis that we go on to explore in this chapter comes not from formally schooled theorists, but from people who have lived through and are intimate with poverty and exclusion. In what follows, dimensions of structural poverty and marginalization are given a uniquely human expression, as paradigms of debate around development are recast and new potentials emerge for an agenda driven by insiders as well as outsiders.

The High-Level Panel and its contributions

Even as debates continued on the achievements of the Millennium Development Goals, the United Nations had already initiated discussions on the post-2015 development framework, keeping in mind several shortcomings listed by internal reviews as well as feedback from external organizations. Thematic consultations in countries across the world were organized to incorporate the experiences and learnings of civil society organizations worldwide into the post-2015 development framework. In addition, the 'My World' initiative of the United Nations Development Group collated perspectives on the Millennium Development Goals and their future.

In 2012, the United Nations formed a 27-member panel of eminent people to advise on the global development framework beyond 2015. The High-Level Panel (HLP), as it came to be known, was co-chaired by the presidents of Indonesia and Liberia, and the prime minister of the United Kingdom, and included leaders from civil society, the private sector, academicians and government. The HLP came up with 12 goals in their 'people-centred and planet-sensitive agenda' focusing on eradicating extreme poverty (UN, 2013).

The report stated that 'no one must be left behind' by the post-2015 agenda and stressed the need to tackle causes of poverty, exclusion and equality, even though none of the 12 goals addressed the structural causes of poverty directly. Transforming economies and providing jobs to all through sustainable development, policies of growth begetting more growth, and

Table 9.1 Goals of the High-Level Panel

Goal 1	End poverty
Goal 2	Empower girls and women and achieve gender equality
Goal 3	Provide quality education and lifelong learning
Goal 4	Ensure healthy lives
Goal 5	Ensure food security and good nutrition
Goal 6	Achieve universal access to water and sanitation
Goal 7	Secure sustainable energy
Goal 8	Create jobs, sustainable livelihoods, and equitable growth
Goal 9	Manage natural resource assets sustainably
Goal 10	Ensure good governance and effective institutions
Goal 11	Ensure stable and peaceful societies
Goal 12	Create a global enabling environment and catalyse long-term finance

Source: Cameron, D., Bambang Yudhoyono, S. and Johnson Sirleaf, E. (2013) 'A New Global Partnership: Eradicate Poverty And Transform Economies Through Sustainable Development: The Report of the High-Level Panel of Eminent Persons on the Post-2015 Development Agenda', United Nations, New York.

flourishing business were seen as contributing to the ending of extreme poverty. Two of the 12 goals focused on eradicating extreme poverty and hunger. The other goals dealt with access to inclusive opportunities (education, health, water and sanitation, jobs) and services for all, particularly women and girls; practices of good governance; global partnerships; and the creation of sustainable livelihoods and a global enabling environment for growth.

In the run-up to the creation of a development framework to succeed the MDGs, the United Nations has opened up the space for civil society interactions much more than it had during the creation of the MDGs.[3]

This opening up of the global policymaking space also helped to set the stage for communities of poor and vulnerable groups across the world, seen as beneficiaries of internationally framed policies, to enter discussions. Set against this backdrop, the Participate initiative of the Institute of Development Studies (Sussex, UK), aimed to create platforms for marginalized and excluded communities to voice their concerns and needs at a global level in the context of the post-Millennium Development Goals agenda-setting. As part of the Participate initiative, Ground-Level Panels were set up in four countries – Brazil, Uganda, Egypt and India – to provide a counterpoint to professional, political and academic voices' dominance of the High-Level Panel. These panels drew on the experiences of their members' marginalization and poverty and in some cases, as in India, on the experiences of other poor groups and individuals like themselves. Praxis was a part of the steering group of the Participate initiative, and acted as the national secretariat of the Ground-Level Panel.

The idea of turning to the expertise of people living in conditions of poverty is not new. In the late 1990s, for example, the Government of India and the United Nations Development Program (UNDP) initiated a Community-Based Pro-Poor Initiatives Programme (CBPPI) that created spaces for communities to play a role in poverty reduction. At the end of the four-year programme, representatives of these communities became evaluators in a process facilitated by Praxis. The initiative leveraged the power of experience to challenge conventional understandings of who were the 'right' people to conduct evaluations and filter this feedback to decision-makers (See Chapter 7).

Voices of the people

Initiatives around the globe have gradually understood the importance of bringing direct voices into policy framing rather than resorting to representational advocacy. However, there was little space within the policymaking system to include voices of excluded groups – whether they are children, dalits, sexual minorities or others. Praxis felt a need to hand over the stick to people who have experienced challenging issues first-hand so that they have the opportunity to contribute to policy formation.

As part of the Participate initiative, Praxis had already initiated in 2012 a research and advocacy campaign called Voice for Change through participatory video and digital story-telling processes and action research, which complemented the Ground-Level Panel's findings.

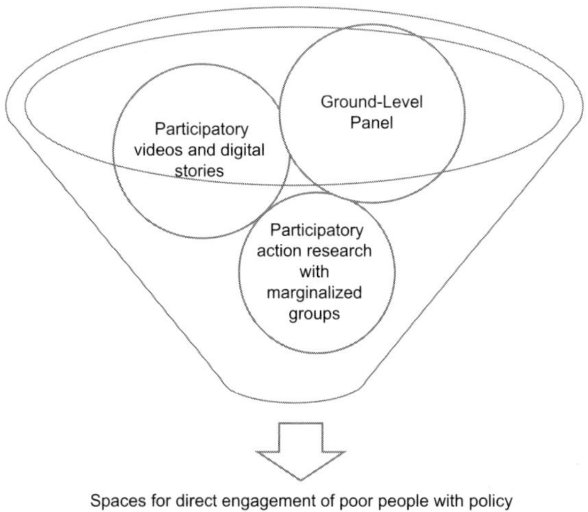

Figure 9.1 Voice for Change advocacy campaign

The Voice for Change initiative aimed to build evidence-based knowledge to facilitate 'direct talk' between communities and policy makers; among and between communities and in different geographical and socio-political contexts. Through thematic studies, audio-visual processes and the facilitation of a Ground-Level Panel, a space was opened up for people facing poverty and exclusion to deliberate on and contribute to policy formation and global discourse in the post-2015 context.

The initiative was significant on two counts. Firstly, it gave excluded groups space to voice their own narratives rather than have their stories told by someone else. This was very visible in a participatory video or digital story process where the group owned the product from the conception through execution, right up to review, finalization and dissemination, when technology was used as a medium of introspection for a community rather than just by individuals. In the action research too, narratives from the poor and marginalized groups were collated through various participatory processes. These were then collectively analysed by members of the group. Based on the analysis, the Praxis team evolved a framework into which the community contributed its inputs. These were then presented in the Voice for Change series. Secondly, the initiative gave members of the groups a platform on which they could interact with groups from across the globe, sharing experiences, analyses and suggestions for a way forward. The various processes were carried out with individuals including sexual minorities and sex workers, urban poor, children from tribal and urban slum areas, and sewerage workers.

In the cases of sex workers and sexual minorities, the effort was to increase their influence. The 'We Can' network (a network of sex workers and sexual minorities, also referred to as V-CAN), facilitated by Praxis, wanted to push their agenda of increasing the visibility of their concerns in the global arena. The interactions with sex workers and sexual minorities included at least 100 participants. They included a participatory video process,[4] a community-led analysis process, the collection of case stories for a document highlighting good practices, and sharing these back formally with members of the community. The participatory video process with the urban poor involved at least 60 people living on pavements, slums, a relocation site, and in shelters for the homeless across two cities – Delhi and Chennai (Praxis 2013 a, b). The study with sewerage workers surveyed around 60 sewerage workers and representatives, while 50 children from tribal backgrounds – as well as those living in shelters and care homes – were part of the Voice for Change process.

The processes brought to light discussions around stigma attached to identity, place of dwelling or profession, which manifested as barriers to accessing services and perceptions of insecurity – exacerbated by an apathetic and unaccountable state. In the case of sex workers and sexual minorities, the stigma revealed itself through lack of access to medical facilities or government entitlements and physical, verbal and emotional abuse from family and members of society.

For some participants, it was found that multiple identities of the individual such as belonging to a particular caste, or belonging to a particular region, religion or profession, were subsumed by one overriding identity that was seen as unacceptable to society to the exclusion of everything else – that of being a sex worker or homosexual or transgendered (Praxis, 2013c). This identity was used to mark and isolate, labelling behaviour as deviant and a threat to public morality. For example, the stigma surrounding transgendered identity clearly emerged when participants spoke about how even their partners refused to see them as anything but sex objects or of the ridicule they experienced from their own families.

The process of filming themselves collectively through a participatory video process brought up several questions. 'Why can't I be recruited into the police force? Do I lack the courage or the strength?' asked a transgender participant in the video process. 'What is the issue if I want to adopt a child?,' asked another. They also expressed demands for recognition of transgender people as a third gender that can access opportunities without fear of violence or exploitation.

The urban poor found themselves branded as criminals (Praxis, 2013d). 'Why should I be denied a job because I live in a relocation site?' asked a participant from Kannagi Nagar, a relocation site for the homeless in Chennai. Another wondered about the meaning of development, when it is meant for only a few: 'Why are we being sidelined from the city to whose growth we contribute?'. 'Whenever there is a metro line to be built, or a stadium that has to be built or the city has to be beautified, we are the ones who are removed. Aren't we also citizens?' asked a young participant who had been living in a homeless shelter since his slum was razed to accommodate a flyover in the national capital, Delhi. They demanded permanent residence near the places in which they were currently living, as well as identity documents that could help them access government services and dignity as citizens.

The multiple vulnerabilities of sewerage workers stem from the undignified and inhuman manner in which the profession is practised and the burden of caste associated with it. The rampant violations of safety guidelines and the unaccountable nature of subcontracting emerged as primary concerns: 'I don't even know the name of my contractor. Who will I go to if there is an accident?' asked one sewerage worker. 'People don't even give me water properly if I am thirsty,' said another, reiterating the injustice meted out to sewerage workers. They demanded that citizens should be made aware of sanitation workers' contribution to making cities sustainable, as well as that their jobs be legally recognized, and that they be provided with basic safety equipment and access to medical services (Praxis, 2014a, b, c).

Children from tribal backgrounds – as well as those who live in urban shelters – described an increasingly unsafe and unstable environment, which they experience physically and emotionally. The children detailed their understanding of safety and the lack of it through participatory mapping of their homes and schools, and digital stories and participatory videos expressing their fears and demands for a safe environment.

The process of alienation of some sections within the society has gone on for several centuries, aided and abetted by the patriarchal, casteist practices and a lack of political will to bring to the fore and resolve the above-mentioned issues. The Voice for Change initiative made these invisible citizens visible by channelling their voices so that they could be heard at different forums (see section on Dissemination of People's Voices, below). The Ground-Level Panel contextualised these voices, along with those of the panellists within the existing spaces for post-2015 development debates.

The Ground-Level Panel

Supplementing the Voice for Change discussions, the Ground-Level Panel (Praxis, 2013e) created a space for those who are currently experiencing poverty and exclusion to talk directly to policy makers. The specific focus of the interactions was to present their thoughts and ideas in the form of their recommendations on the post-2015 development agenda. In calling them the Ground-Level Panel, the idea was not just to create an attractive wordplay but to challenge the dominance of the global elite of professional, political and academic voices (represented by the High-Level Panel) that frame these debates.

During the five-day workshop, the members developed an identity as a Ground-Level Panel in the context of a global conversation about the future of development. With this in mind, they looked at the Millennium Development Goals and at how their lives and well-being had evolved since the year 2000; they critically reviewed the High-Level Panel's goals and identified gaps in it; and they deliberated on what should be core elements of a sustainable international development framework, proposing an alternative set of goals. The panel then shared these goals with representatives from the media, the government, the Planning Commission of India, civil society members and the public. These goals also informed the inputs made to the Sustainable Development Goals formulated by the Open Working Group of the General Assembly between March and June 2013.

The India panel brought together 14 people living in contexts of poverty. Hugely diverse in terms of their backgrounds, they had in common an intimacy with difficulty and struggle. All had experience of battling with exclusion from the kind of social, economic and political rights that the Millennium Development Goals sought to guarantee. Some were able to share stories of immense hope from the ashes of grave adversity. Others' lives continued to be marked by severe forms of marginalization. The identification process ensured that the group was diverse in age and gender, free from political affiliation or leadership linkages, and open to the idea of contributing to an alternative development agenda based on their lived experience.

The panel included a 35-year-old transgender person who had migrated from Kolkata to Chennai 26 years ago and had since been working for the welfare of her community. It also included a 17-year-old tribal girl from the western state of Odisha, who had fled home to escape being married when

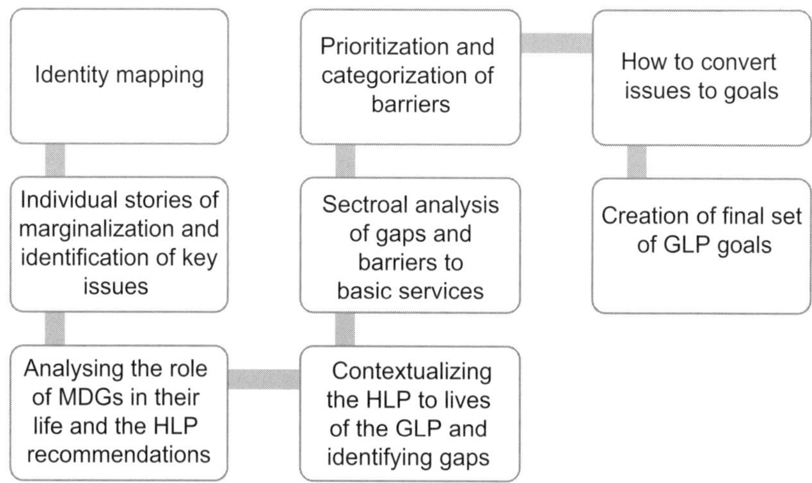

Figure 9.2 Process followed by the GLP

she had just entered her teens; a 42-year-old man who was abandoned by his family at the age of 18 after losing both legs in a truck accident; a young man living with cerebral palsy who recounts the happiest day of his life as the day his telephone booth was inaugurated in the presence of his mother; and the oldest member of the group, a 65-year-old from the exploited and much-excluded Musahar community in Bihar, who was part of a movement to restore land to the poor. (Annex 2 gives a detailed profile of the panelists.)

Each member of the panel brought on board their experience, understanding of issues they had gone through, and unique world-view. The word cloud in Figure 9.3 gives an understanding of the identities of the panelists. The size of each word represents how frequently the identifier was mentioned in the group.

The participants, many of whom had never travelled outside their state, made a journey to Delhi, with some travelling for 48 hours and for the first time by train. They spent the first day exploring some of their shared and individual identities, the vulnerabilities and marginalizations they represented collectively, and how to define some of these terms. Using stories from their own lives, they identified a series of issues and went through a process of converting these issues into goals.

Identifying gaps and barriers and designing a way forward

The panel used different participatory tools to clarify how development goals and targets are set. They contextualized the MDGs to their own lives and came to an understanding of how the goals have progressed nationally and regionally. The panellists provided a reality check on the policy wish list of the High-Level Panel, identifying some interesting gaps.

Rural Muslim Urban Dalit below18 Christian Transgender Disaster-Affected Tribal Man/Boy Hindu Disabled Woman/Girl Over60 Landless

Figure 9.3 Representation of panel identities

The Ground-Level Panel (GLP) review of the High-Level Panel (HLP) goals was systematic and wide-ranging (an exhaustive table listing the gaps identified by the GLP in the HLP's goals can be found in Annex 1). For example, the panel found that the first goal to 'end poverty' lacked an emphasis on tackling corruption. This was expressed through two suggestions seeking adequate action against those wrongly issuing Below Poverty Line certificates to undeserving candidates, and ensuring transparency in the allotment of funds for welfare measures. The ground-level panellists stressed that the goal on gender equality needed to include space for women to express their thoughts and opinions and also brought in the plight of transgender people. The panel also urged that the poor should participate in the framing of laws and policies and highlighted the government-corporate nexus within the ambit of the goal on ensuring good governance and effective institutions. The panellists also noted with concern that one country had a dominant say in the decisions of the United Nations and stressed that all countries should participate equally. They also suggested that a ban on nuclear weapons and armaments was necessary for creating a global enabling environment.

The process of reviewing the HLP report served to create the analytical framework within which the process of alternative goal setting was ensued.

Identifying people's alternatives to Millennium Development Goals

After reviewing the goals, the panellists undertook a detailed sectoral analysis from the perspective of different vulnerabilities to understand access, gaps and barriers to basic services in India. This was done from the points of view of the urban poor; the rural poor; children; the disabled; women and transgender individuals; people affected by disaster and conflict; and dalits, tribal people, and religious minorities. They detailed gaps and barriers associated with society, state and the corporate sector.

Taking this forward, the group listed all the issues that had commonly appeared in several articulations and exercises, and began grouping them into broad categories. They also watched participatory videos produced by members of vulnerable groups as part of the Voice for Change initiatives to understand if any issues had been overlooked. After a final exhaustive process of categorization, they prioritized the issues by distributing a hundred stones (a tool often used in participatory methods, rather than distributing scores, as it's an easier way for many non-academic people to do preferential ranking) across issues based on a consensually agreed order of importance. These priorities laid the foundation for the goals.

One of the group's key viewpoints was that basic needs have been the goals of national Government policy for more than 60 years. Given that these have not been fulfilled for a large section of the population, they suggested that there is a need to identify patterns in the barriers to these being met. The members agreed that all human beings should have access to the basic needs

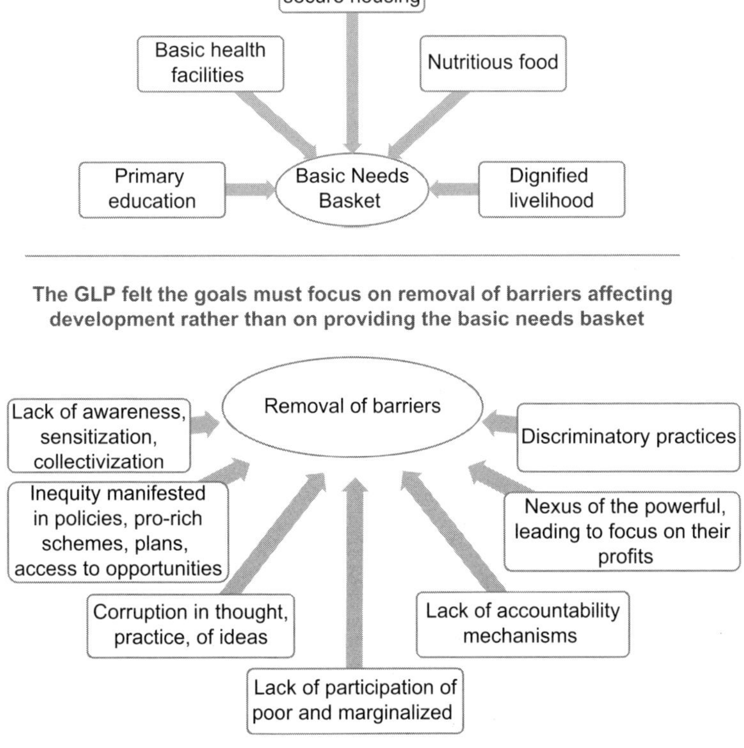

Figure 9.4 The Ground-Level Panel's alternative approach to goal-setting

basket, which contains the five elements shown in Figure 9.4. They argued that these were the rights of every human being and that governments across the world were supposed to ensure these basic rights to all citizens. The panel said that large sums of money should not be allocated towards development goals repeatedly because governments had set the same objectives for themselves within their own fiscal plans.

Instead, the panel suggested that governments should focus on removing these barriers to attaining basic needs. They challenged the way governments and NGOs look at issues in a compartmentalized way – such as health, education, livelihood, and so on – and rarely see the interrelations between them. Through this process, poverty was decisively politicized and represented as a set of issues that implied that the government and society should no longer align with the interests of the powerful. It did not just try to demand technical or investment-based solutions.

This provided the platform for the development of the following 15 goals. In Table 9.5, each goal is listed together with the GLP's comments. These comments give some insight into how the GLP members understood the meaning of each goal and the issues it raises.

Of course, some of the GLP's goals are of particular relevance to the Indian context and not necessarily applicable globally. However, even these can be instructive, as the GLP's goals themselves hinge on the recognition of structural barriers, that – though they manifest very differently in different countries – affect marginalized groups across the world. For instance, the call to end dowry within Goal 7 can be read as a call to challenge gender inequitable norms: a set of structural barriers that reinforce practices deeply discriminatory towards women.[5]

Table 9.5 The Ground-Level Panel's Goals

Goals of the Ground-Level Panel	GLP commentary
GOAL 1. Establish a corruption-free society and state	Corruption is all-pervasive. Political parties have sidelined even national-level movements on tackling corruption.
GOAL 2. Promote Equity	The state shall recognize the need for creating a level-playing field so that everyone has an equal opportunity to realize their dreams. Therefore, there is need for reservation and targeted support for the poor, *dalits*, tribal people, minorities, women, the elderly, transgender people, children, slum-dwellers, and people with disabilities.
GOAL 3. Establish robust accountability mechanisms	There should be more transparency in the way that the state works and more information should be made available to the public for free. This needs to build on the right to information and proactive sharing of information. There should also be better grievance redressal mechanisms. Government should emphasize the collectivization of people.

(Praxis, 2013e)

(Continued)

Table 9.5 The Ground-Level Panel's Goals (Praxis, 2013, e) (Continued)

GOAL 4. Provide identities not doles	Groups that are excluded and marginalized – including the transgender community, people with disabilities, *dalits*, and religious minorities should all be recognised as equal citizens. Care should be taken to ensure that identities, rather than labels, are established.
GOAL 5. Create institutional spaces	To promote people's participation in local governance and policymaking processes.
GOAL 6. End discrimination and stigma	This includes discrimination based on identities such as caste, language, disability, sexual orientation, gender, age, religion, and region.
GOAL 7. Abolish traditions and practices that sustain discrimination in society	These include the caste system, dowry system, female foeticide and *purdah* system.
GOAL 8. Create stringent restrictions on the sale and promotion of alcoholic and other addictive substances.	Sever the profit motive of the state in the sale of alcohol to prevent abuse of alcohol and associated problems.
GOAL 9. Facilitate awareness, sensitization, and collectivization of citizens.	Citizens should be sensitized in respect to issues of excluded and marginalized groups as well as laws and policies. This should be complemented by the establishment of an environment to facilitate the creation of collectives of people to achieve this.
GOAL 10. Promote a safe and secure home environment	This should be done so that vulnerability of households does not expose family members, especially children, to more risk. It is also important to maintain children's emotional health.
GOAL 11. Promoting interests of agricultural labourers, poor farmers, peasants, tribals and slum dwellers and their rights	They should be protected from advancing corporate investments on land and resources.
GOAL 12. Protect the environment	Create stringent systems that deter companies and other business establishments from polluting the environment.
GOAL 13: Enforce mechanisms to prevent tax evasion by corporates	This tax should be rightfully paid to governments who can in turn use this for the development of the poor.
GOAL 14: Creating and implementing rigidly, such systems that protect workers' rights, including their minimum wage and social security	Such systems should apply to all private enterprises and bring parity between government and private wages.
GOAL 15: Promote gender equality and safety in public spaces	This should apply to men, women and transgender individuals.

Many of these goals, such as those relating to corruption, black money, or safe spaces for women made it on to the list because of their immediate relevance in the public mind. Issues concerning agriculture, workers' rights, collectivization, and stigma were born from the day-to-day experiences of those who participated.

Dissemination of people's voices: from being audience members to taking centre stage

The process of collating and channelling people's voices was only one step; the next was the critically important task of enabling otherwise excluded people to engage directly with policy makers. This was organized through several forums.

The Ground-Level Panel chaired a public presentation before an audience comprising the media, several civil society organizations, development agencies, government department functionaries, as well as members of other excluded groups. Through stories and examples from their lives, the panellists engaged in the development discourse in a language they were comfortable using, referencing their realities and speaking from their perspectives. The sharing process reversed the traditional presentation set-up used in contexts across the world, by making the community members whose issues are being discussed the experts and anchors of the whole session.

The Ground-Level Panel shattered the myth that people living in poverty are myopic in their views – that they are only capable of thinking of their basic needs and deprivations. The analysis and inferences generated by the panellists, many of whom were illiterate and belonged to groups frequently written off as under-exposed, generated insights that went beyond the 'expert' panels.

Some of the members participated in webinars and other forums where they shared views with international development workers, representatives of various UN projects and divisions and the larger public, including people facing comparable exclusions from across the world.

Voices of community members who participated in other Voice for Change activities were shared with a global audience through a webinar organized by Participate and at side events organized during the United Nations General Assembly through the participatory videos. Transgender participants shared their participatory video at the Vibgyor International Film Festival in Thrissur, Kerala, drawing attention to their concerns and demands from global policy makers, the Indian Government and society.

A web-chat between urban poor groups who facilitated the participatory video process in Chennai, India, and Nairobi, Kenya, revealed the similarities of the issues faced in both locations. The problem of forcible evictions, which was expressed by a participant from Nairobi, found resonance in the difficulty of relocation faced by slum dwellers in Chennai. Being moved away from places of livelihood, with little facilities and services, were repeatedly mentioned by the urban poor in Chennai as well as Delhi during the participatory video processes.

Further, the issue of street children not getting access to education, medicine and being seen as 'forgotten people' in Nairobi was very similar to the problem of the 'invisibility' of the urban poor in Chennai and Delhi. Sanitation was also a major issue in both countries.

The common nature of the ways in which marginalization played out across continents stressed the need for excluded groups from across the world to come together to influence global development frameworks and discourses through such initiatives.

Limitations and learning

The possibilities of engaging the poor and excluded groups in global development discourse are exciting. However, it was clear from the process that none were representative of any of the excluded groups, nor, indeed, did they aspire to be so. The Ground-Level Panel was not meant to be a representative body. It was an 'expert' body just like the High Level-Panel, but expertise mainstreamed here is of 'experiencing poverty and marginalization'. Rather, these were voices of people who experienced a significant degree of poverty, exclusion, or both, who had come together to analyse common issues from the standpoint of their experience.

A significant limitation was that it was beyond the control of Praxis to be able to determine the reach and impact of the various processes. As a civil society agency, Praxis was able to work with individuals and groups and set up spaces in which they could express themselves as authentically as possible and, further, to arrange for audiences for these participants who were themselves engaged in significant processes of planning and decision-making at national and global levels. They serve, therefore, as contributions of people with this direct experience to a debate, among other contributions that have also been heard within India and beyond. However, their potential efficacy is constrained by the extent to which key decision-makers are prepared to listen and act upon their concerns.

However, the limitations cannot take away from the potential of the process. The aim of setting up the GLP was to allow poor and marginalized people to contribute to the national and global debate: not as representatives of entire communities or areas of Indian society, but as people with personal histories very different to those who normally lead these discussions. Crucially, the legitimacy of their contributions was founded not on received knowledge, but on their intimacy with conditions that post-2015 decision-makers need to deeply understand to ably guide an international movement to end poverty. Here, the baton was handed over to people who, through their lived experience, had become experts in understanding barriers to equity and opportunity, and were thus uniquely placed to be able to chart a way forward for all of us.

Notable emergent learning included:

- **Using up-to-date technology can be an effective way of engaging with otherwise excluded citizens**
  In this engagement with the global development agenda-setting process in the context of the post-Millennium Development Goals debates, the attempt was made to involve community members through progressive processes. From participatory action research, facilitated with communities of marginalized people, the results of which were then shared at different forums, to the use of technology to create a medium where the communities themselves speak directly to their audience through various mediums, the progress has not just been in terms of the use of technology. It also showed a change in the ownership of processes involving poorer and excluded people.

  The community members took over the discussion space by leading the discussion and shaping the direction it took, chairing the process, rather than depending on an external organization. As seen in the web-chats, exposure to new technology and in a language that is not one's own is not necessarily limiting. Rather, it can offer a platform to connect with groups facing similar problems in another continent. Similarly, the Ground-Level Panel created the space for itself to discuss policy issues and share visions for an alternate development agenda before an audience of sector experts, media persons and government functionaries. Our experiences also pointed to the need for constantly energizing and sustaining the effort to create and institutionalize spaces for people living in poverty especially on the global platform, by keeping track of new and developing technologies and the scope they provide.

- **Lived experience is a form of expertise that can be applied to policy discussions**
  Praxis took forward learnings from the community-led evaluation of the UNDP project (see Chapter 3) and other participatory initiatives to create a space for excluded communities to take over policy spaces. There was a clear shift from representational participation with the community as validators of theories or policies to direct participation, in which the community representatives were formulators of policy strategies.

  The Voice for Change initiative saw the communities understand existing and potential policy frames through various factors to which they applied the lens of lived experience, analysed and critiqued it. Especially in the context of the Ground-Level Panel, participants went beyond their immediate concerns to look at how global policy had affected their lives. The rich analysis of the participants lends weight to the argument that academic interest and in-depth research, though very valuable, is no replacement for the voices of people whom development agendas are supposed to benefit. It demonstrates that community-based goal setting can be a reality and that communities can contribute to global decision-making and goal setting by virtue of experiences which few of the people that the sector widely regards as experts can lay claim to. As we move forward now to a post-MDG era, there is good reason to consider ways of giving otherwise excluded people opportunities to contribute to policy discussions.

- **Barriers to goals warrant serious and sustained attention**
  There was a marked change in tone from the upbeat, sector-oriented goals in the HLP framework to goals relating to critical socio-economic, political and governance issues that were of concern to the GLP. Complex issues may get filtered out in the process of making them acceptable to a mainstream audience; and what remains in the process are targets separated from associated social, economic and political complexities. The GLP reminded us that talk of *barriers to* development is inseparable from talk of the *goals of* development.

  Issues such as discrimination, corruption, stigma and identity-politics, which can get dissolved in the established discourse of goal-setting and development frameworks, were formally acknowledged by the Ground-Level Panel. Uncomfortable questions and issues are not evaded, but explicitly located within the language of the goals themselves. In this way, the inclusion of socially excluded people in spaces they may have hitherto been excluded from ensures that goals challenge both political expediency and naïve optimism, and begin to do at least some justice to the size and scope of the task at hand.

- **Addressing power relations is an integral part of setting equitable goals**
  The Ground-Level Panel's goals draw attention to established power relations within local, national and international fora, and call for a need to address the power dynamics at all levels. The GLP's criticism of the dominance of some countries in global development discourse and of the government-corporate nexus within the national scenario brings the focus on the need for introspection and to openness to change.

  The threat of existing power relations to equity is brought out by several goals on the theme – Goal 11 demands action against increasing encroachment of corporate entities on lands and resources owned by the poor and marginalized; and Goal 13 demands stringent action against tax-evasion by corporate entities. The goals were motivated by an authentic experience of inequity and driven by an understanding that development efforts need to take seriously both power relations and the political causes of poverty and exclusion.

Way forward

Seen within the broader history of participatory innovations, not least community-led evaluations and audits, the initiatives discussed in this chapter encourage a new way of understanding accountability to the poor. Here, participants acted not just as national citizens, but in their capacity as global citizens. Their work was tied not to any one project, but to the broader struggles of those who suffer oppression and injustice in India and across the world.

Their approach to understanding goals reflected a conviction that development is impossible without social justice. Their recognition of barriers to development made poverty a fundamentally political problem and in the process implicated a far wider citizenry whose actions help to perpetuate the marginalization of them and others like them. Without constraining the radical authenticity that participants can bring to such exercises, there is a need now to institutionalize community participation in the policy arena. Through initiatives like the Voice for Change, Ground-Level Panel, Beyond 2015 and the World We Want (Wada Na Todo, 2012) campaigns, there is an opportunity for communities to make a substantial contribution to the global development discourse.

It is imperative such opportunities are not missed. As the world sets new frameworks for development, there is immense scope to revisit community involvement, to get inspired by the multiplicity of participatory approaches that have been tried and tested (Chambers, 1997; Estrella and Gaventa et al., 1998); and to go beyond representational voices and towards direct involvement of the excluded, marginalized and poorest in policies that will affect them the most. As seen in this chapter, these initiatives offer the additional dimension of lived experience. Now, there is a need to adopt these initiatives not as one-off experiences, but to institutionalize direct community participation in every aspect of development discourse, be it planning, policy making, implementation or review. The way forward, as we step into what could be a new order of development frameworks, must be one that acknowledges and creates spaces where marginalized people play a central role in re-imagining development.

About the authors

Pradeep Narayanan. Pradeep has close to two decades of experience working Government and non-government institutions as a rights focussed activist-researcher on community mobilisation and participation across several thematic spheres.

Sowmyaa Bharadwaj. Sowmyaa has over a decade's experience in the development sector as a facilitator and practitioner of participatory methods and approaches.

Anusha Chandrasehkaran. Anusha has a background in journalism, later moving to communications work in the development sector

Endnotes

1. The chapter is based on the Ground-Level Panel's Report and the Voice for Change Series developed in the course of a series of activities facilitated to inform Post-2015 debates. The initiative was supported by Participate. The

authors would like to acknowledge the contribution of Eva Watkinson in reviewing this chapter.

2. The Participate initiative of the Institute of Development Studies, (Sussex, UK), which aimed to bring voices from the margins to the forefront of development debates, facilitated the setting-up of Ground-Level Panels through partner organizations in four countries: India, Egypt, Brazil and Uganda.
3. The World We Want and its People's Voice Series are platforms created by the United Nations and civil society to ensure community participation in global policy development.
4. Participatory video is a process of groups using audio-visual technology to come together to analyse their issues and experiences and showcase the same. It is a process where the community is the owner of the process as well as the product, from the stage of ideating, to writing a script, to shooting the film, to editing it. The process focuses as much, if not more, on the process of a community coming together to collectively analyse, decide, and share knowledge, rather than on the output that is created. The output may be used a powerful tool of advocacy as a form of self-expression.
5. Incidentally, the 'Indianness' of some of the demands also reminds us of the limitations of universal formulas and the merits of insisting on contextual interpretations of globally recognized development goals – even to the national level. This is almost uniquely true in the case of India which, in some global development reports, is clubbed together with the rest of South Asia, and sometimes West Asia too, but which is home to more than one-third of the world's poorest people (World Bank, 2013), and has a total population larger than the entire continent of Africa. This lends itself to the suggestion that policy makers should be mindful of setting universal goals that risk obscuring internal diversity and different national and sub-national challenges. Readers interested in sub-national level data on India can start with the most recent national census (2011), available at <http://censusindia.gov.in/>.

Annex 1: Ground-Level Panel's criticism of High-Level Panel's goals

HLP Goals	What it contains	What GLP thought was missing
End Poverty	1. End people living in extreme poverty (less than $1.25 per day) and reduce share of people below national poverty line. 2. Increase share of women and men, communities, and businesses with secure rights to land, property, and other assets. 3. Cover people with social protection systems and build resilience and reduce deaths from natural disasters.	1. The officials who issue below-poverty-line cards to those who are above the poverty line should be dismissed. 2. The government should provide the poor with good houses instead of plastic sheets. 3. The government should provide the poor with housing and shelter. 4. Poverty is an indication of government indifference and apathy. 5. The poor should be provided with government jobs. 6. Effective steps must be taken by to reduce poverty. 7. There should be a platform to get the voices of poor women heard. 8. There should be transparency in the funds allocated for public welfare.
Empower Girls & Women & Achieve Gender Equality	1. Prevent and eliminate all forms of violence against girls and women. 2. End child marriage. 3. Ensure women's right to own and inherit property and transact business. 4. Eliminate discrimination against women in all walks of life.	1. Extend support to single women. 2. Improve the sex ratio [currently more boys than girls caused by female infanticide] 3. Abolish the payment of dowries. 4. Equal rights for men and women. 5. Take steps towards the safety and security of women and girls. 6. Women should be allowed to express their thoughts and opinions. 7. A right for transgender people to live with dignity. 8. Equal opportunity for women to fulfil their dreams and aspirations.
Provide Quality Education and Lifelong Learning	1. Increase proportion of children completing pre-primary education. 2. Ensure quality of education at primary level. 3. Improve access to secondary education and learning outcomes. 4. Increase work-related skills, technical and vocational education.	1. Free secondary education for girls to prevent them from dropping out because of limited family resources. 2. Common school system for all, rich and poor. 3. Parents and family should encourage children to go to school (and those who discourage them should be punished). 4. Establish more schools in villages and rural areas.

HLP Goals	What it contains	What GLP thought was missing
		5. Admission to schools should be on the basis of merit and not bribery. 6. Education should be provided until an individual becomes self-reliant. 7. Teachers should be competent and efficient.
Ensure Healthy Lives	1. End preventable infant and under-five deaths. 2. Increase vaccination coverage for children, adolescents, at-risk adults and older people. 3. Decrease maternal mortality. 4. Universalise sexual and reproductive health and rights. 5. Reduce disease from HIV/AIDS, tuberculosis, malaria, neglected tropical diseases, and priority non-communicable diseases.	1. Reduce corruption in accessing health services. 2. Health counselling for all, once in three months and provide medicines accordingly. 3. Hospital within a radius of 20km in villages so that people get timely treatment. 4. There should be concessions in medical expenses for the poor and needy in private hospitals. 5. Healthcare for all. 6. Compulsory premarital HIV testing so that couples can lead a healthy life.
Ensure Food Security and Good Nutrition	1. End hunger and protect the right of everyone to have access to sufficient, safe, affordable, and nutritious food. 2. Reduce child malnutrition and anaemia. 3. Increase agricultural productivity by sustainably increasing smallholder yields and access to irrigation. 4. Adopt sustainable agricultural, ocean and freshwater fishery practices and rebuild designated fish stocks to sustainable levels. 5. Reduce post-harvest loss and food waste.	1. Use of natural manure in crops. 2. Transparency in public distribution system and enquiries should be made against cases of malpractices. 3. The government should plan properly to ensure fair distribution of food for all. 4. Good-quality food rations at a reasonable price in the public distribution system. 5. Clean, free drinking water for all.
Achieve Universal Access to Water and Sanitation	1. Provide universal access to safe drinking water. 2. End open defecation. 3. Ensure universal access to sanitation at school and work, and improve access at home. 4. Align freshwater withdrawals in line with supply and increase water efficiency in agriculture, industry and urban areas. 5. Recycle or treat all municipal and industrial wastewater prior to discharge.	1. Toilets in each household so that open defecation is avoided. 2. Free availability of drinking water. 3. Rainwater harvesting and conservation of water resources. 4. Steps to derive drinking water from sea-water. 5. Adequate water supply in railway stations. 6. Clean toilets and sanitation

(Continued)

HLP Goals	What it contains	What GLP thought was missing
Secure Sustainable Energy	1. Double the share of renewable energy in the global energy mix. 2. Ensure universal access to modern energy services. 3. Double the global rate of improvement in energy efficiency in buildings, industry, agriculture and transport. 4. Phase out inefficient fossil fuel subsidies that encourage wasteful consumption.	1. Those who have livestock should promote the use of biogas. 2. Use windmills to produce energy. 3. Solar energy options should be made available even to the poor. 4. Encourage solar cars and vehicles. 5. Rainwater harvesting.
Create Jobs, Sustainable Livelihoods, and Equitable Growth	1. Increase jobs and livelihoods. 2. Decrease the number of young people not in education, employment or training. 3. Providing universal access to financial services and infrastructure (transportation and ICT). 4. Increase new start-ups with an enabling business environment and boosting entrepreneurship.	1. The poor should have employment, livelihood and a life with dignity. 2. End corruption. 3. Surveys should be carried out responsibly to guarantee employment to the poor. 4. Right to employment and reservation for the disabled. 5. Employment on the basis of merit. 6. Financial assistance to the unemployed. 7. Create an enabling work environment for women and transgenders. 8. Secure government jobs to more families.
Manage Natural Resource Assets Sustainably	1. Publish and use economic, social and environmental accounts in all governments and major companies. 2. Increase consideration of sustainability in government procurements. 3. Safeguard ecosystems, species and genetic diversity. 4. Reduce deforestation and increase reforestation. 5. Improve soil quality, reduce soil erosion and combat desertification.	1. Promote afforestation and prohibit deforestation. 2. Use of natural manures. 3. Trees should not be cut by the government or private enterprises in the name of development. 4. Control the population explosion. 5. Each household should plant at least one tree. 6. Rivers and other natural resources should not be polluted. 7. Trees should be planted in spaces where roads or any other infrastructure cannot be built. 8. More botanical gardens should be encouraged.

HLP Goals	What it contains	What GLP thought was missing
Ensure Good Governance and Effective Institutions	1. Provide free and universal legal identity (as birth registrations). 2. Ensure freedom of speech, association, peaceful protest and access to independent media and information. 3. Increase public participation in political processes and civic engagement at all levels. 4. Guarantee the public's right to information and access to government data. 5. Reduce bribery and corruption and ensure that officials can be held accountable.	1. Participation of the poor in framing laws and policies. 2. The poor should not be treated like dirt or filth. 3. Government–corporate nexus should be broken. 4. Land acquisition by private companies should be controlled. 5. Policies are implemented only on paper and not in practice. 6. Responsive and accountable government. 7. Cooperation and collaboration with NGOs and voluntary organizations.
Ensure Stable and Peaceful Societies	1. Reduce violent deaths and eliminate all violence against children. 2. Ensure justice institutions are accessible, independent, well-resourced and respect due-process rights. 3. Stem the external stressors that lead to conflict, including organised crime 4. Enhance the capacity, professionalism and accountability of the security forces, police and judiciary.	1. A society without caste, creed, or religion-based discrimination. 2. Equal rights and a right to a life with dignity for transgender people. 3. Food, clothing, shelter, education, and health should be available for all for a peaceful society. 4. A spiritual mind and tolerance towards others. 5. No party politics and discrimination along party lines.
Create a Global Enabling Environment and Catalyse Long-Term Finance	1. Support an open trading system and reduce trade-distorting. 2. Implement reforms to ensure stability of the global financial system and encourage long-term private foreign investment. 3. Hold the increase in global average temperature in line with international agreements. 4. Developed countries that have not done so to make concrete efforts towards the target official development assistance to developing countries and to least developed countries. 5. Other countries should move toward voluntary targets for complementary financial assistance. 6. Reduce illicit flows and tax evasion and increase stolen-asset recovery. 7. Promote collaboration on and access to science, technology, innovation, and development data.	1. Foster cordial relations with foreign countries. 2. Ban on nuclear weapons and armaments. 3. No domination of the United States and equal participation of other nations in the UN. 4. Promote Indian handicrafts overseas for better trade. 5. People's participation and consultation in issues of public concern.

Annex 2: Profile of Ground-Level Panel Members

Amrita Naik, a 17-year-old tribal girl from Odisha, cherishes the achievement of her project on the future solution of soil conservation in mountain areas being selected for the National Science Congress. Her life took a turn for the worse when her mother died when she was 11 years old. Her father, who was unemployed and an alcoholic, married another woman. She had to fend for herself by working on construction sites. She ran away fearing that her father would marry her off, as is customary in her community. A woman at the house she lived in brought her to Kalinga Institute of Social Studies, a residential school for tribal children that provides free education. Amrita feels she is fortunate in having had the opportunity to complete her schooling, and wants to be a lawyer.

Joshna Pradan, 22, fought for her family's right over their one acre of land in their village in Odisha. She studied up to Class 10 and now works as an agricultural labourer in her village. She works hard to take care of her mother and younger siblings. When Joshna lost her father at a very young age, her uncle took possession of the one acre of land their family owned, which was their only means of survival. He also separated her elder brothers from them. She, her mother and her younger siblings went without food for days on end, surviving on the wild roots she brought from the forest. When she grew up, Joshna summoned the village *panchayat* and fought for their land; they have got back a small portion of the land.

Mayavati, 29, is a woman from Uttar Pradesh state who has combated poverty and discrimination to educate her children. As a *dalit*, her father was unfairly paid for work he did in the fields of the landlord. She longed to go out of her house alone, but was never allowed to by her strict father. She was married at 15. She had to work in a rice mill from where she saved up the residue of broken rice mixed with stones to feed her husband and two children. Eventually she got involved with a savings group in her village, which helped her save money and take loans to put her children in school. She also set up her own petty shop. She wants to help other women and believes that no amount of cash transfers will help alleviate poverty.

Mohammad Akbar, 40, lives in Baramula district of Kashmir, and is proud of having helped the people of his village get various benefits since he became the president of the Village Development Committee six years ago. He dropped out of school after Class 10 to support his family, and now works in a local shop to sustain his family of 10. Prior to 2007, conflict between the army and militants in Kashmir disrupted life and frequent strikes took a toll on his children's education. Akbar always wanted to work for the welfare of his community and his dream came true when an NGO approached their village to improve local governance and livelihood opportunities. He helped BPL families in the village access various government benefits.

Mohammad Ismail, aged 29, was a member of a rescue team that helped people to safety during the 2004 tsunami. He lives in Chennai and was diagnosed with 70% disability because of polio at the age of eight. His disability did not deter his spirit. He completed Class 12 and started looking for a job to support his family. In 2002, his already impoverished family suffered a jolt when the slum in which they were living was notified for eviction to make way for a commercial boating site. Despite protests, 1500 houses including his own were demolished, and the inhabitants were moved to a relocation site called Kannagi Nagar on the outskirts of Chennai. Ismail has been desperately looking for a job with private companies but without luck, because where he comes from is considered notorious.

Mohammad Samsul Haque, 45, is a migrant labourer from Assam, who has studied up to Class 5 but managed to educate his two sons. His elder son is graduating.Haque, who was a farmer from NimuaLatima village in Nalbari district of Assam, migrated to Guwahati to work as a daily wage labourer, after regular floods disrupted his fields. He works at a garage as a screen painter during the day and spends his nights as a caretaker in the shop of a local businessman. He goes home during the harvest season to help his family in the fields. There have been a significant improvements there over the past few years because of an NGO that renovated the irrigation canals in his village – a task the government failed to do for 25 years. However, he still finds it difficult to get a job in the city, especially in the rainy season.

Nandlal, 42, from Uttar Pradesh, has overcome the discrimination he faced because of his disability to work for the rights of people with disabilities. Nandlal started driving a truck at a young age; but at the age of 18 he lost both legs in a road accident. Taunted by family members and neighbours because of his disability, he left his village and came to Delhi. He started living on the footpath near India Gate (a popular tourist site) and has worked with several NGOs. He educated himself, read many spiritual books and derived the confidence to face life.

Pinki is a 17-year-old girl from Uttar Pradesh, who is among the few girls in her village who have had the opportunity to study. She belongs to a *dalit* family and is the second of seven siblings. Pinki had to assert her desire to study quite aggressively with her parents before she was allowed to go to school. She feels that the biggest problem in her village is the lack of health facilities, the limited availability of electricity, and absence of employment opportunities for adults. At a seminar on human rights, Pinki was amazed to learn that women in other places have the right to choose whom they want to marry.

Raghunath Sada, 65, led a land rights movement against local landlords in Bihar state. Thanks to his relentless fight, the community to which he belongs, the Musahars, acquired 62 acres of land. The Musahar community is the most disadvantaged community of Bihar, and Sada has been voicing their issues through his writings and discussions in various fora.

Ravikant Redkar, 32, is affected by cerebral palsy and lives in a slum in North Mumbai. The happiest day of his life was when the he was appointed to run a telephone booth, and the inauguration was in the presence of his mother. Ravikant points out how mobile telephony has put his sole livelihood option under threat. However, Ravikant still hopes to overcome the present challenge as he thinks there are some good people in society who believe people with disabilities can be part of the development process. Ravikant is currently also associated with an NGO through which he advocates for the rights of people with disabilities.

Sunita Devi, 28, belongs to the Paswan community and was born in Bihar. She studied till Class 12 and moved to Samastipur where she lives with her four daughters and her husband. Sunita is a tailor and earns a living stitching clothes for women and small children in her village to supplement her husband's meagre income. She believes that she is an independent woman as she does not have to ask people for help.

Ushaben Dineshbhai Vasava, 33, is a tribal woman from Gujarat state, who is leading a team managing an agricultural tool library in her village. Through her initiatives, the village has road access, water supply to individual households, construction of biogas plants and a vermi-compost unit shared among the group members. Ushaben recalls the time when many people did not have access to drinking water.

Uzma is a 16-year-old girl from Delhi who takes care of her mentally ill mother with pride, as well as her three younger siblings. She used to live and beg on the streets along with her mother and siblings. Since 2010, she and her siblings have been staying in a shelter home run by an NGO. She is now learning to operate a computer and attends spoken English classes. With the help of a educational course, she has completed studying till Class 6.

Vineetha, a 35-year-old transgender person, migrated from Kolkata to Chennai 26 years ago, and has been working for the welfare for her community members. She lived with her partner for 13 years and brought up a destitute girl along with him. Five years ago, she was forced to leave her partner and her adopted girl in a crisis. She started life from scratch and since then has been making ends meet by begging and dancing. She lives in rented accommodation, and advises other transgender people not to become addicted to alcohol and tobacco.

CHAPTER 10

Conclusion: pathways to post-2015

Tom Thomas and Pradeep Narayanan

It would be an overstatement to say that 'participation' and participatory methods are in themselves subversive. However, the open endedness and adaptive nature of the approach gives it the potential to be subversive, as we have seen through the experiences outlined in this book. Is it subversive enough to, as Foucault put it in his *Lectures on the Will to Know* 'cut off the head of the king'? Probably not. That would require as he suggests, 'a bold sense of abandon, transgression and excess equal to that of the king it seeks to toss into the sea.' However, it does have the potential to open the lid a bit more on the real but suppressed history of struggles. It has the potential to engage in 'empowered deliberative democracy' in an attempt to, as Thomas Isaac (2003) says 'produce superior outcomes to a traditional representative-techno bureaucratic democracy' in promoting equity and improving the quality of citizenship, to keep the government accountable, the state equitable, and society alive and kicking.

The experiences have also shown that people living in poverty have the capacity to engage and that what is required is the space to do so – whether invited or claimed. Experience also shows that participation does pay in the short run by challenging existing data, myths, cultural instruments of oppression such as stigma, identity-based discrimination, blind spots and internal power dynamics within the sector. In the long run, it raises critical consciousness to deepen democracy and imagine another world.

As governments across the world begin to negotiate and agree on a framework for the development agenda post-2015, it is heartening to note that – unlike the Millennium Development Goals that were developed in a top-down manner – development of the post-2015 framework has been consultative, at least via CSO-mediated processes. Efforts such as the Ground-Level Panel by Participate and Praxis attempted to push the consultation to the next level of direct conversations by people living in poverty. A wealth of inspiring, deep, and often remarkably outward looking recommendations have emerged from people living in poverty.

These welcome beginnings notwithstanding, the larger question that begs an answer is how participation will be placed in the post-2015 framework. Will it be rhetoric as usual, or will the UN and governments be more sensitive or CSOs sufficiently imaginative to infuse into the framework subversive participation that has the potential to deepen democracies and produce superior outcomes? This is a tall order, and is quite unlikely given the nature of UN and governmental processes. However, if equity is a concern and reducing

http://dx.doi.org/10.3362/9781780448695.010

inequalities is a goal, the process requires participation of a different kind, not one that limits it to an invited space where participants pick from a pre-decided menu. In addition to challenging existing data sets and busting myths, providing alternate paradigms would require a participation that can challenge and change the way production relations are tilted in favour of the elite, a participation that can subvert the power equation in favour of the poor, and a participation that can also challenge and make consumption more equitable. In short, it would require participation that is capable of subverting for good. If a space for that isn't envisioned in the post-2015 framework, it is important to do what it takes to help communities and even civil society organizations to claim those spaces. Having seen the experience of the Millennium Development Goals, it doesn't take much to know that a business-as-usual post-2015 framework will miss the targets and fail the people miserably.

In what could be termed as fringe benefits of globalization, newer spaces where participation can intersect with technology have emerged, including spaces created by but not limited to social media. These spaces also offer newer opportunities for local and global solidarity. This is critical in a world increasingly characterized by repulsive corporate greed that seeks to make the world into one big mall with high-appetite consumers. Participation and solidarity hold the key to imagining our world and our development differently, and not confining it to the grand scheme of the markets or mere project frameworks of the UN, governments, or donors. As people living in poverty claim more spaces for direct talk, it is imperative that participation and solidarity are seen as the twinned drivers for a more equitable world.

About the authors

Tom Thomas has over 20 years of experience in the development sector and has led Praxis on several tasks that have provided critical inputs into development policy and thinking on social development, in India and in several countries across South Asia.

Pradeep Narayanan has close to two decades of experience working Government and non-government institutions as a rights-focused activist-researcher on community mobilization and participation across several thematic spheres.

References

Foucault, M. Edited by Arnold I. Davidson (2013) *Lectures on the Will to Know*, <http://www.palgraveconnect.com/pc/doifinder/10.1057/97811370-44860.0001> [Accessed: 4 February 2015].

Isaac, T.M.T., and Heller, P. (2003) *Democracy and Development: Decentralized Planning in Kerala in Deepening Democracy Institutional Innovations in Empowered Participatory Governance*, Verso, London and New York.

Index

accountability
  equity and 66–7
  knowledge for 67–75
  leadership and 53–5
Avahan Initiative 42–4, 102

benaami landholdings 12–13
beneficiary identification process 31–2, 36
Bhoodan movement 6, 16, 19
Bihar *see* land rights
Bill and Melinda Gates Foundation 42–3, 102
British Red Cross Society (BRCS) 25–6, 29, 30–1, 32, 33, 35

castes
  coastal communities 86–7
  infrastructure and services access 72, 77–9, 82–3, *84*
  land disputes 5, 13–14
  see also marginalized groups
Chambers, R. 129–30
cobweb analysis *122*
collaborative knowledge-building 11, 14–15, 16, 29–31
community mobilization monitoring (CMM) 44–5
Community Ownership and Preparedness Index (COPI) 44–5
community representatives, evaluation experience and role 117–27, 129–30
community-based organizations (CBOs) role in HIV prevention *see* monitoring system; sex workers and stigma
Community-Based Pro-Poor Initiatives (CBPPI) Programme 115–17

data-gathering
  beneficiary identification process 31–2, 36
  Community Ownership and Preparedness Index (COPI) 44–5
  digital storytelling (DST) 52–3, 54
  family profiles 32, 34–5
  questionnaires 45
  stories of stigma 106
  see also knowledge
decision-making approaches 26–31, 35–6, *37*
development agenda, future 157–8
digital storytelling (DST) 52–3, 54
disaster relief and reconstruction *see* Maldives; Tamil Nadu
drinking water *see* infrastructure and services access, rural India

Ekta Parishad movement 9, 19
empowerment, power relations and 17–18, 20–1, 35–9, 41–2, 109–10
evaluation
  by agencies *vs* beneficiaries 113–15, 128–31
  cobweb analysis *122*
  community representatives, experience and role 117–27, 129–30
  Community-Based Pro-Poor Initiatives (CBPPI) Programme 115–17

constraints, challenges and institutional learning 127–8
findings 124–6
government departments 115, 116, 126–7
indicators
categorizing 119–20
generating 119, *120*
identifying 118–19
languages *127*
NGOs 114, 126, 127, 128, 130
Praxis 116, 121
scope 133–6
synthesising and speaking out 126–7
tools *123*
facilitating use 121–4
piloting 120–1
UNDP 115, 116, 126
equity audit 72, *73*, *74*
external agencies
vs beneficiaries, evaluation by 113–15, 128–31
inappropriate interventions 26–9, *37*, 88–92
see also governments/government departments; NGOs

family profiles, Maldives 32, 34–5
fishing community *see* Tamil Nadu
focus group discussions (FGDs) 74, 77, 94, 96–7
Foucault, M. 163

Gates Foundation 42–3, 102
gender discrimination
social exclusion and social distance, India 68
see also sex workers and stigma; women
governments/government departments
evaluation 115, 116, 126–7
post-tsunami reconstruction
Maldives (GoM) 25–6, 29, 30, 31, 32–3
Tamil Nadu 92–3, 95
see also under land rights, Bihar
Ground Level Panel 3, 144, 163

healthcare *see* infrastructure and services access, rural India
HIV prevention *see* monitoring system; sex workers and stigma

infrastructure and services access, rural India
equity and accountability 66–7
marginalized groups 68, 72, 77–9, 82–3, *84*
National Infrastructure Equity Audit (NIEA) 67–70, 79–80
attitudes of service providers 75–6
challenges and limitations 77
equity audit 72, *73*, *74*
infrastructure access equity audit 74, *75*
infrastructure audit 70–1
study findings 77–9
policies and programmes (flagship schemes) 63–6, 78–9
privatization 67
social exclusion and social distance 68
social maps 68–9
Issacs, T. 163

Kang, J. et al. 114
knowledge
for accountability 67–75
collaborative 11, 14–15, 16, 29–31
contesting norms of 19–20
from the margins 1–4

land mapping
Maldives 32, 34–5
see also under land rights, Bihar
land rights, Bihar 5–9

Bhoodan movement 6, 16, 19
caste issue 5, 13–14
Ekta Parishad movement 9, 19
extreme poverty 6
general statistics *7*
government action
Land Reform Commission (LRC) 8, 9
legislation 6–7, *8*
land mapping
benaami holdings 12–13
challenges and limitations 18
collaborative knowledge-building 11, 14–15, 16
contesting norms of knowledge and practice 19–20
critical thinking approach 12
government land 16, 17
government records 15, 17, 19–20
landless families' claim 16
marginalized groups 9–11, 18, 19–20
power relations and empowerment potential 17–18, 20–1
unauthorized encroachments 13–14, 17
uses 15–18, 19–21
land use hierarchy *10*
landholdings comparison, Bihar and national figures *6*
Praxis 9, 19
languages *127*
leadership 46, 53–5, 107
learning
evaluation 127–8
monitoring system 55–7
post-disaster reconstruction 38–9

Maldives, post-tsunami reconstruction 25–6
beneficiary identification process 31–2, 36
British Red Cross Society (BRCS) 25–6, 29, 30–1, 32, 33, 35
community engagement concept and methodology 29–31, 34–5
community-led decision-making 35–6
development of community guidelines 37–8
government (GoM) role 25–6, 29, 30, 31, 32–3
land mapping (family profiles) 32, 34–5
learning for future initiatives 38–9
marginalized/vulnerable groups 27–9, 36–7
'normal' practice 26–9, *37*
Partner Representative Steering Committee (PRSC) 29, 31, 32, 33–4, 35–6, 37–8
policy and representation problems and resolutions 32–5
Praxis 26, 29, 30, 32, 36, 37, 38
responses to strategic needs 38
'subversive' empowerment 35–9
marginalized groups
infrastructure and services access 68, 72, 77–9, 82–3, *84*
knowledge from 1–4
land mapping 9–11, 18, 19–20
post-tsunami reconstruction 27–9, 36–7, 86–7, 96–7, 98
monitoring system (CBOs' role in HIV prevention)
action plans and planning cycle activation 49–52
Avahan Initiative 42–4
challenges, learning and risks 55–7
community mobilization monitoring (CMM) 44–5
Community Ownership and Preparedness Index (COPI) 44–5
data dissemination and capacity needs assessment plan 47–9

data interpretation and use 54–5
digital storytelling (DST) 52–3, 54
high-risk groups 43
independence from NGOs 58–9
leadership 46
accountability and responsibilities 53–5
power and sustainability 41–2
Praxis 44, 45–6
responsiveness to communities 53–4
self-assessment framework, development and uses 46–7
transition to new model 45–53
trend identification and strategic planning 53

National Aids Control Organization (NACO) 42
National Aids Control Programme (NACP) 43
National Infrastructure Equity Audit (NIEA) *see under* infrastructure and services access, rural India
NGOs
Coordination and Resource Centre (NCRC) 94
evaluation 114, 126, 127, 128, 130
independence from 58–9

panchayat (fisherman's council) 87–8, 91, 92, 93, 94, 96–7
participatory methods
evaluation process *123*
focus group discussion (FGDs) 74, 77, 94, 96–7
self-help groups (SHGs) 54, 124, 125, 126, 130
social mapping (Village Level People's Plans) 93–8
see also data-gathering; marginalized groups; *specific projects*
power relations and empowerment 17–18, 20–1, 35–9, 41–2, 109–10
post-2015 development agenda 163–4
Praxis
agenda 1–4
evaluation 116, 121
HIV prevention
monitoring system 44, 45–6
sex workers and stigma 106, 107
land rights 9, 19
post-tsunami reconstruction
Maldives 26, 29, 30, 32, 36, 37, 38
Tamil Nadu 93–4, 95, 98, 99

scheduled castes/tribes (SC/ST) 72, 77–9, 82–3, *84*
schools *see* infrastructure and services access, rural India
self-assessment framework, development and uses 46–7
self-help groups (SHGs) 54, 124, 125, 126, 130
sex workers and stigma (CBOs' role in HIV prevention)
Avahan Initiative 102
empowerment 109–10
identification of barriers and strategies 106–8
indicator development 103–4
leadership 107
networking 107
outcomes of participatory processes 109–10
Praxis 106, 107
stakeholder analysis and interaction 104–6, 108
social distance 68
Social Equity Audit 98
Social Equity Watch 67–8, 69
social exclusion 19–20, 68
social mapping 93–8

Social Needs Educational and Human Awareness (SNEHA) 93, 94
South India Federation of Fishermen Societies (SIFFS) 93, 94
stigma *see* sex workers and stigma
storytelling, digital (DST) 52–3, 54
sustainability
  of community participation 41–2, 43–4, 120, 124–5
  of fishing and coastal communities 87, 88

Tamil Nadu, post-tsunami reconstruction
  development of Social Equity Audit 98
  government role and challenges 92–3, 95
  impact on fishing and coastal communities 85–8, 97, 99
  marginalized/vulnerable groups 86–7, 96–7, 98
  NGO Coordination and Resource Centre (NCRC) 94
  panchayat role 87–8, 91, 92, 93, 94, 96–7
  Praxis 93–4, 95, 98, 99
  social mapping (Village Level People's Plans) 93–8
  Social Needs Educational and Human Awareness (SNEHA) 93, 94
  social re-engineering as development 88–92
  South India Federation of Fishermen Societies (SIFFS) 93, 94
transgendered people (TGs) 43, 101, 102, 103, 106, 108
tsunami *see* Maldives; Tamil Nadu

United Nations Development Programme (UNDP) 115, 116, 126

Village Level People's Plans 93–8
Voice for Change (Praxis) 106
vulnerability indices 36–7

women
  evaluation of and by 124, 125, 126
  fishing and coastal communities 88, 96
  land ownership inequality 20